WILLIAM McKINLEY.

FAMOUS AMERICAN STATESMEN & ORATORS

PAST AND PRESENT

WITH

BIOGRAPHICAL SKETCHES

— AND —

THEIR FAMOUS ORATIONS

IN SIX VOLUMES

VOLUME IV

ALEXANDER K. MCCLURE, LL.D.

EDITOR

*Author of "Lincoln and Men of War Times," "Our Presidents
and How We Make Them," etc.*

BYRON ANDREWS

of the "National Tribune," Washington, D. C.

ASSOCIATE EDITOR

*Author of "The Eastern Question," "The Life of Logan," "One of
the People" (McKinley), "Monroe and His Doctrine," etc.*

NEW YORK
F. F. LOVELL PUBLISHING COMPANY

Buchanan, James, an American statesman, sixteenth President of the United States, born at Franklin Co., Pa., April 23, 1791 ; died at Lancaster, Pa., June 1, 1868. Having taken up the profession of law he began practice at Lancaster, Pa., and soon prospered. He was a firm Federalist at the outset of his career, and entered the State Legislature as such in 1814. He was again elected the next year, and in 1820 was sent to Congress, remaining in the House of Representatives five terms. In 1832 he went as minister to Russia, and on his return entered the National Senate, becoming Secretary of State under Polk. In 1853 he was appointed minister to England, and returning in 1856 was elected President as the Democratic candidate. After the expiration of his term of office he lived in retirement. Buchanan was a dignified, polished speaker, with much courtliness of address.

INAUGURAL ADDRESS.

Fellow-Citizens :

I APPEAR before you this day to take the solemn oath " that I will faithfully execute the office of President of the United States and will to the best of my ability preserve, protect, and defend the Constitution of the United States."

In entering upon this great office I must humbly invoke the God of our fathers for wisdom and firmness to execute its high and responsible duties in such a manner as to restore harmony and ancient friendship among the people of the several States, and to preserve our free institutions throughout many generations. Convinced that I owe my election to the inherent love for the Constitution and the Union which

still animates the hearts of the American peole, let me
earnestly ask their powerful support in sustaining all
just measures calculated to perpetuate these, the richest political blessings which Heaven has ever bestowed
upon any nation. Having determined not to become
a candidate for re-election, I shall have no motive to
influence my conduct in administering the government,
except the desire ably and faithfully to serve my
country and to live in the grateful memory of my
countrymen.

We have recently passed through a Presidential contest in which the passions of our fellow-citizens were
excited to the highest degree by questions of deep and
vital importance; but when the people proclaimed their
will the tempest at once subsided and all was calm.

The voice of the majority, speaking in the manner
prescribed by the Constitution, was heard, and instant
submission followed. Our own country could alone
have exhibited so grand and strking a spectacle of the
capacity of man for self-government.

What a happy conception, then, was it for Congress
to apply this simple rule, that the will of the majority
shall govern, to the settlement of the question of
domestic slavery in the Territories! Congress is
neither " to legislate slavery into any Territory or
State, nor to exclude it therefrom, but to leave the
people thereof perfectly free to form and regulate
their domestic institutions in their own way, subject
only to the Constitution of the United States."

As a natural consequence, Congress has also prescribed that when the Territory of Kansas shall be admitted as a State it " shall be received into the Union

with or without slavery, as their Constitution may prescribe at the time of their admission."

A difference of opinion has arisen in regard to the point of time when the people of a Territory shall decide this question for themselves.

This is, happily, a matter of but little practical importance. Besides, it is a judicial question, which legitimately belongs to the Supreme Court of the United States, before whom it is now pending, and will, it is understood, be speedily and finally settled. To their decision, in common with all good citizens, I shall cheerfully submit, whatever this may be, though it has ever been my individual opinion that under the Nebraska-Kansas act the appropriate period will be when the number of actual residents in the Territory shall justify the formation of a Constitution with a view to its admision as a State into the Union. But be this as it may, it is the imperative and indispensable duty of the government of the United States to secure to every resident inhabitant the free and independent expression of his opinion by his vote. This sacred right of each individual must be preserved. That being accomplished, nothing can be fairer than to leave the people of a Territory free from all foreign interference, to decide their own destiny for themselves, subject only to the Constitution of the United States.

The whole Territorial question being settled upon the principle of popular sovereignty—a principle as ancient as free government itself—everything of a practical nature has been decided. No other question remains for adjustment, because all agree that under the Constitution slavery in the States is beyond any human power except that of the respective States themselves wherein it exists. May we not, then, hope that the long agitation on this subject is approaching its end, and that the geographical parties to which it has given birth, so much dreaded by the Father of his Country, will speedily become extinct? Most happy will it be for the country when the public mind shall be diverted from this question to others of more pressing and practical importance. Throughout the whole progress of this agitation, which has scarcely known any intermission for more than twenty years, while it has been productive of no positive good to any human being, it has been the prolific source of great evils to the master, to the slave, and to the whole country. It has alienated and estranged the people of the sister States from each other, and has even seriously endangered the very existence of the Union. Nor has the danger yet entirely ceased. Under our system there is a remedy for all mere political evils in the sound sense and sober judgment of the people. Time is a great corrective. Political subjects which but a few years ago excited and exasperated the public mind have passed away and are now entirely forgotten. But this question of domestic slavery is of far graver importance than any mere political question, because, should the agitation continue, it may eventually endanger the personal safety of a large portion of our countrymen where the institution exists. In that event no form of government, however admirable in itself, and however productive of material benefits, can compensate for the loss of peace and domestic security around the family altar. Let every Union-loving man, therefore, exert his best influence to suppress this agitation, which, since the recent legislation of Congress, is without any legitimate object.

It is an evil omen of the times that men have undertaken to calculate the mere material value of the Union. Reasoned estimates have been presented of the pecuniary profits and local advantages which would result to the different States and sections from its dissolution, and of the comparative injuries which such an event would inflict on other States and sections. Even descending to this low and narrow view of the mighty question, all such calculations are at fault. The bare reference to a single consideration will be conclusive on this point. We at present enjoy a free trade throughout our extensive and expanding country such as the world has never witnessed. This trade is conducted on railroads and canals, on noble rivers and arms of the sea, which bind together the North and South, the East and West, of our confederacy. Annihilate this trade, arrest its free progress by the geographical lines of jealous and hostile States, and you destroy the prosperity and onward march of the whole and every part, and involve all in a common ruin. But such considerations, important as they are in themselves, sink into insignificance when we reflect upon the terrific evils which would result from disunion to every portion of the confederacy—to the North not more than to the South, to the East not more than to the West. These I shall not attempt to portray, because I feel a humble confidence that the kind Providence which inspired our fathers with wisdom to frame the most perfect form of government and union ever

devised by man, will not suffer it to perish until it
shall have been peacefully instrumental, by its example,
in the extension of civil and religious liberty throughout the world.

Next in importance to the maintenance of the Constitution and the Union, is the duty of preserving the
government free from the taint or even the suspicion
of corruption. Public virtue is the vital spirit of republics, and history proves that when this has decayed and
the love of money has usurped its place, although the
forms of free government may remain for a season,
the substance has departed forever.

Our present financial condition is without parallel
in history. No nation has ever before been embarrassed from too large a surplus in its Treasury. This
almost necessarily gives birth to extravagant legislation. It produces wild schemes of expenditure, and
begets a race of speculators and jobbers, whose in-
genuity is exerted in contriving and promoting ex-
pedients to obtain public money. The purity of official
agents, whether rightfully or wrongfully, is suspected,
and the character of the government suffers in the
estimation of the people. This is in itself a very great
evil.

The natural mode of relief from this embarrassment
is to appropriate the surplus in the Treasury to great
national objects for which a clear warrant can be
found in the Constitution. Among these I might men-
tion the extinguishment of the public debt, a reason-
able increase of the navy, which is at present inadequate to the protection of our vast tonnage afloat, now

greater than any other nation, as well as the defence of our extended seacoast.

It is beyond all question the true principle that no more revenue ought to be collected from the people than the amount necessary to defray the expense of a wise, economical, and efficient administration of the government. To reach this point it was necessary to resort to a modification of the tariff, and this has, I trust, been accomplished in such a manner as to do as little injury as may have been practicable to our domestic manufactures, especially those necessary for the defence of the country. Any discrimination against a particular branch for the purpose of benefiting favored corporations, individuals, or interests, would have been unjust to the rest of the community and inconsistent with that spirit of fairness and equality which ought to govern in the adjustment of a revenue tariff.

But the squandering of the public money sinks into comparative insignificance as a temptation to corruption when compared with the squandering of the public lands.

No nation in the tide of time has ever been blessed with so rich and noble an inheritance as we enjoy in the public lands. In administering this important trust, while it may be wise to grant portions of them for the improvement of the remainder, yet we should never forget that it is our cardinal policy to reserve these lands, as much as may be, for actual settlers, and this at moderate prices. We shall thus not only best promote the prosperity of the new States and Territories, by furnishing them a hardy and independent race of honest and industrious citizens, but shall secure homes for our children and our children's children, as well as for those exiles from foreign shores who may seek in this country to improve their condition and to enjoy the blessings of civil and religious liberty. Such immigrants have done much to promote the growth and prosperity of the country. They have proved faithful both in peace and in war. After becoming citizens they are entitled, under the Constitution and laws, to be placed on a perfect equality with native-born citizens, and in this character they should ever be kindly recognized.

The Federal Constitution is a grant from the States to Congress of certain specific powers, and the question whether this grant should be liberally or strictly construed has more or less divided political parties from the beginning. Without entering into the argument, I desire to state at the commencement of my administration that long experience and observation have convinced me that a strict construction of the powers of the government is the only true, as well as the only safe, theory of the Constitution. Whenever in our past history doubtful powers have been exercised by Congress, these have never failed to produce injurious and unhappy consequences. Many such instances might be adduced if this were the proper occasion. Neither is it necessary for the public service to strain the language of the Constitution, because all the great and useful powers required for a successful administration of the government, both in peace and in war, have been granted, either in express terms or by the plainest implication.

While deeply convinced of these truths, I yet consider it clear that under the war-making power Congress may appropriate money toward the construction of a military road when this is absolutely necessary for the defence of any State or Territory of the Union against foreign invasion. Under the Constitution Congress has power " to declare war," " to raise and support armies," " to provide and maintain a navy," and to call forth the militia to " repel invasions." Thus endowed, in an ample manner, with the war-making power, the corresponding duty is required that " the United States shall protect each of them [the States] against invasion." Now, how is it possible to afford this protection to California and our Pacific possessions, except by means of a military road through the territories of the United States, over which men and munitions of war may be speedily transported from the Atlantic States to meet and to repel the invader? In the event of war with a naval power much stronger than our own, we should then have no other available access to the Pacific coast, because such a power would instantly close the route across the isthmus of Central America. It is impossible to conceive that while the Constitution has expressly required Congress to defend all the States, it should yet deny to them, by any fair construction, the only possible means by which one of these States can be defended. Besides, the government, ever since its origin, has been in the constant practice of constructing military roads. It might also be wise to consider whether the love for the Union which now animates our fellow-citizens on the Pacific coast may not be impaired by our neglect or refusal to provide for them, in their remote and isolated condition, the only means by which the power of the States on this side of the Rocky Mountains can reach them in sufficient time to "protect" them "against invasion." I forbear for the present from expressing an opinion as to the wisest and most economical mode in which the government can lend its aid in accomplishing this great and necessary work. I believe that many of the difficulties in the way, which now appear formidable, will in a great degree vanish as soon as the nearest and best route shall have been satisfactorily ascertained.

It may be proper that on this occasion I should make some brief remarks in regard to our rights and duties as a member of the great family of nations. In our intercourse with them there are some plain principles, approved by our own experience, from which we should never depart. We ought to cultivate peace, commerce, and friendship with all nations, and this not merely as the best means of promoting our own material interests, but in a spirit of Christian benevolence toward our fellow-men, wherever their lot may be cast. Our diplomacy should be direct and frank, neither seeking to obtain more nor accepting less than is due. We ought to cherish a sacred regard for the independence of all nations, and never attempt to interfere in the domestic concerns of any unless this shall be imperatively required by the great law of self-preservation. To avoid entangling alliances has been a maxim of our policy ever since the days of Washington, and its wisdom no one will attempt to dispute. In short, we ought to do justice in a kindly spirit to all nations, and require justice from them in return.

It is our glory that while other nations have extended their dominions by the sword, we have never acquired any territory except by fair purchase, or, in the case of Texas, by the voluntary determination of a brave, kindred, and independent people to blend their destinies with our own. Even our acquisitions from Mexico form no exception. Unwilling to take advantage of the fortune of war against a sister republic, we purchased these possessions under the treaty of peace for a sum which was considered at the time a fair equivalent. Our past history forbids that we shall in the future acquire territory unless this be sanctioned by the laws of justice and honor. Acting on this principle, no nation will have a right to interfere or to complain if, in the progress of events, we shall still further extend our possessions. Hitherto in all our acquisitions the people, under the protection of the American flag, have enjoyed civil and religious liberty as well as equal and just laws, and have been contented, prosperous, and happy. Their trade with the rest of the world has rapidly increased, and thus every commercial nation has shared largely in their successful progress.

I shall now proceed to take the oath prescribed by the Constitution, while humbly invoking the blessing of Divine Providence on this great people.

March 4, 1857.

Hayne, Robert Y., an American politician, of prominence as an orator, born in St. Paul's Parish, Colleton
District, S. C., Nov. 10, 1791 ; died at Asheville, N. C.,
Sept. 24, 1839. He was admitted to the bar in 1812, served
in a Carolina regiment during the second war with England,
and after its close entered the State Legislature, and was
speaker of the House, 1818-22. Hayne became attorney-
general of his State in 1822, and was soon after elected to
the National Senate where he vehemently opposed the protective system, declaring in a notable speech that a tariff
was unconstitutional. He engaged in an impassioned debate
with Daniel Webster in January, 1830, upon constitutional
principles, and excitedly proclaimed the constitutional right
of secession. He was chairman of the South Carolina convention which adopted the ordinance of nullification in 1832,
and the same year was elected governor, holding office till
1834. He was mayor of Charleston, 1835-37. Hayne's
oratory was of the most fiery, impassioned character, calculated to produce an overmastering impression upon all but
the coolest spirits.

ON FOOT'S RESOLUTION.*

DELIVERED IN THE UNITED STATES SENATE, JANUARY
21, 1830.†

Mr. President,—When I took occasion, two days
ago, to throw out some ideas with respect to the policy

* The following is the resolution of Mr. Foot : "Resolved, that
the Committee on Public Lands be instructed to inquire and report
the quantity of the public lands remaining unsold within each
State and Territory, and whether it be expedient to limit, for a

† See Mr. Webster's answer to this speech.

of the government in relation to the public lands, nothing certainly could have been further from my thoughts than that I should have been compelled again to throw myself upon the indulgence of the Senate. Little did I expect to be called upon to meet such an argument as was yesterday urged by the gentleman from Massachusetts [Mr. Webster].

Sir, I questioned no man's opinions; I impeached no man's motives; I charged no party or State or section of country with hostility to any other, but ventured, as I thought in a becoming spirit, to put forth my own sentiments in relation to a great national question of public policy.

Such was my course. The gentleman from Missouri [Mr. Benton], it is true, had charged upon the Eastern States an early and continued hostility toward the West, and referred to a number of historical facts and documents in support of that charge. Now, sir, how have these different arguments been met? The honorable gentleman from Massachusetts, after deliberating a whole night upon his course, comes into this chamber to vindicate New England, and instead of making up his issue with the gentleman from Missouri on the charges which he had preferred, chooses to consider me as the author of those charges, and, losing sight entirely of that gentleman, selects me as

certain period, the sales of the public lands to such lands only as have heretofore been offered for sale, and are now subject to entry at the minimum price. And, also, whether the office of surveyor-general, and some of the land offices, may not be abolished without detriment to the public interest; or whether it be expedient to adopt measures to hasten the sales and extend more rapidly the surveys of the public lands."

his adversary and pours out all the vials of his mighty wrath upon my devoted head. Nor is he willing to stop there.

He goes on to assail the institutions and policy of the South, and calls in question the principles and conduct of the State which I have the honor to represent. When I find a gentleman of mature age and experience, of acknowledged talents and profound sagacity, pursuing a course like this, declining the contest offered from the West, and making war upon the unoffending South, I must believe, I am bound to believe, he has some object in view which he has not ventured to disclose.

Mr. President, why is this? Has the gentleman discovered in former controversies with the gentleman from Missouri that he is overmatched by that senator? And does he hope for an easy victory over a more feeble adversary? Has the gentleman's distempered fancy been disturbed by gloomy forebodings of " new alliances to be formed " at which he hinted? Has the ghost of the murdered Coalition come back, like the ghost of Banquo, to " sear the eyeballs of the gentleman," and will it not " down at his bidding?" Are dark visions of broken hopes, and honors lost forever, still floating before his heated imagination? Sir, if it be his object to thrust me between the gentleman from Missouri and himself, in order to rescue the East from the contest it has provoked with the West, he shall not be gratified. Sir, I will not be dragged into the defence of my friend from Missouri. The South shall not be forced into a conflict not its own. The gentleman from Missouri is able to fight his own bat-

tles. The gallant West needs no aid from the South
to repel any attack which may be made on them from
any quarter. Let the gentleman from Massachusetts
controvert the facts and arguments of the gentleman
from Missouri if he can, and if he win the victory let
him wear the honors; I shall not deprive him of his
laurels.

The gentleman from Massachusetts, in reply to my
remarks, on the injurious operations of our land system on the prosperity of the West, pronounced an extravagant eulogium on the paternal care which the
government had extended toward the West, to which
he attributed all that was great and excellent in the
present condition of the new States.

The language of the gentleman on this topic fell
upon my ears like the almost forgotten tones of the
Tory leaders of the British Parliament at the commencement of the American revolution. They, too,
discovered that the colonies had grown great under
the fostering care of the mother country; and I must
confess, while listening to the gentleman, I thought the
appropriate reply to his argument was to be found in
the remark of a celebrated orator made on that occasion: "They have grown great in spite of your
protection."

The gentleman, in commenting on the policy of the
government in relation to the new States, has introduced to our notice a certain Nathan Dane, of Massachusetts, to whom he attributes the celebrated Ordinance of 1787, by which, he tells us, " slavery was forever excluded from the new States north of the Ohio."
After eulogizing the wisdom of this provision in terms

of the most extravagant praise he breaks forth in admiration of the greatness of Nathan Dane—and great indeed he must be if it be true, as stated by the senator from Massachusetts, that " he was greater than Solon and Lycurgus, Minos, Numa Pompilius, and all the legislators and philosophers of the world," ancient and modern.

Sir, to such high authority it is certainly my duty, in a becoming spirit of humility, to submit. And yet the gentleman will pardon me when I say that it is a little unfortunate for the fame of this great legislator that the gentleman from Missouri should have proved that he was not the author of the Ordinance of 1787, on which the senator from Massachusetts has reared so glorious a monument to his name.

Sir, I doubt not the senator will feel some compassion for our ignorance when I tell him that, so little are we acquainted with the modern great men of New England, that until he informed us yesterday that we possessed a Solon and a Lycurgus in the person of Nathan Dane he was only known to the South as a member of a celebrated assembly called and known by the name of " the Hartford Convention." In the proceedings of that assembly, which I hold in my hand (at page 19), will be found, in a few lines, the history of Nathan Dane ; and a little farther on there is conclusive evidence of that ardent devotion to the interests of the new States which it seems has given him a just claim to the title of " Father of the West." By the second resolution of the Hartford Convention it is declared " that it is expedient to attempt to make provision for restraining Congress in the exercise of an unlimited power to make new States and admitting them to the Union." So much for Nathan Dane, of Beverly, Massachusetts.

In commenting upon my views in relation to the public lands the gentleman insists that, it being one of the conditions of the grants that these lands should be applied to " the common benefit of all the States, they must always remain a fund for revenue;" and adds, " they must be treated as so much treasure."

Sir, the gentleman could hardly find language strong enough to convey his disapprobation of the policy which I had ventured to recommend to the favorable consideration of the country. And what, sir, was that policy, and what is the difference between that gentleman and myself on this subject?

I threw out the idea that the public lands ought not to be reserved forever as " a great fund of revenue;" that they ought not to be " treated as a great treasure;" but, that the course of our policy should rather be directed toward the creation of new States and building up great and flourishing communities.

Now, sir, will it be believed by those who now hear me, and who listened to the gentleman's denunciation of my doctrines yesterday, that a book then lay open before him—nay, that he held it in his hand and read from it certain passages of his own speech delivered to the House of Representatives in 1825, in which speech he himself contended for the very doctrines I had advocated and almost in the same terms. Here is the speech of the Hon. Daniel Webster, contained in the first volume of Gales & Seaton's " Register of Debates " (p. 251), delivered in the House of Repre-

2

sentatives on the 18th of January, 1825, in a debate on
the Cumberland Road—the very debate from which
the senator read yesterday.

I shall read from the celebrated speech two passages, from which it will appear that both as to the
past and the future policy of the government in relation to the public lands the gentleman from Massachusetts maintained in 1825 substantially the same
opinions which I have advanced, but which he now so
strongly reprobates. I said, sir, that the system of
credit sales by which the West had been kept constantly in debt to the United States, and by which their
wealth was drained off to be expended elsewhere, had
operated injuriously on their prosperity. On this point
the gentleman from Massachusetts, in January, 1825,
expressed himself thus :

" There could be no doubt if gentlemen looked at the
money received into the treasury from the sale of the
public lands to the West, and then looked to the whole
amount expended by the government (even including
the whole amount of what was laid out for the army)
the latter must be allowed to be very inconsiderable,
and there must be a constant drain of money from the
West to pay for the public lands. It might indeed be
said that this was no more than the refluence of capital which had previously gone over the mountains. Be
it so. Still its practical effect was to produce incon-
venience, if not distress, by absorbing the money
of the people."

I contend that the public lands ought not to be

treated merely as "a fund for revenue," that they ought not to be hoarded "as a great treasure."

On this point the senator expressed himself thus:

"Government, he believed, had received eighteen or twenty millions of dollars from the public lands, and it was with the greatest satisfaction he adverted to the change which had been introduced in the mode of paying for them; yet he could never think the national domain was to be regarded as any great source of revenue. The great object of the government in respect of these lands was not so much the money derived from their sale as it was the getting them settled. What he meant to say was, he did not think they ought to hug that domain as a great treasure which was to enrich the exchequer."

Now, Mr. President, it will be seen that the very doctrines which the gentleman so indignantly abandons were urged by him in 1825; and if I had actually borrowed my sentiments from those which he then avowed I could not have followed more closely in his footsteps. Sir, it is only since the gentleman quoted this book yesterday that my attention has been turned to the sentiments he expressed in 1825, and, if I had remembered them, I might possibly have been deterred from uttering sentiments here which it might well be supposed I had borrowed from that gentleman.

In 1825 the gentleman told the world that the public lands "ought not to be treated as a treasure." He now tells us that "they must be treated as so much treasure."

What the deliberate opinion of the gentleman on
this subject may be belongs not to me to determine;
but I do not think he can, with the shadow of justice
or propriety, impugn my sentiments while his own recorded opinions are identical with my own.   When
the gentleman refers to the conditions of the grants
under which the United States have acquired these
lands, and insist that, as they are declared to be " for
the common benefit of all the States," they can only be
treated as so much treasure, I think he has applied a
rule of construction too narrow for the case.   If in
the deeds of cession it has been declared that the grants
were intended for " the common benefit of all the
States," it is clear from other provisions that they
were not intended merely as so much property; for it
is expressly declared that the object of the grants is
the erection of new States; and the United States, in
accepting this trust, bind themselves to facilitate the
foundation of these States to be admitted into the
Union with all the rights and privileges of the original
States.

This, sir, was the great end to which all parties
looked, and it is by the fulfillment of this high trust
that " the common benefit of all the States " is to be
best promoted.   Sir, let me tell the gentleman that in
the part of the country in which I live we do not
measure political benefits by the money standard.   We
consider as more valuable than gold—liberty, principle, and justice.   But, sir, if we are bound to act on
the narrow principles contended for by the gentleman,
I am wholly at a loss to conceive how he can reconcile
his principles with his own practice.   The lands are,

it seems, to be treated " as so much treasure," and must be applied to the " common benefit of all the States."

Now, if this be so, whence does he derive the right to appropriate them for partial and local objects? How can the gentleman consent to vote away immense bodies of these lands for canals in Indiana and Illinois, to the Louisville and Portland canal, to Kenyon College in Ohio, to schools for the deaf and dumb, and other objects of a similar description?

If grants of this character can fairly be considered as made " for the common benefit of all the States," it can only be because all the States are interested in the welfare of each—a principle which, carried to the full extent, destroys all distinction between local and national objects, and is certainly broad enough to embrace the principles for which I have ventured to contend.

Sir, the true difference between us I take to be this: the gentleman wishes to treat the public lands as a great treasure, just as so much money in the treasury, to be applied to all objects, constitutional and unconstitutional, to which the public money is constantly applied. I consider it as a sacred trust, which we ought to fulfil, on the principles for which I have contended.

The senator from Massachusetts has thought proper to present in strong contrast the friendly feelings of the East towards the West, with sentiments of an opposite character displayed by the South in relation to appropriations for internal improvements. Now, sir, let it be recollected that the South have made no professions; I have certainly made none in their behalf of regard for the West. It has been reserved for the gentleman from Massachusetts, while he vaunts over his own personal devotion to Western interests, to claim for the entire section of country to which he belongs an ardent friendship for the West as manifested by their support of the system of internal improvement, while he casts in our teeth the reproach that the South has manifested hostility to Western interests in opposing appropriations for such objects. That gentleman at the same time acknowledged that the South entertains constitutional scruples on this subject.

Are we then, sir, to understand that the gentleman considers it a just subject of reproach that we respect our oaths by which we are bound " to preserve, protect, and defend the constitution of the United States?" Would the gentleman have us manifest our love to the West by trampling under foot our constitutional scruples? Does he not perceive, if the South is to be reproached with unkindness to the West in voting against appropriations which the gentleman admits they could not vote for without doing violence to their constitutional opinions, that he exposes himself to the question whether, if he was in our situation, he could not vote for these appropriations regardless of his scruples?

No, sir, I will not do the gentleman so great injustice. He has fallen into this error from not having duly weighed the force and effect of the reproach which he was endeavoring to cast upon the South. In relation to the other point, the friendship manifested by New England towards the West in their support of the system of internal improvement, the gentleman will pardon me for saying that I think he is equally unfortunate in having introduced that topic.

As that gentleman has forced it upon us, however, I cannot suffer it to pass unnoticed. When the gentleman tells us that the appropriations for internal improvement in the West would in almost every instance have failed but for New England votes, he has forgotten to tell us the when, the how, and the wherefore this new-born zeal for the West sprang up in the bosom of New England.

If we look back only a few years we will find in both Houses of Congress a uniform and steady opposition on the part of the members from the eastern States generally to all appropriations of this character. At the time I became a member of this House, and for some time afterward, a decided majority of the New England senators were opposed to the very measures which the senator from Massachusetts tells us they now cordially support. Sir, the journals are before me, and an examination of them will satisfy every gentleman of that fact.

It must be well known to every one whose experience dates back as far as 1825 that up to a certain period New England was generally opposed to appropriations for internal improvements in the West. The gentleman from Massachusetts may be himself an exception, but if he went for the system before 1825 it is certain that his colleagues did not go with him. In the session of 1824 and 1825, however (a memorable era in the history of this country), a wonderful change took place in New England in relation to Western interests.

Sir, an extraordinary union of sympathies and of interests was then effected which brought the East and West into close alliance. The book from which I have before read contains the first public annunciation of that happy reconciliation of conflicting interests, personal and political, which brought the East and West together and locked in a fraternal embrace the two great orators of the East and the West.

Sir, it was on the 18th of January, 1825, while the result of the presidential election in the House of Representatives was still doubtful, while the whole country was looking with intense anxiety to that legislative hall where the mighty drama was so soon to be acted, that we saw the leaders of two great parties in the House and in the nation "taking sweet counsel together," and in a celebrated debate on the Cumberland Road fighting side by side for Western interests.

It was on that memorable occasion that the senator from Massachusetts held out the white flag to the West and uttered those liberal sentiments which he yesterday so indignantly repudiated. Then it was that that happy union between the members of the celebrated coalition was consummated, whose immediate issue was a president from one quarter of the Union with the succession (as it was supposed) secured to another.

The "American System," before a rude, disjointed, and misshapen mass, now assumed form and consistency: then it was that it became the "settled policy of the government" that this system should be so administered as to create a reciprocity of interest and a reciprocal distribution of government favors East and

West (the tariff and internal improvements), while the South—yes, sir, the impracticable South—was to be " out of your protection."

The gentleman may boast as much as he pleases of the friendship of New England for the West as displayed in their support of internal improvement; but when he next introduces that topic I trust that he will tell us when that friendship commenced, how it was brought about, and why it was established.

Before I leave this topic I must be permitted to say that the true character of the policy now pursued by the gentleman from Massachusetts and his friends in relation to appropriations of land and money for the benefit of the West is in my estimation very similar to that pursued by Jacob of old toward his brother Esau —it robs them of their birthright for a mess of pottage.

The gentleman from Massachusetts, in alluding to a remark of mine that before any disposition could be made of the public lands the national debt (for which they stand pledged) must be first paid, took occasion to intimate " that the extraordinary fervor which seems to exist in a certain quarter (meaning the South, sir) for the payment of the debt arises from a disposition to weaken the ties which bind the people to the Union."

While the gentleman deals us this blow he professes an ardent desire to see the debt speedily extinguished. He must excuse me, however, for feeling some distrust on that subject until I find this disposition manifested by something stronger than professions. I shall look for acts, decided and unequivocal acts, for the performance of which an opportunity will very soon (if I am not greatly mistaken) be afforded.

Sir, if I were at liberty to judge of the course which that gentleman would pursue from the principles which he has laid down in relation to this matter, I should be bound to conclude that he will be found acting with those with whom it is a darling object to prevent the payment of the public debt. He tells us he is desirous of paying the debt, "because we are under an obligation to discharge it."

Now, sir, suppose it should happen that the public creditors with whom we have contracted the obligation should release us from it so far as to declare their willingness to wait for payment for fifty years to come, provided only that the interest shall be punctually discharged. The gentleman from Massachusetts will then be released from the obligation which now makes him desirous of paying the debt; and let me tell the gentleman the holders of the stock will not only release us from this obligation, but they will implore, nay, they will even pay us not to pay them.

But, adds the gentleman, so far as the debt may have an effect in binding the debtors to the country, and thereby serving as a link to hold the States together, he would be glad that it should exist forever. Surely, then, sir, on the gentleman's own principles, he must be opposed to the payment of the debt.

Sir, let me tell that gentleman that the South repudiates the idea that a pecuniary dependence on the federal government is one of the legitimate means of holding the States together. A moneyed interest in the government is essentially a base interest; and just so far as it operates to bind the feelings of those who are subjected to it to the government,—just so far as it operates in creating sympathies and interests that would not otherwise exist,—is it opposed to all the principles of free government and at war with virtue and patriotism.

Sir, the link which binds the public creditors, as such, to their country, binds them equally to all governments, whether arbitrary or free. In a free government this principle of abject dependence, if extended through all the ramifications of society, must be fatal to liberty.

Already have we made alarming strides in that direction. The entire class of manufacturers, the holders of stock, with their hundreds of millions of capital, are held to the government by the strong link of pecuniary interests; millions of people—entire sections of country, interested, or believing themselves to be so, in the public lands and the public treasure, are bound to the government by the expectation of pecuniary favors.

If this system is carried much farther no man can fail to see that every generous motive of attachment to the country will be destroyed, and in its place will spring up those low, groveling, base, and selfish feelings which bind men to the footstool of a despot by bonds as strong and enduring as those which attach them to free institutions. Sir, I would lay the foundation of this government in the affections of the people—I would teach them to cling to it by dispensing equal justice, and, above all, by securing the " blessings of liberty " to " themselves and to their posterity."

The honorable gentleman from Massachusetts has gone out of his way to pass a high eulogium on the State of Ohio. In the most impassioned tones of eloquence he described her majestic march to greatness. He told us that, having already left all the other States far behind, she was now passing by Virginia and Pennsylvania and about to take her station by the side of New York. To all this, sir, I was disposed most cordially to respond. When, however, the gentleman proceeded to contrast the State of Ohio with Kentucky, to the disadvantage of the latter, I listened to him with regret; and when he proceeded further to attribute the great, and, as he supposed, acknowledged superiority of the former in population, wealth, and general prosperity, to the policy of Nathan Dane, of Massachusetts, which had secured to the people of Ohio (by the Ordinance of 1787) a population of freemen, I will confess that my feelings suffered a revulsion which I am now unable to describe in any language sufficiently respectful toward the gentleman from Massachusetts. In contrasting the State of Ohio with Kentucky for the purpose of pointing out the superiority of the former and of attributing that superiority to the existence of slavery in the one State and its absence in the other, I thought I could discern the very spirit of the Missouri question intruded into this debate for objects best known to the gentleman himself.

Did that gentleman, sir, when he formed the determination to cross the Southern border in order to invade the State of South Carolina, deem it prudent or necessary to enlist under his banners the prejudices of the world, which, like Swiss troops, may be engaged in any cause and are prepared to serve under any leader?

Did he desire to avail himself of those remorseless allies, the passions of mankind, of which it may be more truly said than of the savage tribes of the wilderness, "that their known rule of warfare is an indiscriminate slaughter of all ages, sexes, and conditions?"

Or was it supposed, sir, that in a premeditated and unprovoked attack upon the South it was advisable to begin by a gentle admonition of our supposed weakness in order to prevent us from making that firm and manly resistance due to our own character and our dearest interest? Was the significant hint of the weakness of slaveholding States when contrasted with the superior strength of free States, like the glare of the weapon half drawn from its scabbard, intended to enforce the lessons of prudence and patriotism which the gentleman had resolved, out of his abundant generosity, gratuitously to bestow upon us?

Mr. President, the impression which has gone abroad of the weakness of the South as connected with the slave question exposes us to such constant attacks, has done us so much injury, and is calculated to produce such infinite mischiefs, that I embrace the occasion presented by the remarks of the gentleman from Massachusetts to declare that we are ready to meet the question promptly and fearlessly. It is one from which we are not disposed to shrink in whatever form or under whatever circumstances it may be pressed upon us.

We are ready to make up the issue with the gentleman as to the influence of slavery on individual and national character, on the prosperity and greatness either of the United States or of particular States. Sir, when arraigned before the bar of public opinion on this charge of slavery we can stand up with conscious rectitude, plead not guilty, and put ourselves upon God and our country. Sir, we will not consent to look at slavery in the abstract. We will not stop to inquire whether the black man, as some philosophers have contended, is of an inferior race, nor whether his color and condition are effects of a curse inflicted for the offences of his ancestors? We deal in no abstractions. We will not look back to inquire whether our fathers were guiltless in introducing slaves into this country? If an inquiry should ever be instituted in these matters, however, it will be found that the profits of the slave-trade were not confined to the South. Southern ships and Southern sailors were not the instruments of bringing slaves to the shores of America, nor did our merchants reap the profits of that " accursed traffic."

But, sir, we will pass over all this. If slavery, as it now exists in this country, be an evil, we of the present day found it ready made to our hands. Finding our lot cast among a people whom God had manifestly committed to our care we did not sit down to speculate on abstract questions of theoretical liberty. We met it as a practical question of obligation and duty. We resolved to make the best of the situation in which Providence had placed us, and to fulfill the high trusts which had devolved upon us as the owners of slaves in the only way in which such a trust could be fulfilled without spreading misery and ruin throughout the land.

We found that we had to deal with a people whose physical, moral, and intellectual habits and character totally disqualified them from the enjoyment of the blessings of freedom. We could not send them back to the shores from whence their fathers had been taken; their numbers forbade the thought, even if we did not know that their condition here is infinitely preferable to what it possibly could be among the barren sands and savage tribes of Africa; and it was wholly irreconcilable with all our notions of humanity to tear asunder the tender ties which they had formed among us to gratify the feelings of a false philanthropy.

What a commentary on the wisdom, justice, and humanity of the Southern slave-owner is presented by the example of certain benevolent associations and charitable individuals elsewhere! Shedding weak tears over sufferings which had existence only in their own sickly imaginations, these " friends of humanity " set themselves systematically to work to seduce the slaves of the South from their masters. By means of missionaries and political tracts the scheme was in a great measure successful. Thousands of these deluded victims of fanaticism were seduced into the enjoyment of freedom in our northern cities.

And what has been the consequence? Go to these cities now and ask the question. Visit the dark and narrow lanes and obscure recesses which have been assigned by common consent as the abodes of those outcasts of the world—the free people of color. Sir, there does not exist on the face of the whole earth a population so poor, so wretched, so vile, so loathsome, so utterly destitute of all the comforts, conveniences, and decencies of life as the unfortunate blacks of Philadelphia, New York, and Boston. Liberty has been to them the greatest of calamities, the heaviest of curses.

Sir, I have had some opportunities of making comparison between the condition of the free negroes of the north and the slaves of the south, and the comparison has left not only an indelible impression of the superior advantages of the latter, but has gone far to reconcile me to slavery itself. Never have I felt so forcibly that touching description, " The foxes have holes, and the birds of the air have nests, but the Son of Man hath not where to lay his head," as when I have seen this unhappy race, naked and houseless, almost starving in the streets, and abandoned by all the world. Sir, I have seen, in the neighborhood of one of the most moral, religious, and refined cities of the north, a family of free blacks driven to the caves of the rocks, and there obtaining a precarious subsistence from charity and plunder.

When the gentleman from Massachusetts adopts and reiterates the old charge of weakness as resulting from slavery I must be permitted to call for the proof of those blighting effects which he ascribes to its influence. I suspect that when the subject is closely examined it will be found that there is not much force even on the plausible objection of the want of physical power in slave-holding States. The power of a country is compounded of its population and its wealth, and in modern times, where, from the very form and structure of society, by far the greater portion of the people must, even during the continuance of the most desolating wars, be employed in the cultivation of the soil and other peaceful pursuits, it may be well doubted whether slave-holding States, by reason of a superior value of their productions are not able to maintain a number of troops in the field fully equal to what could be supported by States with a larger white population but not possessed of equal resources. . . .

Mr. President, I wish it to be distinctly understood that all the remarks I have made on this subject are intended to be exclusively applied to a party which I have described as the " Peace Party of New England," embracing the political associates of the senator from Massachusetts—a party which controlled the operations of that State during the embargo and the war, and who are justly chargeable with all the measures I have reprobated. Sir, nothing has been further from my thoughts than to impeach the character or conduct of the people of New England. For their steady habits and hardy virtues I trust I entertain a becoming respect. I fully subscribe to the truth of the description given before the Revolution by one whose praise is the highest eulogy, " that the perseverance of Holland, the activity of France, and the dexterous and firm sagacity of English enterprise have been more than equalled by this recent people." Hardy, enterprising, sagacious, industrious, and moral, the people of New England of the present day are worthy of their ancestors. Still less, Mr. President, has it been my intention to say anything that could be construed into a want of respect for that party who, trampling on all narrow, sectional feelings, have been true to their

3

principles in the worst times,—I mean the Democracy of New England.

Sir, I will declare that, highly as I appreciate the Democracy of the South, I consider even higher praise to be due to the Democracy of New England, who have maintained their principles " through good and through evil report," who at every period of our national history have stood up manfully for " their country, their whole country, and nothing but their country." In the great political revolution of '98 they were found united with the Democracy of the South, marching under the banner of the constitution, led on by the patriarch of liberty in search of the land of political promise which they lived not only to behold but to possess and to enjoy.

Again, sir, in the darkest and most gloomy period of the war, when our country stood single-handed against " the conqueror of the conquerors of the world," when all about and around them was dark, and dreary, disastrous and discouraging, they stood a Spartan band in that narrow pass where the honor of their country was to be defended or to find its grave.

And in the last great struggle, involving, as we believe, the very existence of the principle of popular sovereignty, where were the Democracy of New England? Where they always have been found, sir, struggling side by side with their brethren of the South and the West for popular rights, and assisting in that glorious triumph by which the man of the people was elevated to the highest office in their gift.

Who, then, Mr. President, are the true friends of

the Union? Those who would confine the federal government strictly within the limits prescribed by the constitution; who would preserve to the States and the people all powers not expressly delegated; who would make this a federal and not a national union, and who, administering the government in a spirit of equal justice, would make it a blessing and not a curse. And who are its enemies? Those who are in favor of consolidation, who are constantly stealing power from the States and adding strength to the federal government. Who, assuming an unwarrantable jurisdiction over the States and the people, undertake to regulate the whole industry and capital of the country. But, sir, of all descriptions of men, I consider those as the worst enemies of the Union who sacrifice the equal rights which belong to every member of the confederacy to combinations of interested majorities for personal or political objects.

But the gentleman apprehends no evil from the dependence of the States on the federal government; he can see no danger of corruption from the influence of money or of patronage. Sir, I know that it is supposed to be a wise saying " that patronage is a source of weakness," and in support of that maxim it has been said that " every ten appointments made a hundred enemies."

But I am rather inclined to think, with the eloquent and sagacious orator now reposing on his laurels on the banks of the Roanoke, that " the power of conferring favors creates a crowd of dependents;" he gave a forcible illustration of the truth of the remark, when he told us of the effect of holding up the savory morsel to the eager eyes of the hungry hounds gathered around his door. It mattered not whether the gift was bestowed on Towser or Sweetlips, " Tray, Blanche, or Sweetheart;" while held in suspense they were all governed by a nod, and when the morsel was bestowed the expectation of the favors of to-morrow kept up the subjection of to-day.

The senator from Massachusetts, in denouncing what he is pleased to call the Carolina doctrine, has attempted to throw ridicule upon the idea that a State has any constitutional remedy, by the exercise of its sovereign authority, against " a gross, palpable, and deliberate violation of the constitution." He calls it " an idle " or " ridiculous notion," or something to that effect, and added that it would make the Union " A mere rope of sand."

Now, sir, as the gentleman has not condescended to enter into any examination of the question, and has been satisfied with throwing the weight of his authority into the scale, I do not deem it necessary to do more than to throw into the opposite scale the authority on which South Carolina relies; and there for the present I am perfectly willing to leave the controversy. The South Carolina doctrine—that is to say, the doctrine contained in an exposition reported by a a committee of the legislature in December, 1828, and published by their authority—is the good old Republican doctrine of '98—the doctrine of the celebrated " Virginia Resolutions " of that year, and of " Madison's Report " of '99.

It will be recollected that the legislature of Virginia, in December, 1898, took into consideration the

Alien and Sedition Laws, then considered by all republicans as a gross violation of the constitution of the United States, and on that day passed, among others, the following resolution:

" The General Assembly doth explicitly and peremptorily declare that it views the powers of the federal government as resulting from the compact to which the States are parties, as limited by the plain sense and intention of the instrument constituting that compact, as no further valid than they are atuhorized by the grants enumerated in that compact; and that in case of a deliberate, palpable, and dangerous exercise of other powers not granted by the said compact, the States who are parties thereto have the right and are in duty bound to interpose for arresting the progress of the evil, and for maintaining within their respective limits the authorities, rights, and liberties appertaining to them."

In addition to the above resolution the General Assembly of Virginia " appealed to the other States in the confidence that they would concur with that commonwealth, that the act aforesaid (the Alien and Sedition Laws) are unconstitutional, and that the necessary and proper measures would be taken by each for co-operating with Virginia in maintaining unimpaired the authorities, rights, and liberties reserved to the States respectively or to the people."

The legislatures of several of the New England States, having, contrary to the expectation of the legislature of Virginia, expressed their dissent from these doctrines; the subject came up again for consideration during the session of 1799-1800, when it was referred to a select committee by whom was made that celebrated report which is familiarly known as " Madison's Report," and which deserves to last as long as the constitution itself.

In that report, which was subsequently adopted by the legislature, the whole subject was deliberately re-examined, and the objection urged against the Virginia doctrines carefully considered. The result was that the legislature of Virginia reaffirmed all the principles laid down in the resolutions of 1798, and issued to the world that admirable report which has stamped the character of Mr. Madison as the preserver of that constitution which he had contributed so largely to create and establish.

I will here quote from Mr. Madison's report one or two passages which bear more immediately on the point in controversy:

" The resolution, having taken this view of the federal compact, proceeds to infer ' that in case of a deliberate, palpable, and dangerous exercise of other powers not granted by the said compact, the States who are parties thereto have the right, and are in duty bound, to interpose for arresting the progress of the evil, and for maintaining within their respective limits the authorities, rights, and liberties appertaining to them.'

" It appears to your committee to be a plain principle, founded in common sense, illustrated by common practice, and essential to the nature of compacts, that, where resort can be had to no tribunal superior to the authority of the parties, the parties themselves must be the rightful judges in the last resort whether the bargain made has been pursued or violated. The constitution of the United States was formed by the sanction of the States, given by each in its sovereign capacity. It adds to the stability and dignity as well as to the authority of the constitution that it rests upon this legitimate and solid foundation. The States, then, being the parties to the constitutional compact, and in their sovereign capacity, it follows of necessity, that there can be no tribunal above their authority to decide in the last resort whether the compact made by them be violated; and, consequently, that, as the parties to it they must themselves decide in the last resort such questions as may be of sufficient magnitude to require their interposition.

" The resolution has guarded against any misapprehension of its object by expressly requiring for such an interposition ' the case of a deliberate, palpable, and dangerous breach of the constitution by the exercise of powers not granted by it.' It must be a case, not of a light and transient nature, but of a nature dangerous to the great purposes for which the constitution was established.

" But the resolution has done more than guard against misconstruction by expressly referring to cases of a deliberate, palpable, and dangerous nature. It specifies the object of the interposition which it contemplates to be solely that of arresting the progress of the evil of usurpation, and of maintaining the authori-

ties, rights, and liberties appertaining to the States as
parties to the constitution.

"From this view of the resolution it would seem inconceivable that it can incur any just disapprobation
from those who, laying aside all momentary impressions and recollecting the genuine source and object of
the federal constitution, shall candidly and accurately
interpret the meaning of the general assembly. If the
deliberate exercise of dangerous powers, palpably
withheld by the constitution, could not justify the parties to it in interposing, even so far as to arrest the
progress of the evil and thereby to preserve the constitution itself as well as to provide for the safety of
the parties to it there would be an end to all relief
from usurped power, and a direct subversion of the
rights specified or recognized under all the State constitutions, as well as a plain denial of the fundamental
principles on which our independence itself was declared."

But, sir, our authorities do not stop here. The State
of Kentucky responded to Virginia, and on the 10th of
November, 1798, adopted those celebrated resolutions
well known to have been penned by the author of the
Declaration of American Independence. In those resolutions the legislature of Kentucky declare—

"That the government created by this compact was
not made the exclusive or final judge of the extent of
the powers delegated to itself, since that would have
made its discretion and not the constitution the measure of its powers; but that, as in all other cases of compact among parties having no common judge, each

party has an equal right to judge for itself as well of infractions as of the mode and measure of redress."

At the ensuing session of the legislature the subject was re-examined, and on the 14th of November, 1799, the resolutions of the preceding year were deliberately reaffirmed, and it was among other things solemnly declared:

"That if those who administer the general government be permitted to transgress the limits fixed by that compact, by a total disregard to the special delegations of power therein contained, an annihilation of the State governments and the erection upon their ruins of a general consolidated government will be the inevitable consequence. That the principles of construction contended for by sundry of the State legislatures, that the general government is the exclusive judge of the extent of the powers delegated to it, stop nothing short of despotism; since the discretion of those who administer the government, and not the constitution, would be the measure of their powers. That the several States who formed that instrument, being sovereign and independent, have the unquestionable right to judge of its infraction, and that a nullification, by those sovereignties, of all unauthorized acts done under color of that instrument, is the rightful remedy."

Time and experience confirmed Mr. Jefferson's opinion on this all-important point. In the year 1821 he expressed himself in this emphatic manner:

"It is a fatal heresy to suppose that either our State

governments are superior to the federal or the federal to the State; neither is authorized literally to decide which belongs to itself or its copartner in government; in differences of opinion between their different sets of public servants the appeal is to neither, but to their employers peaceably assembled by their representatives in convention."

The opinion of Mr. Jefferson on this subject has been so repeatedly and so solemnly expressed that they may be said to have been among the most fixed and settled convictions of his mind.

In the protest prepared by him for the legislature of Virginia in December, 1825, in respect to the powers exercised by the federal government in relation to the tariff and internal improvements, which he declares to be " usurpations of the powers retained by the States, mere interpolations into the compact and direct infractions of it," he solemnly reasserts all the principles of the Virginia resolutions of '98—protests against " these acts of the federal branch of the government as null and void, and declares that, although Virginia would consider a dissolution of the Union as among the greatest calamities that could befall them, yet it is not the greatest. There is one yet greater—submission to a government of unlimited powers. It is only when the hope of this shall become absolutely desperate that further forbearance could not be indulged."

In his letter to Mr. Giles, written about the same time, he says:

" I see, as you do, and with the deepest affliction,

the rapid strides with which the federal branch of our government is advancing toward the usurpation of all the rights reserved to the States, and the consolidation in itself of all powers, foreign and domestic, and that too by constructions which leave no limits to their powers, etc. Under the power to regulate commerce they assume indefinitely that also over agriculture and manufactures, etc. Under the authority to establish post-roads they claim that of cutting down mountains for the construction of roads and digging canals, etc. And what is our resource for the preservation of the constitution? Reason and argument? You might as well reason and argue with the marble columns encircling them, etc. Are we then to stand to our arms with the hot-headed Georgian? No [and I say no, and South Carolina has said no], that must be the last resource. We must have patience and long endurance with our brethren, etc., and separate from our companions only when the sole alternatives left are a dissolution of our union with them or submission to a government without limitation of powers. Between these two evils, when we must make a choice, there can be no hesitation."

Such, sir, are the high and imposing authorities in support of " the Carolina doctrine," which is, in fact, the doctrine of the Virginia resolutions of 1798.

Sir, at that day the whole country was divided on this very question. It formed the line of demarcation between the federal and republican parties; and the great political revolution which then took place turned upon the very question involved in these resolutions.

That question was decided by the people, and by that decision the constitution was, in the emphatic language of Mr. Jefferson, " saved at its last gasp."

I should suppose, sir, it would require more self-respect than any gentleman here would be willing to assume to treat lightly doctrines derived from such high resources. Resting on authority like this, I will ask gentlemen whether South Carolina has not manifested a high regard for the Union, when, under a tyranny ten times more grievous than the Alien and Sedition Laws, she has hitherto gone no further than to petition, remonstrate, and to solemnly protest against a series of measures which she believes to be wholly unconstitutional and utterly destructive of her interests. Sir, South Carolina has not gone one step further than Mr. Jefferson himself was disposed to go in relation to the present subject of our present complaints; not a step further than the statesmen from New England were disposed to go under similar circumstances; no further than the senator from Massachusetts himself once considered as within " the limits of a constitutional opposition." The doctrine that it is the right of a State to judge of the violations of the constitution on the part of the federal government and to protect her citizens from the operations of unconstitutional laws was held by the enlightened citizens of Boston who assembled in Faneuil Hall on the 25th of January, 1809. They state in that celebrated memorial that " they looked only to the State legislature, who were competent to devise relief against the unconstitutional acts of the general government. That your power (say they) is adequate to that object is evident from the organization of the confederacy."

A distinguished senator from one of the New England States [Mr. Hillhouse], in a speech delivered here on a bill for enforcing the embargo declared:

" I feel myself bound in conscience to declare (lest the blood of those who shall fall in the execution of this measure shall be on my head) that I consider this to be an act which directs a mortal blow at the liberties of my country; an act containing unconstitutional provisions to which the people are not bound to submit, and to which in my opinion they will not submit."

And the senator from Massachusetts himself, in a speech delivered on the same subject in the other House, said:

" This opposition is constitutional and legal; it is also conscientious. It rests on settled and sober conviction that such policy is destructive to the interests of the people and dangerous to the being of government. The experience of every day confirms these sentiments. Men who act from such motives are not to be discouraged by trifling obstacles nor awed by any dangers. They know the limit of constitutional opposition; up to that limit, at their own discretion, they will walk, and walk fearlessly."

How " the being of the government " was to be endangered by " constitutional opposition " to the embargo I leave to the gentleman to explain.

Thus it will be seen, Mr. President, that the South

Carolina doctrine is the republican doctrine of '98; that it was promulgated by the fathers of the faith; that it was maintained by Virginia and Kentucky in the worst of times; that it constituted the very pivot on which the political revolution of that day turned; that it embraces the very principles the triumph of which at that time saved the constitution at its last gasp, and which New England statesmen were not unwilling to adopt when they believed themselves to be the victims of unconstitutional legislation. Sir, as to the doctrine that the federal government is the exclusive judge of the extent as well as the limitations of its powers, it seems to me to be utterly subversive of the sovereignty and independence of the States.

It makes but little difference in my estimation whether Congress or the Supreme Court are invested with this power. If the federal government in all or any of its departments is to prescribe the limits of its own authority, and the States are bound to submit to the decision and are not allowed to examine and decide for themselves when the barriers of the constitution shall be overleaped, this is practically " a government without limitation of powers."

The States are at once reduced to mere petty corporations and the people are entirely at your mercy. I have but one word more to add. In all the efforts that have been made by South Carolina to resist the unconstitutional laws which Congress has extended over them, she has kept steadily in view the preservation of the Union by the only means by which she believes it can be long preserved—a firm, manly, and steady resistance against usurpation.

The measures of the federal government have, it is true, prostrated her interests, and will soon involve the whole South in irretrievable ruin. But even this evil, great as it is, is not the chief ground of our complaints. It is the principle involved in the contest, a principle which, substituting the discretion of Congress for the limitations of the constitution, brings the States and the people to the feet of the federal government and leaves them nothing they can call their own.

Sir, if the measures of the federal government were less oppressive we should still strive against this usurpation. The South is acting on a principle she has always held sacred—resistance to unauthorized taxation.

These, sir, are the principles which induced the immortal Hampden to resist the payment of a tax of twenty shillings. Would twenty shillings have ruined his fortune? No! but the payment of half twenty shillings on the principle on which it was demanded would have made him a slave.

Sir, if in acting on these high motives, if animated by that ardent love of liberty which has always been the most prominent trait in the Southern character, we should be hurried beyond the bounds of a cold and calculating prudence, who is there with one noble and generous sentiment in his bosom that would not be disposed, in the language of Burke, to exclaim, " You must pardon something to the spirit of liberty !"

Stevens, Thaddeus, an American statesman and orator, born at Peacham, Vt., April 4, 1792 ; died in Washington, D. C., August 11, 1868. After graduation from Dartmouth College he removed to Pennsylvania in 1814, and was there admitted to the bar. He was for several terms a member of the State Legislature, and in 1848 was sent to Congress as a Whig member from Lancaster. While there he strenuously opposed the compromise measures proposed by Henry Clay, and especially the Fugitive Slave Law. From 1853 to 1858 Stevens practised his profession in Lancaster, but in the latter year was again returned to Congress as a Representative, and served there uninterruptedly until his death. During this period he was foremost among Republican leaders. He was a vigorous, powerful debator, with much eloquence at his ready command, and an opponent not to be lightly encountered. His speech against Webster and the Northern Compromisers affords a worthy example of his style. In his own day he was frequently termed " The Great Commoner."

AGAINST WEBSTER AND NORTHERN COMPROMISERS.

HOUSE OF REPRESENTATIVES, JUNE 10, 1850.

DANTE, by actual observation, makes hell consist of nine circles, the punishments of each increasing in intensity over the preceding. Those doomed to the first circle are much less afflicted than those in the ninth, where are tortured Lucifer and Judas Iscariot— and I trust, in the next edition, will be added, the traitors to liberty. But notwithstanding this difference in degree, all, from the first circle to the ninth, inclusive, is hell—cruel, desolate, abhorred, horrible hell! If I might venture to make a suggestion, I would advise these reverend perverters of Scripture to devote their subtlety to what they have probably more interest in—to ascertaining and demonstrating (perhaps an accompanying map might be useful) the exact spot and location where the most comfort might be enjoyed —the coolest corner in the lake that burns with fire and brimstone!

But not only by honorable gentlemen in this House, and right honorable gentlemen in the other, but throughout the country, the friends of liberty are reproached as "transcendentalists and fanatics." Sir, I do not understand the terms in such connection. There can be no fanatics in the cause of genuine liberty. Fanaticism is excessive zeal. There may be, and have been, fanatics in false religion; in the bloody religion of the heathen. There are fanatics in superstition. But there can be no fanatics, however warm their zeal, in true religion, even although you sell your goods, and bestow your money on the poor, and go and follow your Master. There may be, and every hour shows around me, fanatics in the cause of false liberty—that infamous liberty which justifies human bondage; that liberty whose cornerstone is slavery. But there can be no fanaticism, however high the enthusiasm, in the cause of rational, universal liberty—the liberty of the Declaration of Independence.

This is the same censure which the Egyptian tyrant cast upon those old abolitionists, Moses and Aaron, when they "agitated" for freedom, and, in obedience to the command of God, bade him let the people go.

4

But we are told by these pretended advocates of liberty in both branches of Congress, that those who preach freedom here and elsewhere are the slave's worst enemies; that it makes the slaveholder increase their burdens and tighten their chains; that more cruel laws are enacted since this agitation began in 1835. Sir, I am not satisfied that this is the fact. I will send to the clerk, and ask him to read a law of Virginia enacted more than fifty years before this agitation began. It is to be found in the sixth volume of " Hening's Statutes at Large of Virginia," published in 1819, " pursuant to an act of the General Assembly of Virginia, passed on the fifth day of February, 1808."

" Sec. xxiv. And that when any slave shall be notoriously guilty of going abroad in the night, or running away and laying out, and cannot be reclaimed from such disorderly courses by common methods of punishment, it shall be lawful for the county court, upon complaint and proof thereof to them made by the owner of such slave, to order and direct such punishment by dismembering, or any other way, not touching life, as the court shall think fit. And if such slave shall die by means of such dismembering, no forfeiture or punishment shall be thereby incurred."

I have had that law read to see if any gentleman can turn me to any more cruel laws passed since the " agitation." I did not read it myself, though found on the pages of Old Virginia's law books, lest it should make the modest gentleman from Virginia [Mr. Millson], and the gentleman from North Carolina [Mr. Stanly], and his gray-headed negro, blush!

Mr. Bayly of Virginia—That law is repealed, or not now in force.

Mr. Stevens—Then I am glad that the agitation has produced some amelioration of your laws, although I still find it on your statute book.

But suppose it were true that the masters had become more severe; has it not been so with tyrants in every age? The nearer the oppressed is to freedom, and the more hopeful his struggles, the tighter the master rivets his chains. Moses and Aaron urged the emancipation of the enslaved Jews. Their master hardened his heart. Those fanatical abolitionists, guided by Heaven, agitated anew. Pharaoh increased the burden of the slaves. He required the same quantity of brick from them without straw, as when the straw had been found them. They were seen dispersed and wandering to gather stubble to make out their task. They failed, and were beaten with stripes. Moses was their worst enemy, according to these philanthropic gentlemen. Did the Lord think so, and command him to desist, lest he should injure them? No; he directed him to agitate again, and demand the abolition of slavery from the king himself. That great slaveholder still hardened his heart, and refused. The Lord visited him with successive plagues—lice, frogs, locusts, thick darkness—until, as the agitation grew higher, and the chains were tighter drawn, he smote the firstborn of every house in Egypt; nor did the slaveholder relax the grasp on his victims, until there was wailing throughout the whole land, over one dead in every family, from the king that sat on the throne to the captive in the dungeon. So I fear it will be in this land of wicked slavery. You have already among you what is equivalent to the lice and the locusts, that wither up every green thing where the foot of slavery treads. Beware of the final plague. And you, in the midst of slavery, who are willing to do justice to the people, take care that your works testify to the purity of your intentions, even at some cost. Take care that your door-posts are sprinkled with the blood of sacrifice, that when the destroying angel goes forth, as go forth he will, he may pass you by.

Aside from the principle of Eternal Right, I will never consent to the admission of another slave State into the Union (unless bound to do so by some constitutional compact, and I know of none such), on account of the injustice of slave representation. By the Constitution, not only the States now in the Union, but all that may hereafter be admitted, are entitled to have their slaves represented in Congress, five slaves being counted equal to three white freemen. This is unjust to the free States, unless you allow them a representation in the compound ratio of persons and property. There are twenty-five gentlemen on this floor who are virtually the representatives of slaves alone, having not one free constituent. This is an outrage on every representative principle, which supposes that representatives have constituents, whose will they are bound to obey and whose interest they protect. . . .

I shall not now particularly refer to the features of the most extraordinary conspiracy against liberty in the Senate, called the Compromise Bill. If it should survive its puerperal fever, we shall have another opportunity of knocking the monster in the head. I pass over what is familiarly known as the "ten-million bribe," which was evidently inserted for no other purpose than to create public opinion on 'change, and carry the bill.

But it is proposed to propitiate Virginia by giving her two hundred million dollars out of the public treasury, the proceeds of the public lands. If this sum were to be given for the purpose of purchasing the freedom of her slaves, large as it is, it should have my hearty support. It is, I think, at least fifty millions more than would pay for them all at a fair market price. But it is designed for no purpose of emancipation. The cool-headed, cool-hearted, philosophic author had no such "transcendental" object. It is to be specifically appropriated to exile her free people of color, and transport them from the land of their birth to the land of the stranger! Sir, this is a proposition not "fit to be made."

Mr. Averett of Virginia here asked: Did not New England sell slaves?

Mr. Stevens—Yes, she sold, she imported slaves; she was very wicked; she has long since repented. Go ye and do likewise.

It is my purpose nowhere in these remarks to make personal reproaches; I entertain no ill-will toward any human being, nor any brute, that I know of, not even the skunk across the way, to which I referred. Least of all would I reproach the South. I honor her courage and fidelity. Even in a bad, a wicked cause, she

shows a united front. All her sons are faithful to the
cause of human bondage, because it is their cause. But
the North—the poor, timid, mercenary, drivelling
North—has no such united defenders of her cause, although it is the cause of human liberty. None of the
bright lights of the nation shine upon her section.
Even her own great men have turned her accusers.
She is the victim of low ambition—an ambition which
prefers self to country, personal aggrandizement to
the high cause of human liberty. She is offered up a
sacrifice to propitiate Southern tyranny—to conciliate
Southern treason.

We are told that she has not done her duty in restoring fugitive slaves, and that more stringent laws
must be passed to secure that object. A distinguished
Senator from Kentucky [Mr. Clay] says it is the duty,
not only of officers in the free States, but of all the
people who happen to be present, to give active aid
to the slaveowner to run down, arrest, and restore
the man who is fleeing from slavery. An equally distinguished Senator from Massachusetts [Mr. Web-
ster] unites with him in denouncing the aggressions
of the North in this particular; and they both declare
their determination to vote for the bill, with its amend-
ments, now on file, and which has become a part of
the "Compromise."

It may be well to look a little at the law as it now
stands on the subject, and then at the one which has
enlisted such powerful support. By the Constitution
alone, without any legislation, the slaveholder may go
into a free State, take with him such force as he
pleases, and take his slave and carry him back. If the

fact of his slavery be disputed, either by the alleged slave or any one for him, the claimant may issue his writ *de homine repligiando,* and unless the defendant give ample bail for his forthcoming on the final issue, and for the payment of all costs and damages (which include the value of his services in the meantime), the plaintiff may take him into his possession, and retain him until final trial by a court and jury. Is not this sufficient? It is all the right which he would have if he claimed property in a horse or other property which he might allege had strayed over the line. Why should he have any greater right when he claims property in man? Is a man of so much less value than a horse, that he should be deprived of the ordinary protection of the law? Sir, in my judgment, the remedy ought to be left where the Constitution places it, without any legislation. The odious law of 1793 ought to be repealed.

By that law, the slaveholder may not only seize his slave and drag him back, but he may command the aid of all the officers of the United States Court; take his alleged slave before the judge, and after summary examination, without trial by jury, may obtain a certificate of property; which, for the purpose of removal, is conclusive of his slavery, takes away the writ of Habeas Corpus, and the right of trial by jury, and sends the victim to hopeless bondage. If an inhabitant of a free State see a wretched fugitive, who he learns is fleeing from bondage, and gives him a meal of victuals to keep him from starving, and allows him to sleep in his outhouse, although his master is not in pursuit of him, he is liable to the penalty of five hun-

dred dollars. A judge in Pennsylvania lately held
that a worthy citizen of Indiana County incurred such
penalty by giving a cup of water and a crust of bread
to a famishing man whom he knew to be fleeing from
bondage. A slave family escaped from Maryland,
went into Cumberland County, Pennsylvania, and obtained the reluctant consent of a worthy farmer to
sleep in his hayloft. Their owner did not pursue them
for a week afterward. It was held by a State court
that the farmer was liable for the full value of the
slaves, besides the five hundred dollars penalty, and
a jury returned a verdict for two thousand dollars and
costs. Such are some of the provisions of the law
of 1793 now in force, which these great expounders of
constitutional freedom hold to be too mild! And more
stringent laws are to be passed to punish Northern
men who have hearts! . . .

The distinguished Senator from Kentucky [Mr.
Clay] wishes further to make it the duty of all bystand-
ers to aid in the capture of fugitives; to join the chase
and run down the prey. This is asking more than my
constituents will ever grant. They will strictly abide
by the Constitution. The slaveholder may pursue his
slave among them with his own foreign myrmidons,
unmolested, except by their frowning scorn. But no
law that tyranny can pass will ever induce them to
join the hue and cry after the trembling wretch who
has escaped from unjust bondage. Their fair land,
made by nature and their own honest toil as fertile and
as lovely as the vale of Tempe, shall never become
the hunting-ground on which the bloodhounds of

slavery shall course their prey, and command them to join the hunt.

Sir, this tribunal would be more odious than the Star Chamber—these officers more hateful than the Familiars of the Inquisition.

Can the free North stand this? Can New England stand it? Can Massachusetts stand it? If she can, she has but one step further to take in degradation, and that is to deliver her own sons in chains to Southern masters! What would the bold Barons of Runnymede have said to such defenders of liberty? What would the advocates of English freedom, at any time, have said to those who would strike down the writ of Habeas Corpus and the right of trial by jury, those vital principles of Magna Charta and the Bill of Rights? They would have driven them forth as enemies in disguise.

Sir, I am aware of the temerity of these remarks. I know how little effect they will have, coming from so obscure a quarter, and being opposed by the mighty influences that create public opinion. I was struck with the sound sense of the remark made to-day by the gentleman from Tennessee [Mr. Gentry]. He said that the " Compromise " Bill was winning favor with the people, most of whom had never read it, merely because it is advocated by great names in whom they are accustomed to confide.

Late events have convinced me that it were better in republican, representative governments, where the people are to judge and decide on every measure, if there were no great, overshadowing names, to give factitious force to their views, and lead the public mind captive. If the people were to put faith in no man's argument, they would examine every question for themselves, and decide according to their intrinsic merit. The errors of the small do but little harm; those of the great are fatal. Had Lucifer been but a common angel, instead of the Chief of the morning stars, he had not taken with him to perdition the third of the heavenly hosts, and spread disunion and discord in celestial, and sin and misery in earthly, places.

Sir, so long as man is vain and fallible, so long as great men have like passions with others, and, as in republics, are surrounded with stronger temptations, it were better for themselves if their fame acquired no inordinate height, until the grave had precluded error. The errors of obscure men die with them, and cast no shame on their posterity. How different with the Great!

How much better had it been for Lord Bacon, that greatest of human intellects, had he never, during his life, acquired glory, and risen to high honors in the State, than to be degraded from them by the judgment of his peers. How much better for him and his, had he lived and died unknown, than to be branded through all future time as the

> " Wisest, brightest, meanest of mankind."

So now, in this crisis of the fate of liberty, if any of the renowned men of this nation should betray her cause, it were better that they had been unknown to fame. It need not be hoped that the brightness of their past glory will dazzle the eyes of posterity, or illumine the pages of impartial history. A few of its rays may still linger on a fading sky; but they will soon be whelmed in the blackness of darkness. For, unless progressive civilization, and the increasing love of freedom throughout the Christian and civilized world, are fallacious, the Sun of Liberty, of universal Liberty, is already above the horizon, and fast coursing to his meridian splendor, and no advocate of slavery, no apologist of slavery, can look upon his face and live.

THE ISSUE AGAINST ANDREW JOHNSON.

ON THE FIRST RECONSTRUCTION BILL; DELIVERED IN
THE HOUSE OF REPRESENTATIVES,
JANUARY 3, 1867.

Mr. Speaker:

WHAT are the great questions which now divide the nation? In the midst of the political Babel which has been produced by the intermingling of secessionists, rebels, pardoned traitors, hissing Copperheads, and apostate Republicans, such a confusion of tongues is heard that it is difficult to understand either the questions that are asked or the answers that are given. Ask what is the " President's policy," and it is difficult to define it. Ask what is the " policy of Congress," and the answer is not always at hand. A few moments may be profitably spent in seeking the meaning of each of these terms.

In this country the whole sovereignty rests with the people, and is exercised through their representatives in Congress assembled. The legislative power is the sole guardian of that sovereignty. No other branch of the government, no other department, no other

officer of the government, possesses one single particle
of the sovereignty of the nation. No government official, from the President and Chief-Justice down, can
do any one act which is not prescribed and directed by
the legislative power. . . .

Since, then, the President cannot enact, alter, or
modify a single law; cannot even create a petty office
within his own sphere of operations; if, in short, he
is the mere servant of the people, who issue their commands to him through Congress, whence does he derive the constitutional power to create new States, to
remodel old ones, to dictate organic laws, to fix the
qualifications of voters, to declare that States are republican and entitled to command Congress to admit
their Representatives. To my mind it is either the
most ignorant and shallow mistake of his duties, or the
most brazen and impudent usurpation of power. It
is claimed for him by some as Commander-in-Chief of
the army and navy. How absurd that a mere executive officer should claim creative powers. Though
Commander-in-Chief by the Constitution, he would
have nothing to command, either by land or water,
until Congress raised both army and navy. Congress
also prescribes the rules and regulations to govern the
army; even that is not left to the Commander-in-Chief.

Though the President is Commander-in-Chief, Congress is his commander; and, God willing, he shall
obey. . . .

There are several good reasons for the passage of
this bill. In the first place, it is just. I am now con-
fining my argument to negro suffrage in the rebel
States. Have not loyal black quite as good a right to

choose rulers and make laws as rebel whites? In the second place, it is a necessity in order to protect the loyal white men in the seceded States. With them the blacks would act in a body; and it is believed then, in each of said States, except one, the two united would form a majority, control the States, and protect themselves. Now they are the victims of daily murder. They must suffer constant persecution, or be exiled.

Another good reason is that it would insure the ascendency of the Union party. "Do you avow the party purpose?" exclaims some horror-stricken demagogue. I do. For I believe, on my conscience, that on the continued ascendency of that party depends the safety of this great nation. If impartial suffrage is excluded in the rebel States, then every one of them is sure to send a solid rebel representation to Congress, and cast a solid rebel electoral vote. They, with their kindred Copperheads of the North, would always elect the President and control Congress. While Slavery sat upon her defiant throne, and insulted and intimidated the trembling North, the South frequently divided on questions of policy between Whigs and Democrats, and gave victory alternately to the sections. Now, you must divide them between loyalists, without regard to color, and disloyalists, or you will be the perpetual vassals of the free trade, irritated, revengeful South. For these, among other reasons, I am for negro suffrage in every rebel State. If it be just, it should not be denied; if it be necessary, it should be adopted; if it be a punishment to traitors, they deserve it.

Dallas, George M., an American diplomatist and orator, born in Philadelphia, July 10, 1792; died there, Dec. 31, 1864. He studied law with his father, who was Secretary of the Treasury under Madison, and was for a time private secretary to Gallatin during his mission to Russia. In 1829 he was Attorney-General for Philadelphia, and of the State, 1833-35. He sat in the United States Senate, 1831-33, and was minister to Russia, 1837-39. Dallas was Vice-President during the administration of Polk, and minister to England, 1856-61. Upon his recall in the latter year he retired to private life. His oratory was polished and well considered in its cast, his speeches and addresses exhibiting the impress of the cultured man of affairs.

EULOGY ON ANDREW JACKSON.

DELIVERED AT PHILADELPHIA, JUNE 26, 1845.

FELLOW CITIZENS AND FRIENDS,—The sorrows of a nation on the loss of a great and good man are alike confirmed and assuaged by recurring to the virtues and services which endeared him. While funeral solemnities such as are now in progress attest the pervading regrets of communities, and swelling tears betray the anguish of individual friendship; while the muffled drum, the shrouded ensign, and the silent march of mingled processions of citizens and soldiery address their impressive force to the hearts of all, it is well to seek solace in remembrances which must brighten forever the annals of our country, and which add more to the list of names whose mere utterance exalts the pride and strengthens the foundations of patriotism.

At the epoch when, in September, 1774, the delegates of eleven colonies assembled at our Carpenters' Hall before the first gun was fired at Lexington in the cause of western liberty, or Washington was yet hailed as "General and Commander-in-Chief," there could be seen in the wilds of the Waxhaw settlement in South Carolina, on a farm in dangerous proximity to Indian tribes, and clustering with two elder brothers around a widowed mother, a boy about eight years of age in whose veins coursed the same gallant blood that shortly after gushed from the wounds of Montgomery into the trenches of Quebec: that boy, molded in the spirit of those stern times, clinging with his whole soul to the American people, ripened into athletic manhood, enfeebled by toil, by disease, and by age—is just now dead; and you have invited me to pronounce over his yet loose grave the tribute of your affectionate gratitude and veneration; to soothe you by reminding you of the attributes and exploits of one who lived through all your heroic history and was himself an inseparable part of it; who was born on your soil when in fact it was a mere margin of eastern coast, and had sunk into it when a continent; who knew you when but two millions of scattered, weak, dependent, and disquieted provincialists, and yet saw you, ere he ceased to know you, an immense, united, powerful, and peaceful nation! It is impossible on the present occasion and with short notice to do justice to a task so protracted, complicate, and ennobling; but there are incidents and sentiments connected with the character and career of Andrew Jackson with which his countrymen unanimously sympathize, and which his public obsequies seem as appropriately as irresistibly to call into expression.

The stripling orphan, while mourning over the loss of kindred, smarting under wounds and imprisonment, and hourly witnessing some new cruelty committed upon friends and neighbors, imbibed during the storms of our revolution a deep, uncompromising, almost fierce love of country that never lost its sway over his actions. It became to him an impulse as instinctive and irrepressible as breathing, and cannot but be regarded by those who trace his eventful existence as the master-passion of his nature. He passed through the war of 1776, in all but that too youthful for his trials; nor was there ever a moment in his after-being when this devotion can be said to have waned or slumbered in his breast.

Such a trait, so pure, so ardent, so unvarying—as fresh three weeks ago as seventy years before—as prompt and eager amid the frosts of age as when in the spring of life it first kindled at the voice of Washington—invokes, now that the door of his sepulchre is closed, undissembled and undissenting praise. It is this quality of moral excellence which forms the basis of his fame as it was the stimulant to every achievement.

From his fight under Davie with Bryan's regiment of Tories in 1780, when scarcely thirteen years of age, down to the close of his remarkable campaign in Florida when fifty-two, and thenceforward through all the diplomatic conflicts with foreign powers, it shone with steady intensity.

The peace of 1783 found him the only survivor of

his family; left as it were alone to face the snares of the world uneducated and still a boy. His small patrimony melted away before he could check the reckless and prodigal habits to which he had been trained by eight years of wild and desperate strife. There was no one to counsel or to guide him; no one to inculcate lessons of prudence; no one to lead him into the paths of useful industry and of restored tranquillity—but Jackson wanted no one.

At this, perhaps the most critical period of his life, the " iron will " subsequently attributed to his treatment of others was nobly exercised in governing himself. Energetically entering upon the study of the law, the native force of his intellect enabled him, soon after attaining his majority, not merely to preserve his personal independence but to carve his way to recognized distinction. The sphere of his professional practice, the western district of North Carolina, now the State of Tennessee, exacted labors and teemed with dangers such only as a resolution like this could encounter and surmount.

Infested with enraged Cherokees and Choctaws, its wilderness of two hundred miles, crossed and recrossed by the undaunted public solicitor more than twenty times, inured him to fatigue, to the sense of life constantly in peril, and to attacks and artifices of savage enemies whom he was destined signally to subdue and disperse.

It cannot be necessary to pursue these details further; no doubt it will be recollected that after aiding to form a constitution for the State he has made illustrious General Jackson at the age of thirty became her

5

first and only representative in Congress, was almost immediately transferred in November, 1797, to the Senate of the United States, and, unwilling to prolong his legislative services, became a judge of the Supreme Court of Tennessee.

In all these elevated stations, and especially in the last, his sagacious mind, directed by motives at once pure and lofty and sustained by a spirit of unconquerable firmness, has left monuments of practical wisdom and usefulness in maintaining the rights and ameliorating the condition of his countrymen which time cannot efface.

When the prolonged aggressions of Great Britain upon the maritime rights, commerce, and honor of America, prompted, in 1812, a declaration of hostilities, our hero, though watchful of events and keenly alive to their bearing, had retired from public activity and was engaged in the calm pursuits of agricultural life. That signal sounded with welcome in his seclusion and summoned him to a deathless renown. It came to his quick ear like a long-wished-for permit to avenge the wrongs and re-establish the sullied name of those for whom he was ever ready to sacrifice without stint his repose, his fortune, and his blood.

The warcry of his country scarcely vibrated on the breeze ere he echoed it back as a music with which every chord of his soul was in unison. In less than a week, leaving his plough in its yet opening furrow and his ripe harvest drooping for the sickle, he stood equipped and eager, in front of two thousand five hundred volunteers, awaiting orders from the chief executive.

I must not, I dare not, quit the singleness of my

subject to indulge in reminiscences but partially connected with it, however alluring. Yet had the great and generous champion whom we lament a host of associates, competitors with him in the proud struggle of which would risk most, suffer most, and achieve most, in exemplifying the prowess, securing the safety, and exalting the reputation of their country. That, indeed, may be considered as in itself an ample eulogium upon human merit which depicts him as in the van of a roll emblazoned by such names as Scott, Harrison, Brown, Shelby, Johnson, Gaines, Ripley, Hull, Decatur, Perry, and McDonough.

Most of these have gone to graves over which are blooming in unfading verdure the laurels our gratitude planted. None of them can present to posterity a title to immortal honor more conclusive than that involved in their having shared with Jackson the glories of 1812.

There are some fields of public service from which ordinary patriotism not unusually recoils, and of this kind is military action against the comparatively weak yet fierce and wily tribes of savages still occupying parts of their original domain on our continent. Unregulated by the principles of civilized warfare, Indian campaigns and conflicts are accompanied by constant scenes of revolting and unnecessary cruelty. Neither age nor sex nor condition is spared; havoc and destruction are the only ends at which the tomahawk, once brandished, can be stayed.

In exact proportion, however, to the horrors of such a system is the necessity of perfecting those of our people exposed to it by the most prompt and decisive resorts. When, in the midst of the great struggle

with a European monarchy, the frontiers of Georgia
and Tennessee were suddenly assailed by ferocious
Creeks, all eyes turned, appealing with confidence for
security, to him who was known to the foe themselves
by the descriptive designations of "Long Arrow" and
"Sharp Knife." No one, indeed, exhibited in higher
perfection the two qualities essential to such a contest—sagacity and courage.

The sagacity of General Jackson was the admiration
of the sophist and the wonder of the savage; it un-
ravelled the meshes of both without the slightest seeming effort. Piercing through every subtlety or stratagem it attained the truth with electrical rapidity. It
detected at a glance the toils of an adversary and dis-
cerned the mode by which these toils could best be
baffled.

His courage was equally finished and faultless; quick
but cool; easily aroused but never boisterous; concentrated, enduring and manly. No enemy could intimi-
date, no dangers fright him; no surprise shook his presence of mind as no emergency transcended his self-
control. The red braves of the wilderness confessed
that in these, their highest virtues, General Jackson
equalled the most celebrated of their chiefs. Invoked
to the rescue, he roused from a bed of suffering and
debility among the terrified fugitives, addressing them
with brief but animating exhortation: "Your frontier is threatened with invasion by the savage foe. Already are they marching to your borders with their
scalping-knives unsheathed to butcher your women and
children. Time is not to be lost. We must hasten to
the frontier or we shall find it drenched with the blood

of our citizens. The health of your general is restored; he will command in person."

It was the progress of this exhibition in regions at once desolated and unproductive, that this patient and persevering fortitude overcame obstacles of appalling magnitude; and here it was that, with touching kindness, when suffering the cravings of famine, he offered to divide with one of his own soldiers the handful of acorns he had secretly hoarded! The three victories of Talledega, Emuckfaw and Enotochopco, purchased with incredible fatigue, exposure, and loss of life, are not only to be valued in reference to the population and territory they pacified and redeemed, but as having disclosed, just in time for the crises of the main war, the transcendent ability and fitness of him who was destined to stamp its close with an exploit of unrivalled heroism and consummate generalship.

Shall I abruptly recall the battle of New Orleans?—recall, did I say? Is it ever absent from the memory of an American? Mingled indissolubly with the thought of country it springs to mind as Thermopylæ or Marathon when Greece is named. He who gave that battle with all its splendid preliminaries and results to our chronicles of national valor may cease to be mortal but can never cease to be renowned. He may have a grave, but, like the Father of his Country, he can want no monument but posterity.

The judgment of the world has been irreversibly passed upon that extraordinary achievement of our republican soldier. Analyzed in all its plans, its means, its motives, and its execution; the genius that conceived, the patriotism that impelled, the boldness that never backed, nor paused, nor counted; the skill which trebled every resource, the activity that was everywhere, the end that accomplished everything. It was a masterpiece of work which Cæsar, William Tell, Napoleon, and Washington, could unite in applauding. Even the vanquished, soothed by the magnanimity of their victor, have since laid the tribute of their admiration at his feet. For that battle, in itself and alone, as now passed into the imperishable records of history an exhaustless fund of moral property, our descendants in distant ages will teach their children, as they imbibe heroism from illustration and example, to murmur their blessings.

I have dwelt, fellow citizens, with perhaps unnecessary length upon the martial merits of the deceased. I have done so because these merits are incontestable, and form, apart from every other consideration, an overwhelming claim to the veneration and gratitude we are now displaying. To me personally, as you all know, it would be alike consistent and natural to go much farther; but, entertainig a real deference for the sentiments of others, I should be unable to pardon myself if on an occasion so peculiarly solemn a single word fell from my lips which did not chime with the tone of every bosom present. The time has not come, and among a free, fearless, and frank people such as you are, it may possibly never come, when the civic characteristics of Jackson during his chief magistracy of eight years can be other than topics of sincere differences of opinion.

Springing, however, directly from what I have considered as the great root of his public services is at least one branch of his executive policy and action that need not be avoided. If as a Revolutionary lad he clung to the cause of the colonists; if as a soldier he knew no shrinking from his flag; as a president of these States he stood without budging on the rock of their union. It seemed as if, to him, that was hallowed ground, ungenial to the weeds of party, identical indeed with country. Count the cost of this confederacy, and he was scornfully silent; speak of disregarding her laws, and his remonstrances were vehement; move but a hair's breadth to end the compact and he was in arms. On this vast concern, involving, directly or remotely, all the precious objects of American civilization, his zeal was as uncompromising, perhaps as unrefining and undiscriminating, as his convictions were profound. The extent of our obligation to him in regard to it cannot well be exaggerated. Possessing in his high office the opportunity, he gave to his purpose an impetus and an emphasis that will keep forever ringing in the ears of his successors—" The Union must and shall be preserved !"

Such was the hero we mourn. With a constitution undermined by privations incident to his military labors, and a frame shattered by diseases, he had retired to the seclusion of the Hermitage, long and patiently awaiting the only and final relief from suffering. It came to him on the evening of the 8th instant, in the centre of his home's affectionate circle, while his great mind was calm and unclouded and when his heart was prepared to welcome its dilatory messenger. Yes! Yes! he on whom for half a century his country gazed as upon a tower of strength;

on whom she never called for succor against the desolating savage without being answered by a rushing
shout of " Onward to the rescue!"—who anticipated
her invading foes by destroying them ere their foot-
prints on her soil were cold—he, the iron warrior, the
reproachless patriot, has ceased to be mortal, has
willingly made his single surrender—*the* surrender—
the surrender of his soul to its Almighty claimant!

It may almost be said that General Jackson was constituted of two natures, so admirably and so distinctly
were his qualities adapted to their respective spheres
of action. I have portrayed hurriedly and crudely his
public character—let us for an instant see him, on one
or two points at least, in the other aspect, and perhaps
we may thence catch the secret of his sublime and
beautiful death. The rugged exterior which rough
wars in our early western settlements would naturally
impart was smoothed and polished in him by a spirit of
benevolence deeply seated in his temperament. In social intercourse, though always earnest, rapid, impressive, and upright, his friendship was marked by boundless confidence and generosity; while in domestic life
a winning gentleness seemed to spread from the recesses of his heart over the whole man filling the
scenes around him with smiles of serenity and joy.
No husband loved more ardently, more faithfully, more
unchangeably; no parent could surpass the self-sacri-
ficing kindness with which he reared and cherished his
adopted children; no master could be more certain of
reciprocated fondness than he was, when, as expiring,
he breathed the hope of hereafter meeting in the heav-
en to which he was hastening the servants of his

household, " as well as black as white." The truthfulness of this picture is attested by all who were admitted to the sanctuary of his home, precincts too sacred, even on an occasion equally sacred, for more than this brief intrusion.

But there was a crowning characteristic, from adverting to which I must not shrink, though in the presence in which I stand. General Jackson was fervently, unaffectedly, and submissively pious! Wherever he might be and whatever his absorbing pursuit—wading heavily through the swamps of Florida on the tracks of Hillishago; speeding with the swoop of an eagle to grapple the invader, Pakenham; careering at the head of his victorious legions through throngs of admiring countrymen; in the halls of the executive mansion; or at his hearth in the Hermitage; there and then, everywhere and always, though not ostensible and never obtrusive, his faith was with him. But it was most closely and conspicuously with him as dissolution approached; it was with him to brighten the rays of his mind, to cheer the throbs of his heart, to take the sting from his latest pang, and to give melody to his last farewell. The dying hour of Jackson bears triumphant testimony to the Christian's hope.

" Such was the hero ; such was the man we mourn ! "

Come, then, my countrymen! let us, as it were, gather round the depository of his remains! From those who knew him as it has been my lot to know him the frequent tear of cherished and proud remembrance must fall. To all of us it will be some relief to join in the simple and sacred sentiment of public gratitude.

> " How sleep the brave who sink to rest,
> By all their country's honors blest !
> When Spring, with dewy fingers cold,
> Returns to seek their hallowed mold,
> She there shall dress a sweeter sod
> Than fancy's feet have ever trod ;
> By fairy forms their dirge is sung—
> By hands unseen their knell is rung ;—
> There honor comes, a pilgrim gray,
> To bless the turf that wraps their clay ;
> And freedom shall awhile repair
> To dwell a weeping hermit there ! "

Houston, Samuel, a noted American soldier and politician, born near Lexington, Va., March 2, 1793; died at Huntsville, Texas, July 25, 1863. His youth was mainly spent among the Cherokee Indians, and at twenty he entered the army, serving with Jackson against the Creek Indians. Later he studied law at Nashville, represented Tennessee in Congress, 1823-27, and was governor of Tennessee for the next two years. Subsequently he settled in Texas, and when it was denied admission to the Mexican republic, Houston was appointed commander-in-chief of the Texan forces in the ensuing war between Mexico and Texas. Houston succeeded in securing the independence of Texas, and was its President until its annexion to the United States, representing it in the United States Senate for the twelve years following. He was elected governor of Texas in 1859, but resigned from office on account of his strong opposition to secession. Houston's speech on the Nebraska and Kansas Bill is a fair example of the character of his Congressional addresses.

SPEECH OF THE NEBRASKA AND KANSAS BILL.

DELIVERED IN THE UNITED STATES SENATE, MARCH 3, 1857.

MR. PRESIDENT,—I have very little hope that any appeal which I can make for the Indians will do any good. The honorable senator from Indiana [Mr. Pettit] says in substance that God Almighty has condemned them and has made them an inferior race; that there is no use in doing anything for them. With great deference to that senator, for whom I have never cherished any but kindly feelings, I must be permitted to dissent from his opinions. He says they are not civilized and they are not homogeneous, and cannot be so, with the white race. They cannot be civilized! No! Sir, it is idle to tell me that. We have Indians on our western borders whose civilization is not inferior to our own.

It is within the recollection of gentlemen here that, more than twenty years ago, President Ross, one of them, held a correspondence upon the rights of the Indians to the Cherokee country which they possessed east of the Mississippi, and maintained himself in the controversy with great credit and ability; and the triumph of Mr. Adams, if it was one, was much less than he had obtained over the diplomatist of Spain [Mr. Don Onis] in relation to the occupation of Florida by General Jackson. The senator from Indiana says that in ancient times Moses received a command to go and drive the Canaanites and Moabites out of the land of Canaan, and that Joshua subsequently made the experiment of incorporating one tribe of the heathen with the Israelites, but it finally had to be killed off. Therefore, the senator concludes, the Cherokees cannot be civilized. There may have been something statesmanlike in the policy, but I do not discover the morality of it. I will say, however, that there is no analogy between the two cases. The people of Judea who were killed or exterminated were idolaters, and the object was to keep the people of Israel free from the taint of idols and idolatry under the command of Providence, and therefore the extermination in his dispensation became necessary. But the Cherokees never have been idolaters, neither have the Creeks, nor the Choctaws, nor the Chickasaws. They believe in one Great Spirit —in God—the white man's God. They believe in his Son Jesus Christ, and his atonement and propitiation for the sins of men. They believe in the sanctifying efficacy of the Holy Ghost. They bow at the Christian's altar and they believe the Sacred Volume.

Sir, you may drive these people away and give their lands to the white man; but let it not be done upon the justification of the Scriptures. They have well-organized societies; they have villages and towns; they have their State-houses and their capitols; they have females and men who would grace the drawing-rooms or salons of Washington; they have a well-organized judiciary, a trial by jury, and the writ of habeas corpus.

These are the people for whom I demand justice in the organization of these Territories. They are men of education. They have more than one hundred native preachers in those tribes, as I have heard. They have their colleges, as I remarked in my former address to the Senate on this subject. They become associated in friendship with our young men in the various institutions in the United States; and they are prepared to be incorporated upon equal terms with us. But even if they were wild Indians, untutored, when you deprive them of what would give them knowledge and discourage them from making an effort to become civilized and social beings, how can you expect them to be otherwise than savage?

When you undertake to tame wild horses do you turn them from you and drive them into the desert, or do you take care of them and treat them with humanity? These Indians are not inferior, intellectually, to white men. John Ridge was not inferior in point of genius to John Randolph. His father, in point of native intellect, was not inferior to any man. Look at their social condition. in the nations to which I have alluded. Look at the Chickasaws who remain in the State of Mississippi. Even among white men, with all their prejudices against the Indians, with their transcendent genius and accomplishments, they have been elected to the legislature. Whenever they have had an opportunity they have shown that they are not inferior to white men, either in sense or sensibility.

But the honorable senator from Iowa [Mr. Dodge] characterizes the remarks which I made in reference to the Indians as arising from a feeling of " sickly sentimentality." Sir, it is a sickly sentimentality that was implanted in me when I was young, and it has grown up with me. The Indian has a sense of justice, truth, and honor that should find a responsive chord in every heart. If the Indians on the frontier are barbarous, or if they are cannibals, and eat each other, who are to blame for it? They are robbed of the means of sustenance; and with hundreds and thousands of them starving on the frontier, hunger may prompt to such acts to prevent their perishing. We shall never become cannibals in connection with the Indians; but we do worse than that. We rob them, first of their native dignity and character; we rob them next of what the government appropriates for them. If we do not do it in this hall, men are invested with power and authority, who, officiating as agents or traders, rob them of everything which is designed for them. Not less than one hundred millions of dollars, I learn from statistics, since the adoption of this government, have been appropriated by Congress for purposes of justice and benevolence toward the Indians; but I am satisfied that they have never realized fifteen millions beneficially. They are too remote from the seat of government for their real condition to be understood here; and if the government intends liberality or justice toward them it is often diverted from the intended object and consumed by speculators.

I am a friend to the Indian upon the principle that I am a friend to justice. We are not bound to make them promises; but if a promise be made to an Indian it ought to be regarded as sacredly as if it were made to a white man. If we treat them as tribes, recognize them, send commissioners to form treaties and exchange ratifications with them, and the treaties are negotiated, accepted, ratified, and exchanged—having met with the approval of the Senate—I think they may be called compacts; and how are these compacts regarded? Just as we choose to construe them at the time, without any reference to the wishes of the Indians or whether we do them kindness or justice in the operation or not. We are often prompted to their ratification by persons interested; and we lend ourselves unintentionally to an unjust act of oppression upon the Indians by men who go and get their signatures to a treaty. The Indian's mark is made; the employees of the government certify or witness it; and the Indians do not understand it for they do not know what is written. These are some of the circumstances connected with the Indians.

Gentlemen have spoken here of voting millions to build ships, and placing the army and navy at the disposition of the President in the event that England act inconsistently with treaty stipulations. This is done because, if England violates a treaty with us, our national honor is injured. Now I should like to know if it becomes us to violate a treaty made with the Indians when we please, regardless of every principle of truth and honor? We should be careful if it were with a power able to war with us; and it argues a degree of infinite meanness and indescribable degradation on our part to act differently with the Indians, who confide in our honor and justice, and who call the President their Great Father and confide in him. Mr. President, it is in the power of the Congress of the United States to do some justice to the Indians by giving them a government of their own, and encouraging them in their organization and improvement by inviting their delegates to a place on the floor of the Senate and House of Representatives. If you will not do it, the sin will lie at your door, and Providence, in his own way, mysterious and incomprehensible to us though it is, will accomplish all his purposes, and may at some day avenge the wrongs of the Indians upon our nation. As a people we can save them; and the sooner the great work is begun, the sooner will humanity have cause to rejoice in its accomplishment.

Mr. President, I shall say but little more. My address may have been desultory. It embraces many subjects which it would be very hard to keep in entire order. We have, in the first place, the extensive territory; then we have the considerations due to the

Indians; and then we have the proposed repeal of the Missouri Compromise, which seems to require the most explanation and to be the main point in the controversy. The great principle involved in that repeal is non-intervention, which, we are told, is to be of no practical benefit if the Compromise is repealed. It can have no effect but to keep up agitation. Sir, the friends who have survived the distinguished men who took prominent parts in the drama of the Compromise of 1850 ought to feel gratified that those men are not capable of participating in the events of to-day, but that they were permitted, after they had accomplished their labors and seen their country in peace, to leave the world, as Simeon did, with the exclamation: "Lord, now lettest thou thy servant depart in peace, for mine eyes have seen thy salvation." They departed in peace, and they left their country in peace. They felt, as they were about to be gathered to the tombs of their fathers, that the country they had loved so well and which had honored them—that country upon whose fame and name their doings had shed a bright lustre which shines abroad throughout all Christendom—was reposing in peace and happiness.

What would their emotions be if they could now be present and see an effort made, if not so designed, to undo all their work and to tear asunder the cords that they had bound around the hearts of their countrymen? They have departed. The nation felt the wound; and we see the memorials of woe still in this chamber. The proud symbol (the eagle) above your head remains enshrouded in black, as if it deplored the misfortune which had fallen upon us, or as a fearful

6

omen of future calamities which await our nation in the event this bill should become a law.

Above it I behold the majestic figure of Washington, whose presence must ever inspire patriotic emotions and command the admiration and love of every American heart. By these associations I adjure you to regard the contract once made to harmonize and preserve this Union. Maintain the Missouri Compromise! Stir not up agitation. Give us peace.

This much I was bound to declare, in behalf of my country, as I believe, and I know in behalf of my constituents. In the discharge of my duty I have acted fearlessly. The events of the future are left in the hands of a wise Providence; and, in my opinion, upon the decision which we make upon this question must depend union or disunion.

Hoar, George F., an eminent American statesman and orator, born at Concord, Mass., August 20, 1826. He studied law and entered upon his profession at Worcester, Mass., and his earliest appearance in politics was as chairman of the Free Soil party committee in 1849. From this period he has been a conspicuous member of the Republican party. He sat in the Massachusetts legislature in house and senate successively, from 1852 to 1869, when he was elected to congress. After serving as representative until 1877 he became a member of the national senate, where he still remains. He has often exhibited much independence of party in his political action, and in his latest years has been especially prominent in his opposition to national expansion. He is one of the readiest of speakers in debate, while his more formal speeches and orations are polished and scholarly in style, and forceful and eloquent in substance and delivery. His eulogy of President McKinley is the most notable of his later orations.

ADDRESS AT THE BANQUET OF THE NEW ENGLAND SOCIETY.

DELIVERED DECEMBER 22, 1898, AT CHARLESTON, SOUTH CAROLINA.

I NEED not assure this brilliant company how deeply I am impressed by the significance of this occasion. I am not vain enough to find in it anything of personal compliment. I like better to believe that the ties of common history, of common faith, of common citizenship, and inseparable destiny, are drawing our two sister States together again. If cordial friendship, if warm affection (to use no stronger term), can ever exist between two communities they should exist between Massachusetts and South Carolina. They were both of the " Old Thirteen." They were alike in the circumstances of their origin. Both were settled by those noble fugitives who brought the torch of liberty across the sea, when liberty was without other refuge on the face of the earth. The English Pilgrims and Puritans founded Massachusetts, to be followed soon after by the Huguenot exiles who fled from the tyranny of King Louis XIV., after the revocation of the edict of Nantes. Scotch Presbyterianism founded Carolina, to be followed soon after by the French exiles fleeing from the same oppression. Everywhere in New England are traces of the footsteps of this gentle, delightful, and chivalrous race, All over our six States to-day many an honored grave, many a stirring tradition bear witness to the kinship between our early settlers and the settlers of South Carolina. Faneuil Hall, in Boston, which we love to call the " Cradle of Liberty," attests the munificence and bears the name of an illustrious Huguenot.

These French exiles lent their grace and romance to our history also. Their settlements were like clusters of magnolias in some warm valley in our bleak New England.

We are, all of us, in Massachusetts, reading again the story of the voyage of the "Mayflower," written by William Bradford. As you have heard, that precious manuscript has lately been restored to us by the kindness of His Grace the Lord Bishop of London. It is in the eyes of the children of the Pilgrims the most precious manuscript on earth. If there be anything to match the pathos of that terrible voyage it is found in the story of Judith Manigault, the French Huguenot exile, of her nine months' voyage from England to South Carolina. Her name, I am told, has been honored here in every generation since.

If there be a single lesson which the people of this country have learned from their wonderful and crowded history it is that the North and South are indispensable to each other. They are the blades of mighty shears, worthless apart, but when bound by an indissoluble union, powerful, irresistible, and terrible as the shears of fate; like the shears of Atropos, severing every thread and tangled web of evil, cutting out for humanity its beautiful garments of liberty and light from the cloth her dread sisters spin and weave.

I always delight to think, as I know the people of South Carolina delight to think, of these States of ours, not as mere aggregations of individuals, but as beautiful personalities, moral beings endowed with moral characters, capable of faith, of hope, of memory, of pride, of sorrow, and of joy, of courage, of heroism, of honor, and of shame. Certainly this is true of them. Their power and glory, their rightful place in history, depended on these things, and not on numbers or extent of territory.

It is this that justifies the arrangement of the constitution of the United States for equal representation of States in the upper legislative chamber and explains its admirable success.

The separate entity and the absolute freedom, except for the necessary restraints of the constitution

of our different States, is the cause alike of the greatness and the security of the country.

The words Switzerland, France, England, Rome,
Athens, Massachusetts, South Carolina, Virginia,
America, convey to your mind a distinct and individual meaning and suggest an image of distinct moral
quality and moral being as clearly as do the words
Washington, Wellington, or Napoleon. I believe it
is, and I thank God that I believe it is, something much
higher than the average of the qualities of the men
who make it up. We think of Switzerland as something better than the individual Swiss, and of France
as something better than the individual Frenchman,
and of America as something better than the individual American. In great and heroic individual actions we often seem to feel that it is the country, of
which the man is but the instrument, that gives expression to its quality in doing the deed.

It was Switzerland who gathered into her breast
at Sempach the sheaf of fatal Austrian spears. It
was the hereditary spirit of New England that gave
the word of command by the voice of Buttrick, at
Concord, and was in the bosom of Parker at Lexington. It was South Carolina whose lightning stroke
smote the invader by the arm of Marion and whose
wisdom guided the framers of the constitution
through the lips of Rutledge and Gadsden and Pinckney.

The citizen on great occasions knows and obeys
the voice of his country as he knows and obeys an individual voice, whether it appeal to a base or ignoble
or to a generous or noble passion. " Sons of France,

awake to glory," told the French youth what was the
dominant passion in the bosom of France and it awoke
a corresponding sentiment in his own. Under its
spell he marched through Europe and overthrew her
kingdoms and empires and felt in Egypt that forty
centuries were looking down on him from the Pyramids. But at last, one June morning in Trafalgar Bay,
there was another utterance, more quiet in its tone, but
speaking also with a personal and individual voice,
" England expects every man to do his duty."

At the sight of Nelson's immortal signal duty-lov-
ing England and glory-loving France met as they
have met on many an historic battle-field before and
since, and the lover of duty proved the stronger. The
England that expected every man to do his duty was
as real a being to the humblest sailor in Nelson's fleet
as the mother that bore him.

The title of our American States to their equality
under this admirable arrangement depends not on
area or upon numbers but upon character and upon
personality. Fancy a league or a confederacy in
which Athens or Sparta were united with Persia or
Babylon or Nineveh and their political power were to
be reckoned in proportion to their numbers or their
size.

I have sometimes fancied South Carolina and
Massachusetts, those two illustrious and heroic sisters,
instead of sitting apart, one under her palm trees and
the other under her pines, one with the hot gales
from the tropics fanning her brow and the other on
the granite rocks by her ice-bound shores, meeting
together and comparing notes and stories as sisters

born of the same mother compare notes and stories
after a long separation. How the old estrangements,
born of ignorance of each other, would have melted
away.

Does it ever occur to you that the greatest single
tribute ever paid to Daniel Webster was paid by Mr.
Calhoun? And the greatest single tribute ever paid
to Mr. Calhoun was paid by Mr. Webster?

I do not believe that among the compliments or
marks of honor which attended the illustrious career
of Daniel Webster there is one that he would have
valued so much as that which his great friend, his
great rival and antagonist, paid him from his dying
bed.

" Mr. Webster," said Mr. Calhoun, " has as high
a standard of truth as any statesman whom I have met
in debate. Convince him and he cannot reply; he is
silent; he cannot look truth in the face and oppose it
by argument."

There was never, I suppose, paid to John C. Calhoun during his illustrious life any other tribute of
honor he would have valued so highly as that which
was paid him after his death by his friend, his rival,
and antagonist, Daniel Webster.

" Mr. Calhoun," said Mr. Webster, " had the basis,
the indispensable basis, of all high character; and that
was unspotted integrity—unimpeached honor and
character. If he had aspirations they were high and
honorable and noble. There was nothing grovelling or
low or meanly selfish that came near the head or the
heart of Mr. Calhoun. Firm in his purpose, perfectly
patriotic and honest, as I was sure he was, in the prin-

BENJAMIN HARRISON.

ciples he espoused and in the measures he defended, aside from that large regard for that species of distinction that conducted him to eminent stations for the benefit of the republic, I do not believe he had a selfish motive or a selfish feeling. However he may have differed from others of us in his political opinions or his political principles, those opinions and those principles will now descend to posterity and under the sanction of a great name. He has lived long enough, he has done enough, and he has done it so well, so successfully, so honorably, as to connect himself for all time with the records of the country. He is now an historical character. Those of us who have known him here will find that he has left upon our minds, and upon our hearts, a strong and lasting impression of his person, his character, and his public performances, which, while we live, will never be obliterated. We shall hereafter, I am sure, indulge in it as a grateful recollection that we have lived in his age, that we have been his contemporaries, that we have seen him and known him. We shall delight to speak of him to those who are rising up to fill our places. And when the time shall come that we ourselves shall go, one after another, in succession, to our graves, we shall carry with us a deep sense of his genius and character, his honor and integrity, his amiable deportment in private life, and the purity of his exalted patriotism."

Just think for a moment what this means. If any man ever lived who was not merely the representative but the embodiment of the thought, opinion, principles, character, quality, intellectual and moral, of the people of South Carolina for the forty years from 1810 until his death, it was John C. Calhoun. If any man ever lived who not merely was the representative, but the embodiment of the thought, opinion, principles, character, quality, intellectual and moral, of the people of Massachusetts, it was Daniel Webster. Now if, after forty years of rivalry, of conflict, of antagonism, these two statesmen of ours, most widely differing in opinions on public questions, who never met but to exchange a blow, the sparks from the encounter of whose mighty swords kindled the fires which spread over the continent, thought thus of one another, is it not likely that if the States they represented could have met with the same intimacy, with the same knowledge and companionship during all these years, they, too, would have understood, and understanding would have loved each other?

I should like to have had a chance to hearken to their talk. Why, their gossip would almost make up the history of liberty! How they would boast to each other, as sisters do, of their children, their beautiful and brave! How many memories they would find in common! How the warm Scotch-Irish blood would stir in their veins! How the Puritan and the Presbyterian blood would quicken their pulses as they recounted the old struggles for freedom to worship God! What stories they would have to tell each other of the day of the terrible knell from the bell of the old tower of St. Germain de L'Auxerrois, when the edict of Nantes was revoked and sounded its alarm to the Huguenot exiles who found refuge,

some in South Carolina and some in Massachusetts!
You have heard of James Bowdoin, of Paul Revere,
and Peter Faneuil, and Andrew Sigourney. These
men brought to the darkened and gloomy mind of the
Puritan the sunshine of beautiful France, which South
Carolina did not need. They taught our Puritans the
much needed lesson that there was something other
than the snare of Satan in the song of a bird or
the fragrance of a flower.

The boys and girls of South Carolina and the boys
and girls of Massachusetts went to the same school
in the old days. Their schoolmasters were tyranny
and poverty and exile and starvation. They heard
the wild music of the wolves' howl and the savages'
war-cry. They crossed the Atlantic in midwinter,
when

> " Winds blew and waters rolled,
>   Strength to the brave, and power, and Deity."

They learned in that school little of the grace or the
luxury of life. But they learned how to build States
and how to fight tyrants.

They would have found much, these two sisters, to
talk about of a later time. South Carolina would
have talked of her boy Christopher Gadsden, who
George Bancroft said was like a mountain torrent
dashing on an overshot wheel. And Massachusetts
would try to trump the trick with James Otis, that
flame of fire, who said he seemed to hear the prophetic
song of the Sybil chanting the springtime of the new
empire.

They might dispute a little as to which of these two

sons of theirs was the greater. I do not know how that dispute could be settled unless by Otis's own opinion. He said that " Massachusetts sounded the trumpet. But it was owing to South Carolina that it was assented to. Had it not been for South Carolina no Congress would have been appointed. She was all alive and felt at every pore." So perhaps we will accept the verdict of the Massachusetts historian, George Bancroft. He said that " When we count those who above all others contributed to the great result of the Union, we are to name the inspired madman, James Otis, and the unwavering lover of his country, Christopher Gadsden."

It is the same Massachusetts historian, George Bancroft, who says that " the public men of South Carolina were ever ruled by their sense of honor, and felt a stain upon it as a wound."

" Did you ever hear how those wicked boys of mine threw the tea into the harbor," Massachusetts would say; " Oh, yes," South Carolina would answer, " but not one of mine was willing to touch it. So we let it all perish in a cellar."

Certainly these two States liked each other pretty well when Josiah Quincy came down here in 1773 to see Rutledge and Pinckney and Gadsden to concert plans for the coming rebellion. King George never interfered very much with you. But you could not stand the Boston port bill any more than we could.

There is one thing in which Massachusetts must yield the palm, and that is the courage to face an earthquake, that terrible ordeal in the face of which the bravest manhood goes to pieces, and which your

people met a few years ago with a courage and stead-
fastness which commanded the admiration of all mankind.

If this company had gathered on this spot one
hundred and twenty years ago to-night the toast
would have been that which no gathering at Charleston in those days failed to drink—" The Unanimous
Twenty-six, who would not rescind the Massachusetts
circular."

" The royal governor of South Carolina had invited its assembly to treat the letters of the Massachusetts ' with the contempt they deserved;' a committee, composed of Parsons, Gadsden, Pinckney,
Lloyd, Lynch, Laurens, Rutledge, Eliot, and Dart,
reported them to be ' founded upon undeniable constitutional principles;' and the house, sitting with its
doors locked, unanimously directed its speaker to sig-
nify to that province its entire approbation. The
governor, that same evening, dissolved the assembly
by beat of drums."

Mr. Winthrop compared the death of Calhoun to
the blotting out of the constellation of the Southern
Cross from the sky.

Mr. Calhoun was educated at Yale College, in
New England, where President Dwight predicted
his future greatness in his boyhood. It is one of the
pleasant traditions of my own family that he was a
constant and favorite guest in the house of my grand-
mother, in my mother's childhood, and formed a
friendship with her family which he never forgot.

It is delightful also to remember on this occasion that Mr. Lamar, that most Southern man of Southern men, whose tribute to Mr. Calhoun in this city is among the masterpieces of historical literature, paid a discriminating and most affectionate tribute also to Charles Sumner at the time of his death.

In this matchless eulogy Mr. Lamar disclaims any purpose to honor Mr. Sumner because of his high culture, his eminent scholarship, or varied learning, but he declares his admiration for him because of his high moral qualities and his unquenchable love of liberty. Mr. Lamar adds: " My regret is that I did not obey the impulse often found upon me to go to him and offer him my hand and my heart with it."

Mr. Lamar closes this masterpiece of eulogistic oratory with this significant sentence: " Would that the spirit of the illustrious dead whom we honor to-day could speak to both parties in tones that would reach every home throughout this broad territory,—' My countrymen, know one another, and you will love one another.' "

There is another memorable declaration of Mr. Lamar, whom I am proud to have counted among my friends. In his oration at the unveiling of the statue of Calhoun, at Charleston, he said that the appeal to arms had " led to the indissolubility of the American Union and the universality of American freedom."

Now, can we not learn a lesson also from this most significant fact that this great Southern statesman and orator was alike the eulogist of Calhoun and the eulogist of Sumner?

For myself I believe that whatever estrangements

may have existed in the past, or may linger among us now, are born of ignorance and will be dispelled by knowledge. I believe that of our forty-five States there are no two who, if they could meet in the familiarity of personal intercourse, in the fulness of personal knowledge, would not only cease to entertain any bitterness, or alienation, or distrust, but each would utter to the other the words of the Jewish daughter, in that most exquisite of idylls which has come down to us almost from the beginning of time:

"Entreat me not to leave thee, or to return from following after thee; for whither thou goest, I will go; and where thou lodgest, I will lodge; thy people shall be my people, and thy God my God.

"Where thou diest, will I die, and there will I be buried; the Lord do so to me, and more also, if aught but death part me and thee."

Mr. President, I repeat to-night on Southern soil what I said first in my place in the Senate, and what I repeated in Faneuil Hall, with the full approbation of an enthusiastic and crowded audience, representing the culture and the Puritanism of Massachusetts.

The American people have learned to know as never before the quality of the Southern stock, and to value its noble contribution to the American character; its courage in war, its attachment to home and State, its love of rural life, its capacity for great affection and generous emotion, its aptness for command; above all, its constancy, that virtue above all virtues, without which no people can long be either great or free. After all, the fruit of this vine has a flavor not to be found in other gardens. In the great and magnificent future which is before our country, you are to contribute a large share both of strength and beauty.

The best evidence of our complete reconciliation is that there is no subject that we need to hurry by with our fingers on our lips. The time has come when Americans, north, south, east, and west, may discuss any question of public interest in a friendly and quiet spirit, without recrimination and without heat, each understanding the other, each striving to help the other, as men who are bearing a common burden and looking forward with a common hope. I know that this is the feeling of the people of the North. I think I know that it is the feeling of the people of the South. In our part of the country we have to deal with the great problems of the strife between labor and capital, and of the government of cities where vast masses of men born on foreign soil, of different nationalities and of different races, strangers to American principles, to American ideas, to American history, are gathered together to exercise the unaccustomed functions of self-government in an almost unrestricted liberty. You have to deal with a race problem rendered more difficult still by a still larger difference in the physical and intellectual qualities of the two races whom Providence has brought together.

I should be false to my own manhood if I failed to express my profound regret and sorrow for some occurrences which have taken place recently, both in the North and in the South. I am bound to say that, considering all the circumstances, the Northern community has been the worse offender.

It is well known (or if it be not well known I am willing to make it known) that I look with inexpressible alarm and dread upon the prospect of adding to our population millions of persons dwelling in tropical climes, aliens in race and in religion, either to share in our self-government, or, what is worse still, to set an example to mankind of the subjection of one people to another. We have not yet solved the problem how men of different races can dwell together in the same land in accordance with our principles of republican rule and republican liberty. I am not one of those who despair of the solution of that problem in justice and in freedom. I do not look upon the dark side when I think of the future of our beloved land. I count it the one chief good fortune of my own life that, as I grow older, I look out on the world with hope and not despair. We have made wonderful advances within the lifetime of the youngest of us. While we hear from time to time of occurrences much to be deplored and utterly to be condemned, yet, on the whole, we are advancing quite as rapidly as could be expected to the time when these races will live together on American soil in freedom, in honor, and in peace, every man enjoying his just right wherever the American constitution reigns and wherever the American flag floats—when the influence of intelligence, of courage, of energy, inspired by a lofty patriotism and by a Christian love will have its full and legitimate effect, not through disorder, or force,

7

or lawlessness, but under the silent and sure law by which always the superior leads and the inferior follows. The time has already come when throughout large spaces in our country both races are dwelling together in peace and harmony. I believe that condition of things to be the rule in the South and not to be the exception. We have a right to claim that the country and the South shall be judged by the rule and not the exception.

But we want you to stand by us in our troubles as brethren and as countrymen. We shall have to look, in many perils that are before us in the near future, to the conservatism and wisdom of the South. And if the time shall come when you think we can help you your draft shall be fully honored.

But to-night belongs to the memory of the Pilgrims. The Pilgrim of Plymouth has a character in history distinct from any other. He differed from the Puritan of Salem or Boston in everything but the formula in which his religious faith was expressed. He was gentle, peaceful, tolerant, gracious. There was no intolerance or hatred or bigotry in his little commonwealth. He hanged no witches, he whipped no Quakers, he banished no heretic. His little State existed for seventy-two years, when it was blended with the Puritan Commonwealth of Massachusetts. He enacted the mildest code of laws on the face of the earth. There were but eight capital offences in Plymouth. Sir James Mackintosh held in his hand a list of two hundred and twenty-three when he addressed the House of Commons at the beginning of the present century. He held no foot of land not fairly obtained by honest purchase. He treated the Indian with justice and good faith, setting an example which Vattel, the foremost writer on the law of nations, commends to mankind. In his earliest days his tolerance was an example to Roger Williams himself, who has left on record his gratitude for the generous friendship of Winslow. Governor Bradford's courtesy entertained the Catholic priest, who was his guest, with a fish dinner on Friday. John Robinson, the great leader of the Pilgrims, uttered the world's declaration of religious independence when he told his little flock on the wharf at Delft Haven, as reported by Winslow:

"We are ere long to part asunder and the Lord knoweth whether he should live to see our face again. But, whether the Lord hath appointed it or not, he charged us before God and his blessed angels to follow him no further than he followed Christ; and, if God should reveal anything to us by any other instrument of his, to be as ready to receive it as we were to receive any truth by his ministry, for he was very confident the Lord had more truth and light yet to break out of his Holy Word."

The Pilgrim was a model and an example of a beautiful, simple, and stately courtesy. John Robinson, and Bradford, and Brewster, and Carver, and Winslow differ as much from the dark and haughty Endicott, or the bigoted Cotton Mather as, in the English church, Jeremy Taylor, and George Herbert and Donne, and Vaughn differ from Laud, or Bonner, or Bancroft.

Let us not be misunderstood. I am not myself a descendant from the Pilgrims. Every drop of my blood through every line of descent for three centuries has come from a Puritan ancestor. I am ready to do battle for the name and fame of the Massachusetts Puritan in any field and against any antagonist. Let others, if they like, trace their lineage to Norman pirate or to robber baron. The children of the Puritan are not ashamed of him. The Puritan, as a distinct, vital, and predominant power, lived less than a century in England. He appeared early in the reign of Elizabeth, who came to the throne in 1558, and departed at the restoration of Charles II, in 1660. But in that brief period he was the preserver, aye, the creator of English freedom. By the confession of the historians who most dislike him, it is due to him that there is an English constitution. He created the modern House of Commons. That House, when he took his seat in it, was the feeble and timid instrument of despotism. When he left it, it was what it has ever since been—the strongest, freest, most venerable legislative body the world has ever seen. When he took his seat in it, it was little more than the register of the king's command. When he left it, it was the main depository of the national dignity and the national will. King and minister and prelate who stood in his way he brought to the bar and to the block. In the brief but crowded century he made the name of Englishman the highest title of honor upon the earth. A great historian has said: " The dread of his invincible army was on all the inhabitants of the island. He placed the name of John Milton high on the illustrious roll of the great poets of the world, and the name of Oliver Cromwell highest on the roll of English sovereigns." The historian might have added that the dread of this invincible leader was on all the inhabitants of Europe.

And so, when a son of the Puritans comes to the South, when he visits the home of the Rutledges and the Pinckneys and of John C. Calhoun, if there be any relationship in heroism or among the lovers of constitutional liberty, he feels that he can

" Claim kindred there and have the claim allowed."

The Puritan differs from the Pilgrim as the Hebrew prophet from St. John. Abraham, ready to sacrifice Isaac at the command of God; Jeremiah, uttering his terrible prophecy of the downfall of Judea; Brutus, condemning his son to death; Brutus, slaying his friend for the liberty of Rome; Aristides, going into exile, are his spiritual progenitors, as Stonewall Jackson was of his spiritual kindred. You will find him wherever men are sacrificing life or the delights of life on the altar of duty.

But the Pilgrim is of a gentler and a lovelier nature. He, too, if duty or honor call, is ready for the sacrifice. But his weapon is love and not hate. His spirit is the spirit of John, the Beloved Disciple, the spirit of grace, mercy, and peace. His memory is as sweet and fragrant as the perfume of the little flower which gave its name to the ship which brought him over.

So, Mr. President, responding to your sentiment, I give you mine:

South Carolina and Massachusetts, the Presbyterian
and the Puritan, the Huguenot and the Pilgrim; however separated by distance or by difference, they will
at last surely be drawn together by a common love of
liberty and a common faith in God.

Logan, John A., an American soldier and politician, born in Jackson county, Ill., February 9, 1826; died in Washington, D. C., December 26, 1886. His early education was scanty, and, entering the army, he served as lieutenant during the Mexican war. Taking up later the study of law, he was admitted to the bar in 1851, and the next year entered the Illinois legislature. He sat in congress as representative, 1858–61, and entering the Union army as a private in the year last named soon distinguished himself for bravery and rose to the rank of general. He was a prominent figure in politics after the close of the Civil war, and in 1884 was the unsuccessful candidate for the vice-presidency on the ticket with Blaine. Logan was a popular public speaker, his oratory being fluent and forcible rather than polished and scholarly in character.

———

ON THE INDEPENDENCE OF CUBA.

SPEECH DELIVERED IN THE HOUSE OF REPRESENTATIVES, JUNE 15, 1870.

Cuba, with its broad acres, its beautiful vales, its rich soil, its countless resources, is expected to pass into the hands of a few men, to whom it will be a mine of wealth.

Let me appeal to this House not to allow this scheme to be carried out. While this brave band of patriots are wrestling for the dearest right known to man, the right of self-government, should we hesitate to make the simple and single declaration which will save them from being robbed and murdered day after day? Can we, with all our boasted principles of liberty, justice, and equality to all men, stand tamely by and witness these people, within sight of our own shores, following the example which we have furnished, hanged, drawn, and quartered, with most atrocious brutality, without the protection of any flag on God's earth, and not raise our voice against the inhumanity so much as to declare that there is a contest—a war? This poor boon is all they ask, and in my judgment it can be denied to them by none but heartless men.

In what I am saying I have no contest with the President. I am his friend as I ever have been. I have no contest with Mr. Fish or with anybody else. I have no warfare with those who differ from me; they have their opinions, and I am entitled to mine. I look upon General Grant as a good man, but I think that on this question he is deceived. I think if he had not been fishing up in Pennsylvania when this message was written he would not have signed it so readily as he did. I do not think it was necessary to go to Pennsylvania for more fish. We have all we need here. I think it is a message not well considered, and I do not believe he examined it well before signing it. It does not state the case correctly; and I am sorry to see him put upon the record as misstating the law.

I entertain the highest respect for the President and his administration, and I do not purpose that any man shall put me in a false position. I do not intend to allow myself to be placed in antagonism with the administration, nor do I intend to allow any man or set of men to howl upon my heels that I do not support the administration and am therefore to be denounced.

No, sir, I am supporting the administration; I am

maintaining the former views of the President, and I think his former views on this question are better than his later ones. Once we held like opinions on this question of Cuban belligerency, and I see no reason on my part to change those opinions. If he has changed his I find no fault with him. But I prefer to stand by his former judgment, formed when he was cool, when he deliberated for himself, when he had not men around him to bother and annoy him with their peculiar and interested notions; when he thought for himself and wrote for himself. I believed then as he believed. I believe now as I believed then, and I do not propose to change.

Now, Mr. Speaker, I think the Republicans on this side of the House owe it to themselves to take the side of the oppressed. I wish to say to the Republican party as the friend of this administration, that the most friendly act toward this present administration is to let this message go before the country, so far as the opinion of the President is concerned. Do not let us make any war upon it. Let it appear to the country that we differ from the President in this matter honestly. Let us as Republicans, notwithstanding the message, declare that we will accord to these people all the rights of civilized warfare. Let us do this, and I have no doubt the country will say, " Well done, good and faithful servants."

If your action be taken in the interest of freedom, if you shall help the oppressed and act on the side of liberty and humanity, if in a contest between despotism and a people struggling bravely for independence you give the preference to the latter, if in doing this you should happen to commit error, and that error should happen to be on the side of humanity and liberty, there is no country in the world which can or ought to find fault with you. In questions tried before our juries they are always instructed to give the benefit of the doubt in favor of the prisoner.

In this case, if there be any doubt, I implore the House let it be in favor of Cuba. By taking the side of Cuba against Spain we are true to the instincts of our organization in sympathizing with a people suffering under oppression. It will show that you do not sympathize with despotism. It will show that now, as heretofore, the Republican party sympathize with struggling humanity seeking freedom and independence.

Your record is clear in the past. We have had too much sympathy of late years for great monarchies. Indeed there seems to be too great a disposition in some quarters to sympathize too much with monarchy and to sympathize too much with the exercise of arbitrary power in oppression to justice and liberty. And why is this? Because these are great governments and controlled by the great ones. These monarchical governments have mighty fleets floating upon the high seas. They have ministers residing in our midst. They have pleasant men who can afford to give splendid entertainments. They are genial men at the dinner table, and facile in the artful manœuvres of diplomacy. They are what was known in the time of Louis XIV. and the " Fronde," as *honnête* men. They have all the appliances for making good their cause when they wish to crush out people who are struggling for independence. They are heard, and they have official access to our government, which is denied to all others.

But never let it be said that the Republican party sympathizes with the oppressors against the oppressed. I warn you that no statesman and no political party ever had a long life in this country which did not love liberty, no matter from where the cry came, whether from South America, or from Mexico, or from our own slaves when they were held in bondage. When the South American States raised the standard of rebellion against Spain we sympathized with them; when Mexico did the same thing, she also had our sympathy; and gentlemen should not forget that it was the Republican party that gave freedom and franchise to four million slaves in our own midst. Let gentlemen carefully examine the history of this country before they cast these people off and consign them to the merciless horrors of a Spanish inquisition. Read and mark well that no party ever succeeded which refused justice or sympathized with the oppressor against the oppressed.

If the party which abolished slavery; the party which, in the spirit of justice, gave citzenship to those who were freed by it; the party which has always held itself to be the great exponent of free principles and justice to all, of liberty and humanity—if that party shall now turn its back upon its former glorious record and lend moral support and material aid to Spain in its cruel crusade against the revolutionists of Cuba it must inevitably go down under the indignation of the people who now make up its formidable numbers.

If, however, we shall give the aid which is asked to encourage and sustain struggling humanity; if we shall help these Cubans fighting for independence; if we shall do that which every dictate of justice demands of us in the emergency; in a word, if we are true to the doctrines and principles we have enunciated, then the Republican party will live to ride safely for many years to come through the boisterous storms of politics, and will override in the future, as it has done in the past, all such theories as secession and rebellion in our government, and all that is antagonistic to the universal liberty of man. It will overcome every obstacle that stands in the way of the great advance, the great civilization, the great enlightenment, the great Christianity of this age. And whenever you fail to allow it to march onward in the path in which it has started, and undertake to impede it in its efforts to press onward, you strike a blow at your own party, your own interests and safety.

For I tell you that whenever you halt, or shirk the responsibilities of the hour as Republicans the Democrats will overtake you.

The Democrats were once formidable so far as the questions of the day were concerned. They are far behind you now; and I say to you, Republicans, do not let the Democrats beat you to-day as regards the position they take in favor of liberty. If you do, the country will perhaps give you reason to learn after awhile that you have forgotten the trust that was reposed in you, and have failed to perform the duty with which it has honored you, but allowed it to slip from your hands to be discharged by others.

For these things you must answer before the great forum of the people; and if they adjudge you recreant in the support of the principles reposed in you, and false to the requirements of the present, they will not find you worthy of confidence in the future.

Hawley, Joseph H., an American journalist and politician, born at Stewartsville, N. C., October 31, 1826. He
studied law and practised his profession in Hartford, Conn.,
from 1850 to 1857, entering heartily into politics the while
and being notably prominent as an opponent of slavery.
He took up journalism in 1857 and was the editor of the
" Evening Press " at Hartford. He served in the Federal
army throughout the Civil war, retiring in 1865 with the rank
of brevet major-general. He was elected governor of Con-
necticut in 1866, serving for one term, and then resumed
journalism. In 1872 he entered congress as representative,
and was twice re-elected, and in 1881 became a United States
senator, which position he still holds. He was president of
the Centennial commission, 1875–76.

ON THE PRESS.

SPEECH AT THE BANQUET OF THE NEW ENGLAND
SOCIETY, DECEMBER 22, 1875.

GENTLEMEN,—Our distinguished president paid the
very highest compliment to the press to-night; for,
while he has given at least a fortnight's notice to every
other gentleman, he only told me to-night that I had to
respond to the toast of " The Press." But as I have
attended a good many dinners of the New England
Society, and never knew " The Press " to be called
upon before midnight, I felt entirely safe.

Now, sir, I have spent an evening—some six hours
—here, enjoying all the festivities and hospitalities
of this occasion to the utmost, and at last I am called

upon, at an hour when we are full of jollity and mirth, to respond to a toast that in reality calls upon me for my most serious effort.

I assure you that, had I known that I was to speak upon this subject to-night, I would, contrary to my usual custom, have been deliberately prepared; for I, in reality, have a great deal to say upon that matter; and permit me to add that I have a somewhat peculiar qualification, for I have been a man within the press, " a chiel amang ye takin' notes, and prentin' them; " and I have been again a man altogether outside of the press, not writing for months to his own people, and subject to receive all the jibes and criticisms and attacks of the press. " I know how it is myself."

The " Press of the Republic " is a text worthy of the noblest oration. It has a great, a high, and a holy duty. It is at once the leader and educator, and, on the other hand, the representative of the people. I can only touch on some points that I have in my mind, upon this occasion. It seems to me that we are passing through a period of peculiar importance regarding the value and influence of the press of the American Republic. There are times when I join with them in the most indignant denunciation, in the warmest appeal. There are times when I feel the cutting, cruel, stinging injustice of the American press.

It is the duty of an editor, sitting, as he does, as a judge—and I mean all that the word implies—upon all that goes on about him in public life—it is his duty to hear both sides, and all sides, as deliberately and calmly as he may, and to pronounce a judgment that, so far as he knows, may be the judgment of posterity.

" It is true that he has two duties. We know that it is his duty to condemn the bad. When it be made perfectly clear that the bad man is really a bad man, a corrupter of youth, make him drink the hemlock, expel him, punish him, crush him.

But there is another duty imposed upon the American press, quite as great. If there be a man who loves the Republic, who would work for it, who would talk for it, who would fight for it, who would die for it— there are millions of them, thank God!—it is the duty of the American press to uphold him, and to praise him when the time comes, in the proper place, on the proper occasion.

The press is to deal not alone in censure of the bad, but in praise of the good. I like the phrase, " The independent press." I am an editor myself. I love my calling. I think it is growing to be one of the great professions of the day. I claim as an editor (and that is my chief pursuit in life), to be a gentleman also. If I see or know anything to be wrong in the land, high or low, I will say so. If it be in my own party, I will take special pains to say so; for I suppose it to be true of both parties that we have a very high, a very glorious, a very beautiful, a very lovable idea of the future American Republic. So I will condemn, I say, whatever may be wrong. I hold myself to be an independent journalist.

But, my friends, I hope you will excuse the phrase —I am going to follow it by another—at the same time I do freely avow that I am a partisan; for I never knew anything good, from Moses down to John Brown, that was not carried through by partisanship.

If you believe in anything, say so; work for it, fight for it.

There are always two sides in the world. The good fight is always going on. The bad men are always working. The devil is always busy. And again, on the other side you have your high idea of whatever is beautiful and good and true in the world; and God is always working also. The man who stands between them—who says, "This is somewhat good, and that is somewhat good; I stand between them"—permit me to say, is a man for whom I have very little respect.

Some men say there is a God; some men say there is no God. Some of the independents say that the truth lies between them. I cannot find it between them. Every man has a God. If you believe in your God, he may be another God from mine; but if you are a man, I want you to fight for him, and I may have to fight against you, but do you fight for the God that you believe in.

I do sincerely think (and I wish that this was a congregation of my fellow editors of the whole land, for my heart is in reality full of this thing)—I do sincerely think that there is something of a danger that our eloquent, ready, powerful, versatile, indefatigable, vigorous, omnipresent, omniscient men of the press may drive out of public life—and they will ridicule that phrase—may drive out of public life, not all, but a very considerable class of sensitive, high-minded, honorable, ambitious gentlemen.

Now, I do not say anything about the future for myself. I have got a "free lance," I have got a newspaper, and I can fight with the rest of them; but I will

8

give you a bit of my experience in public life. I tell you, my friends of the New English Society, that one of the sorest things that a man in public life has to bear is the reckless, unreasonable censure of members of the press whom individually he respects.

That large-hearted man, whom personally I love, with whom I could shake hands, with whom I did shake hands, with whom I sat at the social board time and again, grossly misinterprets my public actions; intimates all manner of dishonorable things, which I would fight at two paces rather than be guilty of; and it would be useless for me to write a public letter to explain or contradict.

Now, I am only one of hundreds. I can stand still and wait the result, in the confidence that, if not all, yet some men believe me to be honorable and true; if they do not, God and I know it, and would "fight it out on that line."

Gentlemen, it is rather my habit to talk in earnest. Next to the evil of having all public men in this land corrupt; next to the evil of having all our governmental affairs in the hands of men venal and weak and narrow, debauching public life and carrying it down to destruction, is the calamity of having all the young men believe it is so, whether it be so or not.

Teach all the boys to believe that every man who goes into public life has his price; teach all the boys to believe that there is no man who enters public life anywhere that does not look out for his own, and is not always scheming to do something for himself or his friends, and seeking to prolong his power; teach every young man who has a desire to go into political life to think—because you have told him so—that the way to succeed is to follow such arts, and by that kind of talk you may ruin your country.

Now, gentlemen, as I have said, this is a matter for an evening oration. I have barely touched some of the points. I have said the press has a twofold duty and fortune: it is the leader, the educator, the director of the people. It is, at the same time, the reflector of the people. I could spend an hour upon the theme. . . .

I cannot cease, however, without thanking the president of the St. Patrick's Society, the only gentleman who has mentioned the word "centennial." When I was leaving Philadelphia, my wife warned me not to use that word, knowing to what it might lead me; and so I shall simply ask you all to come to Philadelphia next year, and join in the great national exhibition, where you will have an opportunity of seeing the progress which this nation has made under the ideas of liberty, government, industry, and thrift which were instilled by the Pilgrim Fathers.

Voorhees, Daniel W., an American politician and orator, born at Liberty, Ohio, September 26, 1827; died in Washington, D. C., April 10, 1897. After studying law and being admitted to the bar in 1861, he began to practise at Covington, Ind., removing to Terre Haute, in the same state, in 1857. He was United States district attorney, 1858–61, and while serving as such his speech in court in defence of John Cook, one of the John Brown raiders, gave him an extended fame as an orator. Voorhees was a Democratic Representative in Congress, 1861–65, and also 1869–71. In 1877 he became a United States Senator, and was re-elected in 1885 and again in 1891. Almost upon his entrance into the Senate he made there an impassioned speech in favor of free silver coinage and the acceptance of greenbacks as full legal tender money, but in 1893 voted for the repeal of the silver purchase portion of the "Sherman Act." To his efforts as chairman of the library committee, 1880–97, is largely due the existence of the present Congressional Library building. Voorhees was strongly partisan in his political utterances, and, though undeniably eloquent, was an impetuous, emotional orator, rather than a convincing one. In allusion to his stature he was sometimes termed "The Tall Sycamore of the Wabash." A volume of his "Speeches" appeared in 1875, and his "Lectures, Addresses and Speeches," with a brief biography, in 1898.

DEFENCE OF JOHN E. COOK.

DELIVERED AT CHARLESTOWN, VIRGINIA, NOVEMBER 8, 1859.

WHO is John E. Cook?

He has the right himself to be heard before you; but I will answer for him. Sprung from an ancestry of loyal attachment to the American government, he inherits no blood of tainted impurity. His grandfather an officer of the Revolution, by which your liberty, as well as mine was achieved, and his grayhaired father, who lived to weep over him, a soldier of the war of 1812, he brings no dishonored lineage into your presence. If the blood which flows in his veins has been offered against your peace, the same blood in the veins of those from whose loins he sprang has been offered in fierce shock of battle and foreign invasion in behalf of the people of Virginia and the Union. Born of a parent stock occupying the middle walks of life, and possessed of all those tender and domestic virtues which escape the contamination of those vices that dwell on the frozen peaks, or in the dark and deep caverns of society, he would not have been here had precept and example been remembered in the prodigal wanderings of his short and checkered life.

Poor deluded boy! wayward, misled child! An evil star presided over thy natal hour and smote it with gloom. The hour in which thy mother bore thee and blessed thee as her blue-eyed babe upon her knee is to her now one of bitterness as she stands near the bank of the chill river of death and looks back on a name hitherto as unspotted and as pure as the unstained snow. May God stand by and sustain her, and preserve the mothers of Virginia from the waves of sorrow that now roll over her! . . .

In an evil hour—and may it be forever accursed!—John E. Cook met John Brown on the prostituted plains of Kansas. On that field of fanaticism, three years ago, this fair and gentle youth was thrown into contact with the pirate and robber of civil warfare.

To others whose sympathies he has enlisted I will leave the task of transmitting John Brown as a martyr and hero to posterity. In my eyes he stands the chief of criminals, the thief of property stolen—horses and slaves—from the citizens of Missouri, a falsifier here in this court, as I shall yet show, and a murderer not only of your citizens, but of the young men who have already lost their lives in his bloody foray of your border. This is not pleasant to say, but it is the truth, and, as such, ought to be and shall be said. You have seen John Brown, the leader.

Now look on John Cook, the follower. He is in evidence before you. Never did I plead for a face that I was more willing to show. If evil is there, I have not seen it. If murder is there, I am to learn to mark the lines of the murderer anew. If the assassin is in that young face, then commend me to the look of an assassin. No, gentlemen, it is a face for a mother to love, and a sister to idolize, and in which the natural goodness of his heart pleads trumpet-tongued against the deep damnation that estranged him from home and its principles.

Let us look at the meeting of these two men. Place them side by side. Put the young face by the old face; the young head by the old head. We have seen somewhat of the history of the young man. Look now for a moment at the history of the old man.

He did not go to Kansas as a peaceable settler with his interests linked to the legitimate growth and prosperity of that ill-fated Territory. He went there in the language of one who has spoken for him since his confinement here, as the Moses of the slaves' deliverance. He went there to fulfil a dream, which had tortured his brain for thirty years, that he was to be the leader of a second exodus from bondage. He went there for war and not for peace. He went there to call around him the wayward and unstable elements of a society in which the bonds of order, law, and religion were loosened, and the angry demon of discord was unchained. Storm was his element by his own showing. He courted the fierce tempest. He sowed the wind that he might reap the whirlwind. He invoked the lightning and gloried in its devastation. Sixty summers and winters had passed over his head, and planted the seeds of spring and gathered the harvests of autumn in the fields of his experience. He was the hero, too, of battles there. If laurels could be gained in such a fratricidal war as raged in Kansas, he had them on his brow.

Ossawatomie was given to him, and added to his name by the insanity of the crazy crew of the North as Napoleon conferred the names of battlefields on his favorite marshals. The action of Black Jack, too, gave him consideration, circumstance, and condition with philanthropists of bastard quality, carpet knight heroes in Boston, and servile followers of fanaticism throughout the country. His courage is now lauded to the skies by men who have none of it themselves. This virtue, I admit, he has—linked, however, with a thousand crimes. An iron will, with which to accomplish evil under the skilful guise of good, I also admit to be in his possession—rendering his influence over the young all the more despotic and dangerous.

Imagine, if you please, the bark on which this young man at the bar, and all his hopes were freighted, laid alongside of the old weather-beaten and murderous man-of-war whose character I have placed before you. The one was stern and bent upon a fatal voyage. Grim-visaged war, civil commotion, pillage and death, disunion and universal desolation thronged through the mind of John Brown. To him law was nothing, the Union was nothing, the peace and welfare of the country were nothing, the lives of the citizens of Virginia were nothing.

Though a red sea of blood rolled before him, yet he lifted up his hand and cried Forward. Shall he now shrink from his prominence, and attempt to shrivel back to the grade of his recruits and subalterns? Shall he deny his bad pre-eminence, and say that he did not incite the revolt which has involved his followers in ruin? Shall he stand before this court and before the country, and deny that he was the master-spirit, and gathered together the young men who followed him to the death in this mad expedition?

No! his own hand signs himself "Commander-in-chief," and shows the proper distinction which should be made between himself and the men who, in an evil moment, obeyed his orders. Now turn to the contrast again and behold the prisoner. Young and new to the rough ways of life, his unsandalled foot, tender and unused to the journey before him, a waif on the ocean, at the mercy of the current which might assail him, and unfortunately endowed with that fearful gift which causes one to walk as in a dream through all the vicissitudes of a lifetime; severed and wandering from the sustaining and protecting ties of kindred, he gave, without knowing his destination or purpose, a pledge of military obedience to John Brown, "Commander-in-chief." . . .

John Brown was the despotic leader and John E. Cook was an ill-fated follower of an enterprise whose horror he now realizes and deplores. I defy the man, here or elsewhere, who has ever known John E. Cook, who has ever looked once fully into his face, and learned anything of his history, to lay his hand on his heart and say that he believes him guilty of the origin or the results of the outbreak at Harper's Ferry.

Here, then, are the two characters whom you are thinking to punish alike. Can it be that a jury of Christian men will find no discrimination should be made between them? Are the tempter and the tempted the same in your eyes? Is the beguiled youth to die the same as the old offender who has pondered his crimes for thirty years? Are there no grades in your estimation of guilt? Is each one, without respect to age or circumstances, to be beaten with the same number of stripes?

Such is not the law, human or divine. We are all to be rewarded according to our works, whether in punishment for evil, or blessings for good that we have done. You are here to do justice, and if justice requires the same fate to befall Cook that befalls Brown, I know nothing of her rules, and do not care to learn. They are as widely asunder, in all that constitutes guilt, as the poles of the earth, and should be dealt with accordingly. It is in your power to do so, and by the principles by which you yourselves are willing to be judged hereafter, I implore you to do it!

Come with me, however, gentlemen, and let us approach the spot where the tragedy of the 17th of October occurred, and analyze the conduct of the prisoner there. It is not true that he came as a citizen to your State and gained a home in your midst to betray you. He was ordered to take his position at Harper's Ferry in advance of his party for the sole purpose of ascertaining whether Colonel Forbes, of New York, had divulged the plan. This order came from John Brown, the "Commander-in-chief," and was doubtless a matter of as much interest to others of prominent station as to himself.

Cook simply obeyed—no more. There is not a particle of evidence that he tampered with your slaves during his temporary residence. On the contrary, it is admitted on all hands that he did not. His position there is well defined. Nor was he from under the cold, stern eye of his leader. From the top of the mountain his chief looked down upon him, and held him as within a charmed circle. Would Cook have lived a day had he tried to break the meshes which environed him?

Happy the hour in which he had made the attempt even had he perished, but in fixing the measure of his guilt, the circumstances by which he was surrounded must all be weighed. At every step we see him as the instrument in the hands of other men, and not as originating or advising anything. . . .

But it has been said that Cook left the scene at Harper's Ferry at an early hour to avoid the danger of the occasion, and thus broke faith with his comrades in wrong. Even this is wholly untrue. Again we find the faithful, obedient subaltern carrying out the orders of his chief, and when he had crossed the river and fulfilled the commands of Brown, he did what Brown's own son would not do—by returning and exposing himself to the fire of the soldiers and citizens for the relief of Brown and his party. We see much, alas! too much, to condemn in his conduct, but nothing to despise; we look in vain for an act that belongs to a base or malignant nature. Let the hand of chastisement fall gently on the errors of such as him, and reserve your heavy blows for such as commit crime from motives of depravity.

Up to this point I have followed the prisoner, and traced his immediate connection with this sad affair. You have everything before you. You have heard his own account of his strange and infatuated wanderings up and down the earth with John Brown and his coadjutors; how like a fiction it all seems, and yet how lamentably true; how unreal to minds like ours; how like the fever dream of a mind warped and disordered to the borders of insanity does the part which the prisoner has played seem to every practical judgment!

Is there nothing in it all that affords you the dearest privilege which man has on earth—the privilege of being merciful? Why, the very thief on the cross, for a single moment's repentance over his crimes, received absolute forgiveness, and was rewarded with paradise.

But, gentlemen, in estimating the magnitude of this young man's guilt, there is one fact which is proven in his behalf by the current history of the day which you cannot fail to consider. Shall John E. Cook perish, and the real criminals who for twenty years have taught the principles on which he acted, hear no voice from this spot? Shall no mark be placed on them? Shall this occasion pass away, and the prime felons who attacked your soil and murdered your citizens at Harper's Ferry escape? The indictment before us says that the prisoner was "seduced by the false and malignant counsels of other traitorous persons."

Never was a sentence written more just and true. "False and malignant counsels" have been dropping for years, as deadly and blighting as the poison of the Bohun upas tree, from the tongues of evil and traitorous persons in that section of the Union to which the prisoner belongs. They have seduced not only his mind, but many others, honest and misguided like him, to regard the crime at Harper's Ferry as no crime, your rights as unmitigated wrongs, and the constitution of the country as a league with hell and a covenant with death. On the skirts of the leaders of abolition fanaticism in the North is every drop of blood shed in the conflict at Harper's Ferry; on their souls rests the crime of murder for every life there lost; and all the waters of the ocean could not wash the stains of slaughter from their treacherous and guilty hands.

A noted Boston abolitionist [Wendell Phillips], a few days ago, at Brooklyn, New York, in the presence of thousands, speaking of this tragic occurrence, says:

" It is the natural result of anti-slavery teaching. For one, I accept it. I expected it." I, too, accept it in the same light, and so will the country. Those who taught, and not those who believed and acted, are the men of crime in the sight of God. And to guard other young men, so far as in my power, from the fatal snare which has been tightened around the hopes and destiny of John E. Cook, and to show who are fully responsible for his conduct, I intend to link with this trial the names of wiser and older men than he; and, if he is to be punished and consigned to a wretched doom, they shall stand beside him in the public stocks; they shall be pilloried forever in public shame as " the evil and traitorous persons who seduced him to his ruin by their false and malignant counsels."

The chief of these men, the leader of a great party, a senator of long standing, has announced to the country that there is a higher law than the constitution, which guarantees to each man the full exercise of his own inclination. The prisoner before you has simply acted on the law of Wm. H. Seward, and not the law of his fathers. He has followed the Mahomet of an incendiary faith.

Come forth, ye sages of abolitionism, who now cower and skulk under hasty denials of your complicity with the bloody result of your wicked and unholy doctrines, and take your places on the witness stand. Tell the world why this thing has happened. Tell this jury why they are trying John E. Cook for his life. You advised his conduct and taught him that he was doing right. You taught him a higher law and then pointed out to him the field of action. Let facts be submitted. Mr. Seward, in speaking of slavery, says: "It can and must be abolished, and you and I must do it."

What worse did the prisoner attempt? Again, he said, upon this same subject, "Circumstances determine possibilities;" and doubtless the circumstance with which John Brown had connected his plans made them possible in his estimation, for it is in evidence before the country, unimpeached and uncontradicted, that the great senator of New York had the whole matter submitted to him, and only whispered back, in response, that he had better not have been told. He has boldly announced an irrepressible conflict between the free and slave States of this Union.

These seditious phrases, "higher law" and "irrepressible conflict," warrant and invite the construction which the prisoner and his young deluded companions placed upon them. Yet they are either in chains, with the frightful gibbet in full view, or sleep in dishonored graves, while the apostle and masterspirit of insurrection is loaded with honors, and fares sumptuously every day. Such is poor, short-handed justice in this world.

An old man, and for long years a member of the national Congress from Ohio, next shall testify here before you that he taught the prisoner the terrible error which now involves his life. Servile insurrection have forever been on the tongue and lips of Joshua R. Giddings. He says "that when the contest shall come, when the thunder shall roll and the lightning flash, and when the slaves shall rise in the South, in imitation of the horrid scenes of the West

Indies, when the Southern man shall turn pale and tremble, when your dwellings shall smoke with the torch of the incendiary, and dismay sit on each countenance, he will hail it as the approaching dawn of that political and moral millennium which he is well assured will come upon the world."

The atrocity of these sentiments chills the blood of honest patriots, and no part of the prisoner's conduct equals their bloody import. Shall the old leader escape and the young follower die? Shall the teacher, whose doctrines told the prisoner that what he did was right, go unscathed of the lightning which he has unchained? If so, Justice has fled from her temples on earth, and awaits us only on high to measure out what is right between man and man.

The men who have misled this boy to his ruin shall here receive my maledictions. They shrink back from him now in the hour of his calamity. They lift up their hands and say, Avaunt! to the bloody spectre which their infernal orgies have summoned up. You hear them all over the land ejaculating through false, pale, coward lips, " Thou canst not say I did it," when their hands are reeking with all the blood that has been shed and which yet awaits the extreme penalty of the law. False, fleeting, perjured traitors, false to friends as well as country, and perjured before the constitution of the Republic—ministers who profess to be of God who told this boy here to carry a Sharpe's rifle to Kansas instead of his mother's Bible—shall this jury, this court, and this country forget their guilt and their infamy because a victim to their precepts is yielding up his life before you?

May God forget me if I here, in the presence of this pale face, forget to denounce with the withering, blighting, blasting power of majestic truth, the tall and stately criminals of the Northern States of this Union.

The visionary mind of the prisoner heard from a member of congress from Massachusetts that a new constitution, a new Bible, and a new God were to be inaugurated and to possess the country. They were to be new, because they were to be anti-slavery, for the old constitution, and the old Bible, and the God of our fathers, the ancient Lord God of Israel, the same yesterday, to-day, and forever, were not on the side of abolitionism.

Is there no mitigation for his doom in the fact that he took his life in his hand, and aimed at that which a coward taught him, but dared not himself attempt? Base, pusillanimous demagogues have led the prisoner to the bar, but while he suffers—if suffer he must—they, too, shall have their recreant limbs broken on the wheel.

I will not leave the soil of Virginia, I will not let this awful occasion pass into history, without giving a voice and an utterance to its true purport and meaning, without heaping upon its authors the load of execration which they are to bear henceforth and forever. Day after day and year after year has the baleful simoon of revolution, anarchy, discord, hostility to the South and her institutions, swept over that section of the country in which the lot of the prisoner has been cast. That he has been poisoned by its breath should not cut him off from human sympathy; rather should it render every heart clement toward him.

He never sought place or station, but sought merely to develop those doctrines which evil and traitorous persons have caused him to believe were true. Ministers, editors, and politicians—Beecher, Parker, Seward, Giddings, Sumner, Hale, and a host of lesser lights of each class—who in this court-room, who in this vast country, who in the wide world who shall read this trial believes them not guilty as charged in the indictment in all the counts to a deeper and far more fearful extent than John E. Cook. Midnight gloom is not more somber in contrast with the blazing light of the meridian sun than is the guilt of such men in comparison with that which overwhelms the prisoner. They put in motion the maelstrom which has engulfed him. They started the torrent which has borne him over the precipice. They called forth from the caverns the tempest which wrecked him on a sunken reef.

Before God, and in the light of eternal truth, the disaster at Harper's Ferry is their act, and not his. May the ghost of each victim to their doctrine of disunion and abomination sit heavy on their guilty souls! May the fate of the prisoner, whatever it may be, disturb their slumbers and paralyze their arms when they are again raised against the peace of the country and the lives of its citizens!

I know by the gleam of each eye into which I look in this jury-box, that if these men could change places with young Cook, you would gladly say to him, " Go, erring and repentant youth, our vengeance shall fall on those who paid their money, urged on the attack, and guided the blow." Let me appeal to you, gentle-

9

men of the jury, in the name of eternal truth and
everlasting right, is nothing to be forgiven to youth,
to inexperience, to a gentle, kind heart, to a wayward
and peculiar though not vicious character, strangely
apt to be led by present influences?

I have shown you what those influences, generally
and specially, have been over the mind of the prisoner.
I have shown you the malign influence of his direct
leader. I have shown you, also, the " false and malignant counsels " in behalf of this sad enterprise, ema-
nating from those in place, power, and position. It
might have been your prodigal son borne away and
seduced by such counsels, as well as my young client.
Do with him as you would have your own child dealt
by under like circumstances. He has been stolen
from the principles of his ancestors and betrayed from
the teachings of his kindred. If he was your own
handsome child, repentant and confessing his wrong
to his country, what would you wish a jury of strangers to do? That do yourselves.

By that rule guide your verdict; and the poor boon
of mercy will not be cut off from him. He thought the
country was about to be convulsed; that the slave was
pining for an opportunity to rise against his master;
that two thirds of the laboring population of the country, north and south, would flock to the standard of
revolt; that a single day would bring ten, fifty—yea, a
hundred thousand men—to arms in behalf of the insurrection of the slaves. This is in evidence.

Who are responsible for such terribly false views?
and what kind of a visionary and dreaming mind is
that which has so fatally entertained them? That the

prisoner's mind is pliant to the impressions, whether for good or for evil, by which it is surrounded, let his first interview in his prison with Governor Willard, in the presence of your senator, Colonel Mason, bear witness. His error was placed before him. His wrong to his family and his country was drawn by a patriotic, and, at the same time, an affectionate hand. His natural being at once asserted its sway. The influence of good, and not of evil, once more controlled him as in the days of his childhood; and now here before you he has the merit at least of a loyal citizen, making all the atonement in his power for the wrong which he has committed. That he has told strictly the truth in his statement is proven by every word of evidence in this cause.

Gentlemen, you have this case. I surrender into your hands the issues of life and death. As long as you live, a more important case than this you will never be called to try. Consider it, therefore, well in all its bearings. I have tried to show you those facts which go to palliate the conduct of the prisoner. Shall I go home and say that in justice you remembered not mercy to him? Leave the door of clemency open; do not shut it by a wholesale conviction. Remember that life is an awful and a sacred thing; remember that death is terrible—terrible at any time, and in any form.

> " Come to the bridal chamber, Death !
>   Come when the mother feels
> For the first time, her first-born's breath ;
>   Come when the blessed seals
> That close the pestilence are broke,
> And crowded cities wail its stroke ;

> Come in consumption's ghastly form,
> The earthquake's shock, the ocean's storm;
> Come when the heart beats high and warm
>   With banquet song, and dance, and wine,
> And thou art terrible. The groan,
> The knell, the pall, the bier,
> And all we know, or dream, or fear
>   Of agony, are thine."

But when to the frightful mien of the grim monster, when to the chill visage of the spirit of the glass and scythe, is added the hated, dreaded spectre of the gibbet, we turn shuddering from the accumulated horror. God spare this boy, and those who love him, from such a scene of woe.

I part from you now, and most likely forever. When we next meet—when I next look upon your faces and you on mine—it will be in that land and before that Tribunal where the only plea that will save you or me from a worse fate than awaits the prisoner, will be mercy. Charity is the paramount virtue; all else is as sounding brass and a tinkling cymbal. Charity suffereth long, and is kind. Forbid it not to come into your deliberation; and, when your last hour comes, the memory that you allowed it to plead for your erring brother, John E. Cook, will brighten your passage over the dark river, and rise by your side as an interceding angel in that day when your trial as well as his shall be determined by a just but merciful God.

I thank the court and you, gentlemen, for your patient kindness, and I am done.

Bayard, Thomas F., an eminent American statesman, diplomat and orator, born in Wilmington, Del., October 29, 1828; died at Deadham, Mass., September 28, 1898. He came of a family which for three generations had been represented in the United States Senate, and after studying law with his father was admitted to the bar in 1851 and began practice in his native city. He succeeded his father in the National Senate in 1869, serving there continuously till 1885. Bayard was Secretary of State during President Cleveland's first administration, and from 1893 to 1897 was ambassador to England, being the first minister to Great Britain to bear that title. He was a polished, eloquent speaker, with a graceful, persuasive delivery, and was especially happy as the orator at occasional semi-public functions. He was popular in England, and his integrity of character won for him the high respect of all parties at home. No collection of his speeches has been made as yet.

ON THE UNITED STATES ARMY.

[From an address on "Unwritten Law," delivered before the Phi Beta Kappa Society of Harvard University, June 28, 1877.]

THE army of the United States, like the militia of the several States, is the creation of their respective legislation; like the "princes and lords" of Goldsmith's verse,—

> "A breath can make them, as a breath hath made."

"He has kept among us, in times of peace, standing armies, without the consent of the legislature," was one of the facts justifying revolution, "submitted to a candid world," by the founders of this government. So long as human nature remains unchanged, the final argument of force cannot be disregarded; but, outside and beyond the will of the people expressed by law, an American army cannot exist; it is but their instrument for their own service. It is wholly dependent upon them; and they are never dependent upon it, and never will be while civil liberty exists in substance among us.

When called into existence, the army represents the military spirit of the whole nation, and is supported by the enthusiasm and pride of all. It is composed of American valor, skill, and energy, and is dedicated to the glory of our common country, whose history contains no brighter pages than those which record the naval and military achievements of her sons; but neither army nor navy stands now, nor ever did, nor ever will, toward the American people in the relation of policem n to a turbulent crowd. And those who would wish to see it placed in such an attitude, and employed in such work, are short-sighted indeed, and little regard the true dignity of the American soldier, or the real security of the American citizen.

The army of the United States is born of the martial spirit of a brave people, and is the product of national courage. This hall is hallowed as a memorial of the valor and devotion of those gallant youths who made themselves part of the army, at a time when they felt their country needed their service, and who freely offered up their lives upon the altar of patriotism.

"O, those who live are heroes now, and martyrs those who sleep."

Their surviving companions have returned to the

paths of civil life, and the community is gladdened by their presence and strengthened by their example. If, to-morrow, the individuals who compose the army of the United States should return to the occupations of civil life, they would be quietly engulfed in the great wave of humanity which rolls around them, and the true forces of the government would move on in their proper orbits as quietly and securely as before the event.

Louis XIV. of France, "Le grand Monarque,"—of whom it was truly said, "his highest praise was that he supported the stage-trick of royalty with effect,"—caused his cannon to be cast with the words, "*Ultima ratio regum;*" and his apothegm has so far advanced that in our day cannon seem, not the last, but the first and only, argument of royal government in Europe.

In the maze of strife, armed diplomacy, and exhausting warfare, in which all Europe now seems about to be involved, how just the picture drawn by Montesquieu nearly a century and a half ago!

"A new distemper has spread itself in Europe, infecting our princes, and inducing them to keep up an exorbitant number of troops. It has its redoublings, and of necessity becomes contagious; for as soon as one prince augments his forces the rest, of course, do the same, so that nothing is gained thereby but public ruin. Each monarch keeps as many armies on foot as if his people were in danger of being exterminated, and they give the name of peace to this effort against all."

But a few weeks ago at Berlin, during a debate in the Imperial Parliament in relation to an increased grant of new captaincies of their army, a remarkable speech was made by General Von Moltke, the venerable master of the science of warfare. The telegram says:

"He insisted on the necessity of the grant. He said he wished for long peace, but the times did not permit such hope. On the contrary, the time was not far distant when every government would be compelled to strain all its strength for securing its existence. The reason for this was the regrettable distrust of governments toward each other. France had made great strides in her defences. Uncommonly large masses of troops were at present between Paris and the German frontier. Everything France did for her army received the undivided approval of her people. She was decidedly in advance of Germany in having her *cadres* for war ready in times of peace. Germany could not avoid a measure destined to compensate for it."

Will it not be well for Americans to comprehend fully the importance of the confession contained in this speech?

To-day the consolidated Empire of Germany is confessedly the best organized and equipped military power on the globe.

To reach this end every nerve has been strained, every resource of that people freely applied. The idea of military excellence, like the rod of Aaron, has swallowed up all others; all others have bent to its service, until upon the shoulder of every man within her borders capable of bearing arms, the hand of the drill-sergeant has been laid, and from centre to circumference of the empire centralized military power reigns supreme.

Whatever of unqualified success a victory of arms can yield, surely it was achieved by Germany in her last memorable campaign against France. And history nowhere else exhibits in such completeness and precision the mathematical demonstration of successful scientific warfare.

With a rapidity and fulness scarcely credible, the student of history saw the "whirligig of time bring in his revenges," whilst the disciples of military art witnessed demonstrations of the problems of war executed upon a scale and with a steady and intelligible certainty that approached the marvellous.

Never was a military campaign more completely and at all points successful,—even to the conquest and dismemberment of the hostile territory as a safeguard for the future, and the exaction of enormous tribute by way of pecuniary reimbursements from the vanquished. Let us note well the fruit of it all, and learn, so far as we may by the costly experience of others, what are the consequences of such a system and policy. Does it secure peace, prosperity, and tranquil happiness? Let the victor answer.

It is Von Moltke, one of the chief architects of the system, himself who confesses,—even whilst the garlands of his great triumph are yet unfaded on his brow, —that he " longs for peace, but the times do not permit such hope. That every government is soon to be compelled to strain all its strength for securing its existence."

To the worshippers of military power and the believers in armed force as the chief instrumentality of human government I commend Von Moltke's speech.

If perfected military rule brings a people to such a pass, may Heaven preserve our country from it.

Well may we exclaim with the sightless apostle of English liberty,—

> " What can war, but endless war still breed."

Even victory must have a future and the only victories which can have permanence, and the fruits of which grow more secure with time, are those of justice and reason; those of mere force are almost certain to contain self-generated seeds for their own subsequent reversal.

The safety and strength of our American government consists in the self-reliant and self-controlling spirit of its people.

It was their courage, their intelligence, their virtues, that enabled our forefathers to build it up; and the same qualities and our sense of its value will inspire their descendants with love and courage to defend it.

> " Full flashing on our dormant souls the firm conviction comes
> That what our fathers did for theirs—we would for our homes."

In 1789, no sooner was the original constitution of our government adopted than the several States and their people hastened unanimously to declare in a second article of amendment that,

" A well-regulated militia being necessary to the security of a free state, the right of the people to keep and bear arms shall not be infringed."

And by article third,

" No soldier shall, in time of peace, be quartered in any house without the consent of the owner; nor in time of war, but in a manner to be prescribed by law."

The right of the people to bear arms was thus sedulously guarded, and the necessary security of a free state was declared to be a " well-regulated militia." By the first article of the original constitution, power was given to Congress to raise and support armies, but coupled with the express condition that no appropriation of money to that purpose should be made for a longer period than two years. When delegating power to Congress to call forth the militia to execute the laws of the Union, and suppress insurrection and invasion, the power was expressly reserved to the States, respectively, to appoint their own officers, and to train the militia according to the discipline prescribed by Congress.

Thus it will be seen that in the martial spirit of a free people, and in their right to bear arms, the founders of our government reposed their trust, and experience has proved how wisely.

The army of the United States is our honorable instrument of self-defence, and its organization, its numbers, its employment, are to be regulated wholly by law. The military is at all times to be subordinate to the civil authority, and dependent upon law for its powers, and the prescription of its duties.

The existence or non-existence of an army makes no change in the character or methods of our government. It would be difficult to imagine a more unwarranted, and, to our American ear, more offensive statement than that " without the army the American people would be a mob."

The army and navy of the United States will be maintained in such strength as convenience, or the necessity of the government, shall dictate; and they will be held in the respect and honor due to valiant and faithful public servants, but there must be no confusion in the public mind as to the nature and proper theatre of their duties, and their true relation to their fellow citizens.

If erroneous ideas on this subject are beginning to take shape and find expression among us, let them be quietly but effectually discouraged.

Military force is always to be regarded with jealousy by a people who would be free.

It is only by military force that usurped power can have its pretensions enforced.

All history tells us that those who aspire to extraordinary power and dominion seldom trouble themselves about anything other than armies to enforce their pretensions, always decided by the possession of the longest sword.

And here, almost in the shadow of Bunker Hill, what words so befitting this grave topic, and the words of what man so proper to be recalled and heeded, as those of the patriot Webster, uttered four-and-thirty years ago, upon the completion of the monument there erected to the valor of the citizen-soldiers of America?

"Quite too frequent resort is made to military force; and quite too much of the substance of the people is consumed in maintaining armies, not for defence against foreign aggression, but for enforcing obedience to domestic authority. Standing armies are the oppressive instruments for governing the people in the ranks of hereditary and arbitrary monarchs.

"A military republic, a government founded on mock elections, and supported only by the sword, is a movement, indeed, but a retrograde and disastrous movement, from the regular and old-fashioned monarchical systems.

"If men would enjoy the blessings of the republican government, they must govern themselves by reason, by mutual counsel and consultation, by a sense and feeling of general interest, and by an acquiescence of the minority in the will of the majority properly expressed; and above all the military must be kept, according to our bill of rights, in strict subordination to the civil authority.

"Wherever this lesson is not both learned and practised, there can be no political freedom. Absurd and preposterous is it, a scoff and satire on free forms of constitutional liberty, for frames of government to be prescribed by military leaders, and the right of suffrage to be exercised at the point of the sword."

The grandeur and glory of our Republic must have its base in the interests and affections of our whole people; they must not be oppressed by its weight, but must see in it the work of their own hands, which they can recognize and uphold with an honest pride, and which every emotion that influences men will induce them to maintain and defend.

They must feel in their hearts "the ever-growing and eternal debt which is due to generous government from protected freedom."

Silently and almost imperceptibly the generations succeed each other, and at the close of every third lustrum it is startling to mark what a new body of men have come into the rank of leadership in our public affairs.

How few of those who to-day guide and influence public measures did so fifteen years ago.

While it may not be in the power of leading men to control the decision of issues, it is in a great degree within their ability to create issues, by pressing forward subjects for public consideration; and herein lies much of the power of the demagogue, that pest of popular government, who, seeking only his own advancement, adroitly presents topics to the public calculated only to arouse their passions and prejudices, to the neglect of matters really vital.

Despite the almost perfect religious liberty in this country, the passions of sectarianism and the prejudices inseparable from such a subject are always to be discovered floating on the surface of society, ready to be seized upon by the shallow and unscrupulous.

The embers of such differences among mankind are

never cold, and the breath of the demagogue can always fan them into flame, until the placid warmth of religion, instead of gently thawing the ice around human hearts, and imparting a glow of comfort to the homes of a happy community, becomes a raging conflagration in which the peace and good will of society are consumed.

In a country so vast in its area, and differing so widely in all the aspects of life and occupation of its inhabitants, antagonism of interest, rivalry in business, and misunderstandings are frequently and inevitably to be expected; and the constant exercise of conciliation and harmony is called for to accommodate differences and soothe exasperation.

It is in the power of unscrupulous self-seekers to raise such issues as shall involve, not the real interest and welfare of their countrymen, but their passions only, which are easily kindled, and can leave nothing but the ashes of disappointment and bitterness as the residuum.

The war between the good and evil influences in human society will never cease, and the champions of the former can never afford to lean idly on their swords, or slumber in their tents.

All around us we see successful men, vigorous and able, but unscrupulous and base, who have engraved success alone upon their banners, and as a consequence do not hesitate to trail them in the dust of low action, and stain them with disrepute, in pursuit of their object.

They keep within the pale of the written law, having its words on their lips, but none of its spirit in their hearts. Audacity and a self-trumpeting assurance are their characteristics. They reach a bad eminence, and contrive to maintain it, by all manner of self-advertisement; utterly immodest and indelicate, but successful in keeping themselves in the public eye. To them, politics is a mere game, in which stratagem and finesse are the means, and self-interest and personal advancement the end. Great aid is given to such characters by the public press, whose columns too often laud their tricky, shifty action, or at least give it the publicity it desires, without accompanying it with the condemnation it deserves.

How shall such influences be overcome? How shall we purge places of public station of men whose open boast is that they may be proven to be knaves, but cannot be called " fools? "

Nothing can effect this but the unwritten law, which shall create a tone on national honesty, truthfulness and honor, to which the people will respond, and which will compel at least an outward imitation of the virtues upon which it is founded.

The armor of the Roman soldier covered only the front of his body. The cuirass shielded his breast, but his back was left unprotected. Each man felt himself to be the representative of the valor and good fame of his legion and his country.

The unwritten law of honor forbade him to turn his back upon danger, and thus became his impenetrable shield.

Such is the spirit and such are the laws that constitute the true safeguards of a nation against dangers from within and without.

Schurz, Carl, an American statesman and orator of eminence, born at Liblar, near Cologne, Prussia, March 2, 1829. While a student at Bonn university he became implicated in the insurrectionary proceedings of 1849, and was consequently obliged to flee the country. He came to America in 1852, and after three years in Philadelphia settled in Wisconsin, and in 1856 became known as a political orator in German. Two years later he delivered his first speech in English, which was widely circulated, and he was presently conspicuous as a lyceum lecturer. He took a keen interest in American politics, and delivered many campaign speeches in the presidential contest of 1860. He was minister to Spain for some months in 1861, and then entering the Union army he distinguished himself as a military commander, attaining the rank of general. Removing to St. Louis, he sat in Congress as Senator from Missouri, 1869–75, and there was conspicuous as an opponent of several administration measures. Schurz was Secretary of the Interior in the cabinet of President Hayes, and edited the " Evening Post " at New York, 1881–84. He succeeded Curtis as president of the Civil Service League, and for a score of years has been conspicuous in his opposition to conventional, partisan politics. He is a polished, eloquent orator, among the latest of whose speeches is a forcible arraignment of The Policy of Imperialism.

THE POLICY OF IMPERIALISM.

ADDRESS AT THE ANTI-IMPERIALISTIC CONFERENCE ·IN CHICAGO, OCTOBER 17, 1899.

MORE than eight months ago I had the honor of addressing the citizens of Chicago on the subject of American imperialism, meaning the policy of annexing to this Republic distant countries and alien popu-

10

lations that will not fit into our democratic system of government. I discussed at that time mainly the baneful effect the pursuit of an imperialistic policy would produce upon our political institutions.

After long silence, during which I have carefully reviewed my own opinions as well as those of others in the light of the best information I could obtain, I shall now approach the same subject from another point of view.

We all know that the popular mind is much disturbed by the Philippine war, and that, however highly we admire the bravery of our soldiers, nobody professes to be proud of the war itself. There are few Americans who do not frankly admit their regret that this war should ever have happened.

In April, 1898, we went to war with Spain for the avowed purpose of liberating the people of Cuba, who had long been struggling for freedom and independence. Our object in that war was clearly and emphatically proclaimed by a solemn resolution of Congress repudiating all intention of annexation on our part and declaring that the Cuban people " are, and of right ought to be, free and independent." This solemn declaration was made to do justice to the spirit of the American people, who were indeed willing to wage a war of liberation, but would not have consented to a war of conquest. It was also to propitiate the opinion of mankind for our action. President McKinley also declared with equal solemnity that annexation by force could not be thought of, because, according to our code of morals, it would be " criminal aggression."

Can it justly be pretended that these declarations

referred only to the island of Cuba? What would the American people, what would the world have said, if Congress had resolved that the Cuban people were indeed rightfully entitled to freedom and independence, but that as to the people of other Spanish colonies we recognized no such right; and if President McKinley had declared that the forcible annexation of Cuba would be criminal, but that the forcible anexation of other Spanish colonies would be a righteous act? A general outburst of protest from our own people, and of derision and contempt from the whole world, would have been the answer. No; there can be no cavil. That war was proclaimed to all mankind to be a war of liberation, and not of conquest, and even now our very imperialists are still boasting that the war was prompted by the most unselfish and generous purposes, and that those insult us who do not believe it.

In the course of that war Commodore Dewey, by a brilliant feat of arms, destroyed the Spanish fleet in the harbor of Manila. This did not change the heralded character of the war—certainly not in Dewey's own opinion. The Filipinos, constituting the strongest and foremost tribe of the population of the archipelago, had long been fighting for freedom and independence, just as the Cubans had. The great mass of the other islanders sympathized with them. They fought for the same cause as the Cubans, and they fought against the same enemy—the same enemy against whom we were waging our war of humanity and liberation. They had the same title to freedom and independence which we recognized as " of right "

in the Cubans—nay, more, for, as Admiral Dewey
telegraphed to our government, "They are far superior in their intelligence, and more capable of self-
government than the natives of Cuba." The Admiral
adds: "I am familiar with both races, and further
intercourse with them has confirmed me in this
opinion."

Indeed, the mendacious stories spread by our imperialists which represent those people as barbarians,
their doings as mere "savagery," and their chiefs as
no better than "cut-throats," have been refuted by
such a mass of authoritative testimony, coming in part
from men who are themselves imperialists, that their
authors should hide their heads in shame; for surely it
is not the part of really brave men to calumniate their
victims before sacrificing them. We need not praise
the Filipinos as in every way the equals of the "em-
battled farmers" of Lexington and Concord, and
Aguinaldo as the peer of Washington; but there is an
overwhelming abundance of testimony, some of it
unwilling, that the Filipinos are fully the equals, and
even the superiors, of the Cubans and the Mexicans.
As to Aguinaldo, Admiral Dewey is credited with
saying that he is controlled by men abler than himself.
The same could be said of more than one of our Presidents. Moreover, it would prove that those are
greatly mistaken who predict that the Filipino uprising would collapse were Aguinaldo captured or killed.
The old slander that Aguinaldo had sold out the revolutionary movement for a bribe of $400,000 has been
so thoroughly exploded by the best authority that it
required uncommon audacity to repeat it.

Now let us see what has happened. Two months before the beginning of our Spanish war our consul at Manila reported to the State Department: "Conditions here and in Cuba are practically alike. War exists, battles are almost of daily occurrence. The crown forces (Spanish) have not been able to dislodge a rebel army within ten miles of Manila. A republic is organized here as in Cuba." When two months later our war of liberation and humanity began, Commodore Dewey was at Hongkong with his ships. He received orders to attack and destroy the Spanish fleet in those waters. It was then that our consul-general at Singapore informed our State Department that he had conferred with General Aguinaldo, then at Singapore, as to the co-operation of the Philippine insurgents, and that he had telegraphed to Commodore Dewey that Aguinaldo was willing to come to Hongkong to arrange with Dewey for "general co-operation, if desired;" whereupon Dewey promptly answered: "Tell Aguinaldo come soon as possible." The meeting was had. Dewey sailed to Manila to destroy the Spanish fleet, and Aguinaldo was taken to the seat of war on a vessel of the United States. His forces received a supply of arms through Commodore Dewey, and did faithfully and effectively co-operate with our forces against the Spaniards, so effectively, indeed, that soon afterward by their efforts the Spaniards had lost the whole country except a few garrisons in which they were practically blockaded.

Now, what were the relations between the Philippine insurgents and this Republic? There is some dispute as to certain agreements, including a promise of Philippine independence, said to have been made between Aguinaldo and our consul-general at Singapore, before Aguinaldo proceeded to co-operate with Dewey. But I lay no stress upon this point. I will let only the record of facts speak. Of these facts the first, of highest importance, is that Aguinaldo was "desired"—that is, invited—by officers of the United States to co-operate with our forces. The second is that the Filipino junta in Hongkong immediately after these conferences appealed to their countrymen to receive the American fleet about to sail for Manila as friends, by a proclamation which had these words:

"Compatriots, divine Providence is about to place independence within our reach. The Americans, not from any mercenary motives, but for the sake of humanity, have considered it opportune to extend their protecting mantle to our beloved country. Where you see the American flag flying assemble in mass. They are our redeemers."

With this faith his followers gave Aguinaldo a rapturous greeting upon his arrival at Cavité, where he proclaimed his government and organized his army under Dewey's eyes.

The arrival of our land forces did not at first change these relations. Brig.-Gen. Thomas M. Anderson, commanding, wrote to Aguinaldo, July 4, as follows: "General, I have the honor to inform you that the United States of America, whose land forces I have the honor to command in this vicinity, being at war with the kingdom of Spain, has entire sympathy and most friendly sentiments for the native people of the Philippine Islands. For these reasons I desire to have the most amicable relations with you, and to have you and your people co-operate with us in military operations against the Spanish forces," etc. Aguinaldo responded cordially, and an extended correspondence followed, special services being asked for by the party of the first part, being rendered by the second, and duly acknowledged by the first. All this went on pleasantly until the capture of Manila, in which Aguinaldo effectively co-operated by fighting the Spaniards outside, taking many prisoners from them, and hemming them in. The services they rendered by taking thousands of Spanish prisoners, by harassing the Spaniards in the trenches, and by completely blockading Manila on the land side, were amply testified to by our own officers. Aguinaldo was also active on the sea. He had ships, which our commanders permitted to pass in and out of Manila Bay, under the flag of the Philippine republic, on their expeditions against other provinces.

Now, whether there was or not any formal compact of alliance signed and sealed, no candid man who has studied the official documents will deny that in point of fact the Filipinos, having been desired and invited to do so, were, before the capture of Manila, acting, and were practically recognized as our allies, and that as such they did effective service, which we accepted and profited by. This is an indisputable fact, proved by the record.

It is an equally indisputable fact that during that

period the Filipino government constantly and publicly, so that nobody could plead ignorance of it or
misunderstand it, informed the world that their object
was the achievement of national independence, and
that they believed the Americans had come in good
faith to help them accomplish that end, as in the case
of Cuba.   It was weeks after various proclamations
and other public utterances of Aguinaldo to that effect
that the correspondence between him and General
Anderson, which I have quoted, took place, and that
the useful services of the Filipinos as our practical
allies were accepted.   It is, further, an indisputable
fact that during this period our government did not
inform the Filipinos that their fond expectations as
to our recognition of their independence were mistaken.

Our secretary of state did, indeed, on June 16 write
to Mr. Pratt, our consul-general at Singapore, that
our government knew the Philippine insurgents, not
indeed as patriots struggling for liberty, and who,
like the Cubans, " are and of right ought to be free
and independent," but merely as " discontented and
rebellious subjects of Spain," who, if we occupied
their country in consequence of the war, would have
to yield us due " obedience."   And other officers of
our government were instructed not to make any
promises to the Filipinos as to the future.   But the
Filipinos themselves were not so informed.   They
were left to believe that, while fighting in co-operation
with the American forces, they were fighting for
their own independence.   They could not imagine
that the government of the great American Repub-

lic, while boasting of having gone to war with Spain under the banner of liberation and humanity in behalf of Cuba, was capable of secretly plotting to turn that war into one for the conquest and subjugation of the Philippines.

Thus the Filipinos went faithfully and bravely on doing for us the service of allies, of brothers-in-arms, far from dreaming that the same troops with whom they had been asked to co-operate would soon be employed by the great apostle of liberation and humanity to slaughter them for no other reason than that they, the Filipinos, continued to stand up for their own freedom and independence.

But just that was to happen. As soon as Manila was taken and we had no further use for our Filipino allies, they were ordered to fall back and back from the city and its suburbs. Our military commanders treated the Filipinos' country as if it were our own. When Aguinaldo sent one of his aides-de-camp to General Merritt with a request for an interview, General Merritt was "too busy." When our peace negotiations with Spain began, and representatives of the Filipinos asked for audience to solicit consideration of the rights and wishes of their people, the doors were slammed in their faces, in Washington as well as in Paris.

And behind those doors the scheme was hatched to deprive the Philippine Islanders of independence from foreign rule and to make them the subjects of another foreign ruler, and that foreign ruler their late ally, this great Republic which had grandly proclaimed to the world that its war against Spain was not a war of conquest, but a war of liberation and humanity.

Behind those doors which were tightly closed to the people of the Philippines a treaty was made with Spain, by the direction of President Mc-Kinley, which provided for the cession of the Philippine Islands by Spain to the United States for a consideration of $20,000,000. It has been said that this sum was not purchase money, but a compensation for improvements made by Spain, or a *solatium* to sweeten the pill of cession, or what not; but stripped of all cloudy verbiage, it was really purchase money, the sale being made by Spain under duress. Thus Spain sold, and the United States bought, what was called the sovereignty of Spain over the Philippine Islands and their people.

Now look at the circumstances under which that "cession" was made. Spain had lost the possession of the country, except a few isolated and helpless little garrisons, most of which were effectively blockaded by the Filipinos. The American forces occupied Cavité and the harbor and city of Manila, and nothing more. The bulk of the country was occupied and possessed by the people thereof, over whom Spain had, in point of fact, ceased to exercise any sovereignty, the Spanish power having been driven out or destroyed by the Filipino insurrection, while the United States had not acquired, beyond Cavité and Manila, any authority of whatever name by military occupation, nor by recognition on the part of the people. Aguinaldo's army surrounded Manila on the land side, and his government claimed organized control over fifteen

provinces. That government was established at Mal-
olos, not far from Manila; and a very respectable government it was. According to Mr. Barrett, our late
minister in Siam, himself an ardent imperialist, who
had seen it, it had a well-organized executive, divided into several departments, ably conducted, and
a popular assembly, a congress, which would favorably
compare with the Parliament of Japan—an infinitely
better government than the insurrectionary government of Cuba ever was.

It is said that Aguinaldo's government was in operation among only a part of the people of the islands.
This is true. But it is also certain that it was recognized and supported by an immeasurably larger part
of the people than Spanish sovereignty, which had
practically ceased to exist, and than American rule,
which was confined to a harbor and a city and which
was carried on by the exercise of military force under
what was substantially martial law over a people that
constituted about one twentieth of the whole population of the islands. Thus, having brought but a very
small fraction of the country and its people under our
military control, we bought by that treaty the sovereignty over the whole from a power which had practically lost that sovereignty and therefore did no
longer possess it; and we contemptuously disdained
to consult the existing native government, which
actually did control a large part of the country and the
people, and which had been our ally in the war with
Spain. The sovereignty we thus acquired may well
be defined as Abraham Lincoln once defined the
" popular sovereignty " of Senator Douglas's doctrine

—as being like a soup made by boiling the shadow of the breastbone of a pigeon that had been starved to death.

No wonder that treaty found opposition in the Senate. Virulent abuse was heaped upon the " statesman who would oppose the ratification of a peace treaty." A peace treaty? This was no peace treaty at all. It was a treaty with half a dozen bloody wars in its belly. It was, in the first place, an open and brutal declaration of war against our allies, the Filipinos, who struggled for freedom and independence from foreign rule. Every man not totally blind could see that. For such a treaty the true friends of peace could, of course, not vote.

But more. Even before that treaty had been assented to by the Senate—that is, even before that ghastly shadow of our Philippine sovereignty had obtained any legal sanction—President McKinley assumed of his own motion the sovereignty of the Philippine Islands by his famous " benevolent-assimilation" order of December 21, 1898, through which our military commander at Manila was directed forthwith to extend the military government of the United States over the whole archipelago, and by which the Filipinos were notified that if they refused to submit, they would be compelled by force of arms. Having bravely fought for their freedom and independence from one foreign rule, they did refuse to submit to another foreign rule, and then the slaughter of our late allies began—the slaughter by American arms of a once friendly and confiding people. And this slaughter has been going on ever since.

This is a grim story. Two years ago the prediction of such a possibility would have been regarded as a hideous nightmare, as the offspring of a diseased imagination. But to-day it is a true tale—a plain recital of facts taken from the official records. These things have actually been done in these last two years by and under the administration of William McKinley. This is our Philippine war as it stands. Is it a wonder that the American people should be troubled in their consciences? . . .

I am not here as a partisan, but as an American citizen anxious for the future of the Republic. And I cannot too earnestly admonish the American people, if they value the fundamental principles of their government and their own security and that of their children, for a moment to throw aside all partisan bias and soberly to consider what kind of a precedent they would set if they consented to, and by consenting approved, the President's management of the Philippine business merely " because we are in it."

We cannot expect all our future Presidents to be models in public virtue and wisdom, as George Washington was. Imagine now in the presidential office a man well-meaning, but, it may be, short-sighted and pliable, and under the influence of so-called " friends " who are greedy and reckless speculators, and who would not scruple to push him into warlike complications in order to get great opportunities for profit; or a man of that inordinate ambition which intoxicates the mind and befogs the conscience; or a man of extreme partisan spirit, who honestly believes the victory of his party to be necessary for the salvation of the universe, and may think that a foreign broil would serve the chances of his party; or a man of an uncontrollable combativeness of temperament which might run away with his sense of responsibility—and that we shall have such men in the presidential chair is by no means unlikely with our loose way of selecting candidates for the presidency.

Imagine, then, a future President belonging to either of these classes to have before him the precedent of Mr. McKinley's management of the Philippine business, sanctioned by the approval or only the acquiescence of the people, and to feel himself permitted—nay, even encouraged—to say to himself that, as this precedent shows, he may plunge the country into warlike conflicts of his own motion, without asking leave of Congress, with only some legal technicalities to cover his usurpation, or even without such, and that he may, by a machinery of deception called a war censorship, keep the people in the dark about what is going on; and that, into however bad a mess he may have got the country, he may count upon the people, as soon as a drop of blood has been shed, to uphold the usurpation and to cry down everybody who opposes it as a "traitor," and all this because "we are in it!" Can you conceive a more baneful precedent, a more prolific source of danger to the peace and security of the country? Can any sane man deny that it will be all the more prolific of evil if in this way we drift into a foreign policy full of temptation for dangerous adventures?

I say, therefore, that if we have the future of the Republic at heart we must not only not uphold the administration in its course because "we are in it," but just because we are in it, have been got into it in such a way, the American people should stamp the administration's proceedings with a verdict of disapproval so clear and emphatic and "get out of it" in such a fashion that this will be a solemn warning to future Presidents instead of a seductive precedent.

What, then, to accomplish this end is to be done? Of course we, as we are here, can only advise. But by calling forth expressions of the popular will by various means of public demonstration and, if need be, at the polls, we can make that advice so strong that those in power will hardly disregard it. We have often been taunted with having no positive policy to propose. But such a policy has more than once been proposed and I can only repeat it.

In the first place, let it be well understood that those are egregiously mistaken who think that if by a strong military effort the Philippine war be stopped everything will be right and no more question about it. No; the American trouble of conscience will not be appeased, and the question will be as big and virulent as ever, unless the close of the war be promptly followed by an assurance to the islanders of their freedom and independence, which assurance, if given now, would surely end the war without more fighting.

We propose, therefore, that it be given now. Let the Philippine islanders at the same time be told that the American people will be glad to see them establish an independent government, and to aid them in that task as far as may be necessary, and even, if required, lend our good offices to bring it about; and that meanwhile we shall deem it our duty to protect them against interference from other foreign powers—in other words, that with regard to them we mean honestly to live up to the righteous principles with the profession of which we commended to the world our Spanish war.

And then let us have in the Philippines, to carry out this program, not a small politician, nor a meddlesome martinet, but a statesman of large mind and genuine sympathy, who will not merely deal in sanctimonious cant and oily promises with a string to them, but who will prove by his acts that he and we are honest; who will keep in mind that their government is not merely to suit us, but to suit them; that it should not be measured by standards which we ourselves have not been able to reach, but be a government of their own, adapted to their own conditions and notions—whether it be a true republic, like ours, or a dictatorship like that of Porfirio Diaz, in Mexico, or an oligarchy like the one maintained by us in Hawaii, or even something like the boss rule we are tolerating in New York and Pennsylvania.

Those who talk so much about "fitting a people for self-government" often forget that no people were ever made "fit" for self-government by being kept in the leading strings of a foreign power. You learn to walk by doing your own crawling and stumbling. Self-government is learned only by exercising it upon one's own responsibility. Of course there will be mistakes and troubles and disorders. We have had and now have these, too—at the beginning our persecution of the Tories, our flounderings before the constitution was formed, our Shay's rebellion, our whisky war, and various failures and disturbances, among them a civil war that cost us a loss of life and treasure horrible to think of, and the murder of two Presidents. But who will say that on account of these things some foreign power should have kept the American people in leading strings to teach them to govern themselves? If the Philippine islanders do as well as the Mexicans, who have worked their way, since we let them alone after our war of 1847; through many disorders, to an orderly government, who will have a right to find fault with the result? Those who seek to impose upon them an unreasonable standard of excellence in self-government do not seriously wish to let them govern themselves at all. You may take it as a general rule that he who wants to reign over others is solemnly convinced that they are quite unable to govern themselves.

Now, what objection is there to the policy dictated by our fundamental principles and our good faith? I hear the angry cry: "What? Surrender to Aguinaldo? Will not the world ridicule and despise us for such a confession of our incompetency to deal with so feeble a foe? What will become of our prestige?" No, we shall not surrender to Aguinaldo. In giving up a criminal aggression we shall surrender only to our own consciences, to our own sense of right and justice, to our own understanding of our own true interests, and to the vital principles of our own Republic. Nobody will laugh at us whose good opinion we have reason to cherish. There will of course be an outcry of disappointment in England. But from whom will

11

it come? From such men as James Bryce or John
Morley or any one of those true friends of this Republic who understand and admire and wish to perpetuate
and spread the fundamental principles of its vitality?
No, not from them.

But the outcry will come from those in England
who long to see us entangled in complications apt to
make this American Republic dependent upon British
aid and thus subservient to British interests. They,
indeed, will be quite angry. But the less we mind
their displeasure as well as their flattery the better
for the safety as well as the honor of our country.

The true friends of this Republic in England, and,
indeed, all over the world, who are now grieving to
see us go astray, will rejoice and their hearts will be
uplifted with new confidence in our honesty, in our
wisdom, and in the virtue of democratic institutions
when they behold the American people throwing aside
all the puerilities of false pride and returning to the
path of their true duty. . . .

Who are the true patriots in America to-day—those
who drag our Republic, once so proud of its high principles and ideals, through the mire of broken pledges,
vulgar ambitions and vanities and criminal aggressions; those who do violence to their own moral sense
by insisting that, like the Dreyfus iniquity, a criminal
course once begun must be persisted in, or those who,
fearless of the demagogue clamor, strive to make the
flag of the Republic once more what it was once—
the flag of justice, liberty, and true civilization—and
to lift up the American people among the nations of

the earth to the proud position of the people that have a conscience and obey it.

The country has these days highly and deservedly honored Admiral Dewey as a national hero. Who are his true friends—those who would desecrate Dewey's splendid achievement at Manila by making it the starting point of criminal aggression, and thus the opening of a most disgraceful and inevitably disastrous chapter of American history, to be remembered with sorrow, or those who strive so to shape the results of that brilliant feat of arms that it may stand in history not as a part of a treacherous conquest, but as a true victory of American good faith in an honest war of liberation and humanity—to be proud of for all time, as Dewey himself no doubt meant it to be.

I know the imperialists will say that I have been pleading here for Aguinaldo and his Filipinos against our Republic. No, not for the Filipinos merely, although, as one of those who have grown gray in the struggle for free and honest government, I would never be ashamed to plead for the cause of freedom and independence, even when its banner is carried by dusky and feeble hands. But I am pleading for more. I am pleading for the cause of American honor and self-respect, American interests, American democracy; aye, for the cause of the American people against an administration of our public affairs which has wantonly plunged this country into an iniquitous war; which has disgraced the Republic by a scandalous breach of faith to a people struggling for their freedom whom we had used as allies; which has been systematically seeking to deceive and mislead the public mind by the manufacture of false news; which has struck at the very foundation of our constitutional government by an Executive usurpation of the war power; which makes sport of the great principles and high ideals that have been and should ever remain the guiding star of our course, and which, unless stopped in time, will transform this government of the people, for the people, and by the people into an imperial government cynically calling itself republican— a government in which the noisy worship of arrogant might will drown the voice of right; which will impose upon the people a burdensome and demoralizing militarism, and which will be driven into a policy of wild and rapacious adventure by the unscrupulous greed of the exploiter—a policy always fatal to democracy.

I plead the cause of the American people against all this, and I here declare my profound conviction that if this administration of our affairs were submitted for judgment to a popular vote on a clear issue it would be condemned by an overwhelming majority.

I confidently trust that the American people will prove themselves too clear-headed not to appreciate the vital difference between the expansion of the Republic and its free institutions over contiguous territory and kindred populations, which we all gladly welcome if accomplished peaceably or honorably, and imperialism which reaches out for distant lands to be ruled as subject provinces; too intelligent not to perceive that our very first step on the road of imperialism has been a betrayal of the fundamental principles of democracy, followed by disaster and disgrace; too enlightened not to understand that a monarchy may do such things and still remain a strong monarchy, while a democracy cannot do them and still remain a democracy; too wise not to detect the false pride, or the dangerous ambitions, or the selfish schemes which so often hide themselves under that deceptive cry of mock patriotism: "Our country, right or wrong!" They will not fail to recognize that our dignity, our free institutions, and the peace and welfare of this and coming generations of Americans will be secure only as we cling to the watchword of true patriotism: "Our country—when right to be kept right; when wrong to be put right."

Conkling, Roscoe, a noted American politician, born
in Albany, N. Y., October 30, 1829; died in New York
City April 18, 1888. He took up the study of law, and
being admitted to the bar in 1850, settled in Utica, N. Y.,
where his abilities as a lawyer soon brought him into prominence. He was mayor of Utica in 1858, and the next year
entered Congress as Representative, remaining till 1862. He
returned in 1864 and became a United States Senator in
1867. He was a Republican of strong partisan sympathies
and exercised an imperious control over many of his party.
Taking offense at some of President Garfield's New York
official appointments, Conkling withdrew from the Senate,
and, declining all inducements to return to public life, continued unreconciled with his party for the rest of his life.
He was an able, brilliant speaker, but vain and self-willed.
His address on nominating Grant for a third term is among
his most characteristic speeches.

SPEECH NOMINATING GRANT.*

DELIVERED JUNE 5, 1880.

IN obedience to instructions I should never dare to
disregard—expressing, also, my own firm convictions
—I rise to propose a nomination with which the country and the Republican party can grandly win. The
election before us is to be the Austerlitz of American
politics. It will decide, for many years, whether the
country shall be Republican or Cossack. The supreme need of the hour is not a candidate who can
carry Michigan. All Republican candidates can do

* Used by permission of A. R. Conkling.

that. The need is not of a candidate who is popular in the Territories, because they have no vote. The need is of a candidate who can carry doubtful States. Not the doubtful States of the North alone, but doubtful States of the South, which we have heard, if I understand it aright, ought to take little or no part here, because the South has nothing to give, but everything to receive.

No, gentlemen, the need that presses upon the conscience of this convention is of a candidate who can carry doubtful States both North and South. And believing that he, more surely than any other man, can carry New York against any opponent, and can carry not only the North, but several States of the South, New York is for Ulysses S. Grant. Never defeated in peace or in war, his name is the most illustrious borne by living man.

His services attest his greatness, and the country— nay, the world—knows them by heart. His fame was earned not alone in things written and said, but by the arduous greatness of things done. And perils and emergencies will search in vain in the future, as they have searched in vain in the past, for any other on whom the nation leans with such confidence and trust. Never having had a policy to enforce against the will of the people, he never betrayed a cause or a friend, and the people will never desert nor betray him.

Standing on the highest eminence of human distinction, modest, firm, simple, and self-poised, having filled all lands with his renown, he has seen not only the high-born and the titled, but the poor and the lowly in the uttermost ends of the earth rise and uncover before him. He has studied the needs and the defects of many systems of government, and he has returned a better American than ever, with a wealth of knowledge and experience added to the hard common sense which shone so conspicuously in all the fierce light that beat upon him during sixteen years, the most trying, the most portentous, the most perilous in the nation's history.

Vilified and reviled, ruthlessly aspersed by unnumbered presses, not in other lands, but in his own, assaults upon him have seasoned and strengthened his hold on the public heart. Calumny's ammunition has all been exploded; the powder has all been burned once; its force is spent; and the name of Grant will glitter a bright and imperishable star in the diadem of the Republic when those who have tried to tarnish that name have moldered in forgotten graves, and when their memories and their epitaphs have vanished utterly.

Never elated by success, never depressed by adversity, he has ever, in peace as in war, shown the genius of common sense. The terms he prescribed for Lee's surrender foreshadowed the wisest prophecies and principles of true reconstruction. Victor in the greatest war of modern times, he quickly signalized his aversion to war and his love of peace by an arbitration of internal disputes, which stands as the wisest, the most majestic example of its kind in the world's diplomacy. When inflation, at the height of its popularity and frenzy, had swept both Houses of Congress, it was the veto of Grant which, single and alone, overthrew expansion and cleared the way for specie resumption. To him, immeasurably more than to any other man, is due the fact that every paper dollar is at last as good as gold.

With him as our leader we shall have no defensive campaign. No! We shall have nothing to explain away. We shall have no apologies to make. The shafts and the arrows have all been aimed at him, and they lie broken and harmless at his feet.

Life, liberty and property will find a safeguard in him. When he said of the colored men in Florida, " Wherever I am, they may come also "—when he so said, he meant that, had he the power, the poor dwellers in the cabins of the South should no longer be driven in terror from the homes of their childhood and the graves of their murdered dead. When he refused to see Dennis Kearney in California, he meant that communism, lawlessness, and disorder, although it might stalk high-headed and dictate law to a whole city, would always find a foe in him. He meant that, popular or unpopular, he would hew to the line of right, let the chips fly where they may.

His integrity, his common sense, his courage, his unequalled experience, are the qualities offered to his country. The only argument, the only one that the wit of man or the stress of politics has devised is one which would dumfounder Solomon, because he thought there was nothing new under the sun. Having tried Grant twice and found him faithful, we are told that we must not, even after an interval of years, trust him again.

My countrymen! my countrymen! what stultification does not such a fallacy involve! The American people exclude Jefferson Davis from public trust! Why? why? Because he was the arch-traitor and would-be destroyer; and now the same people are asked to ostracise Grant and not to trust him. Why? why? I repeat: because he was the arch-preserver of his country, and because, not only in war, but twice as civil magistrate, he gave his highest, noblest efforts to the republic. Is this an electioneering juggle, or is it hypocrisy's masquerade?

There is no field of human activity, responsibility, or reason in which rational beings object to an agent because he has been weighed in the balance and not found wanting. There is, I say, no department of human reason in which sane men reject an agent because he has had experience, making him exceptionally competent and fit.

From the man who shoes your horse to the lawyer who tries your cause, the officer who manages your railway or your mill, the doctor into whose hands you give your life, or the minister who seeks to save your soul, what man do you reject because by his works you have known him and found him faithful and fit? What makes the presidential office an exception to all things else in the common sense to be applied to selecting its incumbent? Who dares—who dares to put fetters on that free choice and judgment which is the birthright of the American people? Can it be said that Grant has used official power and place to perpetuate his term?

He has no place, and official power has not been used for him. Without patronage and without emissaries, without committees, without bureaus, without telegraph wires running from his house to this convention, or running from his house anywhere else, this man is the candidate whose friends have never threatened to bolt unless this convention did as they said. He is a Republican who never wavers. He and his friends stand by the creed and the candidates of the Republican party. They hold the rightful rule of the majority as the very essence of their faith, and they mean to uphold that faith against not only the common enemy, but against the charlatans, jayhawkers, tramps and guerillas—the men who deploy between the lines, and forage now on one side and then on the other. This convention is master of a supreme opportunity. It can name the next President. It can make sure of his election. It can make sure not only of his election, but of his certain and peaceful inauguration. More than all, it can break that power which dominates and mildews the South. It can overthrow an organization whose very existence is a standing protest against progress.

The purpose of the Democratic party is spoils. Its very hope of existence is a Solid South. Its success is a menace to order and prosperity. I say this convention can overthrow that power. It can dissolve and emancipate a Solid South. It can speed the nation in a career of grandeur eclipsing all past achievements.

Gentlemen, we have only to listen above the din and look beyond the dust of an hour to behold the Republican party advancing with its ensigns resplendent with illustrious achievements, marching to certain and lasting victory with its greatest marshal at its head.

Blaine, James G., a celebrated American politician and orator, born at West Brownsville, Pa., January 31, 1830; died in Washington, D. C., January 27, 1893. He taught school for several years at the opening of his career, and although he studied law he never sought admission to the bar. In 1853 he settled in Augusta, Maine, and there engaged in journalism, entering the State Legislature in 1858, and remaining there four years. From 1862 to 1876 he was a Representative in Congress, serving as Speaker for six years, and, then entered the National Senate, to which he was re-elected for a second term. He was Secretary of State, 1881–82, and Secretary of State for a second time during President Harrison's administration, 1889–93. He was twice a candidate for nomination to the presidency, and was the actual candidate of the Republican party for that office in 1884, being defeated after a contest of great bitterness. Blaine was an able, brilliant politician, and was much admired as an orator, His oration on Garfield is one of his finest efforts.

ON THE REMONETIZATION OF SILVER.

UNITED STATES SENATE, FEBRUARY 7, 1878.

The discussion on the question of remonetizing silver, Mr. President, has been prolonged, able, and exhaustive. I may not expect to add much to its value, but I promise not to add much to its length. I shall endeavor to consider facts rather than theories, to state conclusions rather than arguments:

First. I believe gold and silver coin to be the money of the Constitution—indeed, the money of the American people anterior to the Constitution, which that great organic law recognized as quite independent of its own existence. No power was conferred on Congress to declare that either metal should not be money. Congress has therefore, in my judgment, no power to demonetize silver any more than to demonetize gold; no power to demonetize either any more than to demonetize both. In this statement I am but repeating the weighty dictum of the first of constitutional lawyers. " I am certainly of opinion," said Mr. Webster, " that gold and silver, at rates fixed by Congress, constitute the legal standard of value in this country, and that neither Congress nor any State has authority to establish any other standard or to displace this standard." Few persons can be found, I apprehend, who will maintain that Congress possesses the power to demonetize both gold and silver, or that Congress could be justified in prohibiting the coinage of both; and yet in logic and legal construction it would be difficult to show where and why the power of Congress over silver is greater than over gold—greater over either than over the two. If, therefore, silver has been demonetized, I am in favor of remonetizing it. If its coinage has been prohibited, I am in favor of ordering it to be resumed. If it has been restricted, I am in favor of having it enlarged.

Second. What power, then, has Congress over gold and silver? It has the exclusive power to coin them; the exclusive power to regulate their value; very great, very wise, very necessary powers, for the discreet exercise of which a critical occasion has now arisen. However men may differ about causes and processes, all will admit that within a few years a great disturbance has taken place in the relative values of gold and silver, and that silver is worth less or gold is worth more in the money markets of the world in 1878 than in 1873, when the further coinage of silver dollars was prohibited in this country. To remonetize it now as though the facts and circumstances of that day were surrounding us, is to wilfully and blindly deceive ourselves. If our demonetization were the only cause for the decline in the value of silver, then remonetization would be its proper and effectual cure. But other causes, quite beyond our control, have been far more potentially operative than the simple fact of Congress prohibiting its further coinage; and as legislators we are bound to take cognizance of these causes. The demonetization of silver in the great German Empire and the consequent partial, or wellnigh complete, suspension of coinage in the governments of the Latin Union, have been the leading dominant causes for the rapid decline in the value of silver. I do not think the over-supply of silver has had, in comparison with these other causes, an appreciable influence in the decline of its value, because its over-supply with respect to gold in these later years has not been nearly so great as was the over-supply of gold with respect to silver for many years after the mines of California and Australia were opened; and the over-supply of gold from those rich sources did not effect the relative positions and uses of the two metals in any European country.

I believe then if Germany were to remonetize silver and the kingdoms and states of the Latin Union were to reopen their mints, silver would at once resume its former relation with gold. The European countries when driven to remonetization, as I believe they will be, must of necessity adopt their old ratio of fifteen and a half of silver to one of gold, and we shall then be compelled to adopt the same ratio instead of our former sixteen to one. For if we fail to do this we shall, as before, lose our silver, which like all things else seeks the highest market; and if fifteen and a half pounds of silver will buy as much gold in Europe as sixteen pounds will buy in America, the silver, of course, will go to Europe. But our line of policy in a joint movement with other nations to remonetize is very simple and very direct. The difficult problem is what we shall do when we aim to re-establish silver without the co-operation of European powers, and really as an advance movement to coerce them there into the same policy. Evidently the first dictate of prudence is to coin such a dollar as will not only do justice among our citizens at home, but will prove a protection—an absolute barricade—against the gold monometallists of Europe, who, whenever the opportunity offers, will quickly draw from us the one hundred and sixty millions of gold coin still in our midst. And if we coin a silver dollar of full legal tender, obviously below the current value of the gold dollar, we are opening wide our doors and inviting Europe to take our gold. And with our gold flowing out from us we are forced to the single silver standard and our relations with the leading commercial countries of the world are at once embarrassed and crippled.

Third. The question before Congress then—sharply defined in the pending House bill—is, whether it is now safe and expedient to offer free coinage to the

silver dollar of $412\frac{1}{2}$ grains, with the mints of the
Latin Union closed and Germany not permitting silver to be coined as money. At current rates of silver
the free coinage of a dollar containing $412\frac{1}{2}$ grains,
worth in gold about ninety-two cents, gives an ille-
gitimate profit to the owner of the bullion, enabling
him to take ninety-two cents' worth of it to the mint
and get it stamped as coin and force his neighbor to
take it for a full dollar. This is an undue and unfair
advantage which the government has no right to give
to the owner of silver bullion, and which defrauds the
man who is forced to take the dollar. And it assured-
ly follows that if we give free coinage to this dollar
of inferior value and put it in circulation, we do so at
the expense of our better coinage in gold; and unless
we expect the uniform and invariable experience of
other nations to be in some mysterious way suspended
for our peculiar benefit, we inevitably lose our gold
coin. It will flow out from us with the certainty and
resistless force of the tides. Gold has indeed remained
with us in considerable amount during the circulation
of the inferior currency of the legal tender; but that
was because there were two great uses reserved by law
for gold: the collection of customs and the payment
of interest on the public debt. But if the inferior silver
coin is also to be used for these two reserved purposes,
then gold has no tie to bind it to us. What gain, therefore, would we make for the circulating medium, if
on opening the gate for silver to flow in, we open a still
wider gate for gold to flow out? If I were to venture
upon a dictum on the silver question, I would declare
that until Europe remonetizes we cannot afford to coin

a dollar as low as 412½ grains. After Europe remonetizes on the old standard, we cannot afford to coin a dollar above 400 grains. If we coin too low a dollar before general remonetization our gold will flow out from us. If we coin too high a dollar after general remonetization our silver will leave us. It is only an equated value both before and after general remonetization that will preserve both gold and silver to us. . . .

Fifth. The responsibility of re-establishing silver in its ancient and honorable place as money in Europe and America, devolves really on the Congress of the United States. If we act here with prudence, wisdom, and firmness, we shall not only successfully remonetize silver and bring it into general use as money in our own country, but the influence of our example will be potential among all European nations, with the possible exception of England. Indeed, our annual indebtment to Europe is so great that if we have the right to pay it in silver we necessarily coerce those nations by the strongest of all forces, self-interest, to aid us in upholding the value of silver as money. But if we attempt the remonetization on a basis which is obviously and notoriously below the fair standard of value as it now exists, we incur all the evil consequences of failure at home and the positive certainty of successful opposition abroad. We are and shall be the greatest producers of silver in the world, and we have a larger stake in its complete monetization than any other country. The difference to the United States between the general acceptance of silver as money in the commercial world and its destruction as money, will possibly equal within the next half century the

12

entire bonded debt of the nation. But to gain this advantage we must make it actual money—the accepted equal of gold in the markets of the world. Remonetization here followed by general remonetization in Europe will secure to the United States the most stable basis for its currency that we have ever enjoyed, and will effectually aid in solving all the problems by which our financial situation is surrounded.

Sixth. On the much-vexed and long-mooted question of a bimetallic or monometallic standard my own views are sufficiently indicated in the remarks I have made. I believe the struggle now going on in this country and in other countries for a single gold standard would, if successful, produce widespread disaster in the end throughout the commercial world. The destruction of silver as money and establishing gold as the sole unit of value must have a ruinous effect on all forms of property except those investments which yield a fixed return in money. These would be enormously enhanced in value, and would gain a disproportionate and unfair advantage over every other species of property. If, as the most reliable statistics affirm, there are nearly seven thousand millions of coin or bullion in the world, not very unequally divided between gold and silver, it is impossible to strike silver out of existence as money without results which will prove distressing to millions and utterly disastrous to tens of thousands. Alexander Hamilton, in his able and invaluable report in 1791 on the establishment of a mint, declared that " to annul the use of either gold or silver as money is to abridge the quantity of circulating medium, and is liable to all the objections which arise from a comparison of the benefits of a full circulation with the evils of a scanty circulation." I take no risk in saying that the benefits of a full circulation and the evils of a scanty circulation are both immeasurably greater to-day than they were when Mr. Hamilton uttered these weighty words, always provided that the circulation is one of actual money, and not of depreciated promises to pay.

In the report from which I have already quoted, Mr. Hamilton argues at length in favor of a double standard, and all the subsequent experience of wellnigh ninety years has brought out no clearer statement of the whole case nor developed a more complete comprehension of this subtle and difficult subject. "On the whole," says Mr. Hamilton, "it seems most advisable not to attach the unit exclusively to either of the metals, because this cannot be done effectually without destroying the office and character of one of them as money and reducing it to the situation of mere merchandise." And then Mr. Hamilton wisely concludes that this reduction of either of the metals to mere merchandise (I again quote his exact words) "would probably be a greater evil than occasional variations in the unit from the fluctuations in the relative value of the metals, especially if care be taken to regulate the proportion between them with an eye to their average commercial value." I do not think that this country, holding so vast a proportion of the world's supply of silver in its mountains and its mines, can afford to reduce the metal to the "situation of mere merchandise." If silver ceases to be used as money in Europe and America, the great mines of the Pacific

Slope will be closed and dead. Mining enterprises of the gigantic scale existing in this country cannot be carried on to provide backs for looking-glasses and to manufacture cream-pitchers and sugar-bowls. A vast source of wealth to this entire country is destroyed the moment silver is permanently disused as money. It is for us to check that tendency and bring the continent of Europe back to the full recognition of the value of the metal as a medium of exchange.

Seventh. The question of beginning anew the coinage of silver dollars has aroused much discussion as to its effect on the public credit; and the Senator from Ohio (Mr. Matthews) placed this phase of the subject in the very forefront of the debate—insisting, prematurely and illogically, I think, on a sort of judicial construction in advance, by concurrent resolution, of a certain law in case that law should happen to be passed by Congress. My own view on this question can be stated very briefly. I believe the public creditor can afford to be paid in any silver dollar that the United States can afford to coin and circulate. We have forty thousand millions of property in this country, and a wise self-interest will not permit us to overturn its relations by seeking for an inferior dollar wherewith to settle the dues and demands of any creditor. The question might be different from a merely selfish standpoint if, on paying the dollar to the public creditor, it would disappear after performing that function. But the trouble is that the inferior dollar you pay the public creditor remains in circulation, to the exclusion of the better dollar. That which you pay at home will stay there; that which you send abroad will come back.

The interest of the public creditor is indissolubly bound up with the interest of the whole people. Whatever affects him affects us all; and the evil that we might inflict upon him by paying an inferior dollar would recoil upon us with a vengeance as manifold as the aggregate wealth of the Republic transcends the comparatively small limits of our bonded debt. And remember that our aggregate wealth is always increasing, and our bonded debt steadily growing less! If paid in a good silver dollar, the bondholder has nothing to complain of. If paid in an inferior silver dollar he has the same grievance that will be uttered still more plaintively by the holder of the legal-tender note and of the national-bank bill, by the pensioner, by the day laborer, and by the countless host of the poor, whom we have with us always, and on whom the most distressing effect of inferior money will be ultimately precipitated.

But I must say, Mr. President, that the specific demand for the payment of our bonds in gold coin and in nothing else comes with an ill-grace from certain quarters. European criticism is levelled against us and hard names are hurled at us across the ocean, for simply daring to state that the letter of our law declares the bonds to be payable in standard coin of July 14, 1870; expressly and explicitly declared so, and declared so in the interest of the public creditor, and the declaration inserted in the very body of the eight hundred million of bonds that have been issued since that date. Beyond all doubt the silver dollar was included in the standard coins of that public act. Payment at that time would have been as acceptable and as undisputed in silver as in gold dollars, for both were equally valuable in the European as well as in the American market. Seven-eighths of all our bonds, owned out of the country, are held in Germany and in Holland, and Germany has demonetized silver and Holland has been forced thereby to suspend its coinage, since the subjects of both powers purchased our securities. The German Empire, the very year after we made our specific declaration for paying our bonds in coin, passed a law destroying so far as lay in their power the value of silver as money. I do not say that it was specially aimed at this country, but it was passed regardless of its effect upon us, and was followed, according to public and undenied statement, by a large investment on the part of the German Government in our bonds, with a view, it was understood, of holding them as a coin reserve for drawing gold from us to aid in establishing their gold standard at home. Thus, by one move the German Government destroyed, so far as lay in its power, the then existing value of silver as money, enhanced consequently the value of gold, and then got into position to draw gold from us at the moment of their need, which would also be the moment of our own sorest distress. I do not say that the German Government in these successive steps did a single thing which it had not a perfect right to do, but I do say that the subjects of that empire have no right to complain of our government for the initial step which has impaired the value of one of our standard coins. And the German Government, by joining with us in the remonetization of silver, can place that standard coin in its old position and make it as easy for this government to pay and as profitable for their subjects to receive the one metal as the other. . . .

The effect of paying the labor of this country in silver coin of full value, as compared with the irredeemable paper or as compared even with silver of inferior value, will make itself felt in a single generation to the extent of tens of millions, perhaps hundreds of millions, in the aggregate savings which represent consolidated capital. It is the instinct of man from the savage to the scholar—developed in childhood and remaining with age—to value the metals which in all tongues are called precious. Excessive paper money leads to extravagance, to waste, and to want, as we painfully witness on all sides to-day. And in the midst of the proof of its demoralizing and destructive effect, we hear it proclaimed in the Halls of Congress that "the people demand cheap money." I deny it. I declare such a phrase to be a total misapprehension, a total misinterpretation of the popular wish. The people do not demand cheap money. They demand an abundance of good money, which is an entirely different thing. They do not want a single gold standard that will exclude silver and benefit those already rich. They do not want an inferior silver standard that will drive out gold and not help those already poor. They want both metals, in full value, in equal honor, in whatever abundance the bountiful earth will yield them to the searching eye of science and to the hard hand of labor.

The two metals have existed side by side in harmonious, honorable companionship as money, ever since intelligent trade was known among men. It is wellnigh forty centuries since " Abraham weighed to Ephron the silver which he had named in the audience of the sons of Heth—four hundred shekels of silver—current money with the merchant." Since that time nations have risen and fallen, races have disappeared, dialects and languages have been forgotten, arts have been lost, treasures have perished, continents have been discovered, islands have been sunk in the sea, and through all these ages, and through all these changes, silver and gold have reigned supreme, as the representatives of value, as the media of exchange. The dethronement of each has been attempted in turn, and sometimes the dethronement of both; but always in vain. And we are here to-day, deliberating anew over the problem which comes down to us from Abraham's time: *the weight of the silver* that shall be " current money with the merchant."

Garfield, James A., an American statesman, twentieth President of the United States, born in Orange township, Ohio, November 19, 1831; died at Elberon, N. J., September 19, 1881. Obtaining an education with difficulty, he studied law and in 1861 was admitted to the bar. He served with distinction during a part of the Civil war, becoming a general in the Federal army, and in 1863 entered Congress as a representative from Ohio. In 1880 he became a member of the United States Senate, and in the autumn of that year was the successful candidate for the Presidency of the Republican party. He was assassinated by a disappointed office-seeker in July, 1881, and after a long illness died from his wounds in the following September. He was an eloquent, though not a brilliant speaker, and in congressional debates was always able. His speeches and addresses are included in his works edited by B. A. Hinsdale, 1883.

INAUGURAL ADDRESS.

DELIVERED MARCH 4, 1881.

FELLOW CITIZENS,—We stand to-day upon an eminence which overlooks a hundred years of national life—a century crowded with perils, but crowned with the triumphs of liberty and love. Before continuing our onward march, let us pause on this height for a moment, to strengthen our faith and renew our hope, by a glance at the pathway along which our people have travelled. It is now three days more than one hundred years since the adoption of the first written constitution of the United States, the articles of confederation and of perpetual union. The new Republic was then beset with danger on every hand. It had not conquered a place in the family of nations. The decisive battle of the war for independence, whose centennial anniversary will soon be gratefully celebrated at Yorktown, had not yet been fought. The colonists were struggling, not only against the armies of Great Britain, but against the settled opinions of mankind, for the world did not believe that the supreme authority of government could be safely intrusted to the guardianship of the people themselves. We cannot over-estimate the fervent love of liberty, the intelligent courage, and saving common sense, with which our fathers made the great experiment of self-government. When they found, after a short time, that the confederacy of States was too weak to meet the necessities of a vigorous and expanding Republic, they boldly set it aside, and, in its stead, established a national Union, founded directly upon the will of the people, and endowed it with future powers of self-preservation, and with ample authority for the accomplishments of its great objects. Under this constitution the boundaries of freedom have been enlarged, the foundations of order and peace have been strengthened, and the growth, in all the better elements of national life, has vindicated the wisdom of the founders, and given new hope to their descendants. Under this constitution our people long ago made themselves safe against danger from without, and secured for their marines and flag an equality of rights on all the seas. Under the constitution twenty-five States have been added to the Union, with constitutions and laws, framed and enforced by their own citizens, to secure the manifold

blessings of local and self-government. The jurisdiction of this constitution now covers an area fifty
times greater than that of the original thirteen States,
and a population twenty times greater than that of 1870.
The supreme trial of the constitution came at last,
under the tremendous pressure of civil war. We, ourselves, are witnesses that the Union emerged from the
blood and fire of that conflict purified and made
stronger for all the beneficent purposes of good government, and now, at the close of this first century
of growth, with inspirations of its history in their
hearts, our people have lately reviewed the condition
of the nation, passed judgment upon the conduct and
opinions of the political parties and have registered
their will concerning the future administration· of
government. To interpret and execute that will, in
accordance with the constitution, is the paramount
duty of the Executive.

Even from this brief review, it is manifest that the
nation is resolutely facing to the front, resolved to employ its best energies in developing the great possibilities of the future. Sacredly preserving whatever has
been gained to liberty and good government during the
century, our people are determined to leave behind
them all those bitter controversies concerning things
which have been irrevocably settled, and the further
discussion of which can only stir up strife and delay
the onward march. The supremacy of the nation and
its laws should be no longer a subject of debate. That
discussion, which for half a century threatened the
existence of the Union, was closed at last in the high
court of war, by a decree from which there is no ap-

peal, that the constitution and laws made in pursuance thereof shall continue to be the supreme law of the land, binding alike upon the States and upon the people. This decree does not disturb the autonomy of the States, nor interfere with any of their necessary rules of local self-government, but it does fix and establish the permanent supremacy of the Union. The will of the nation, speaking with the voice of battle, and through the amended constitution, has fulfilled the great promise of 1776, by proclaiming, "Liberty throughout the land to all the inhabitants thereof."

The elevation of the negro race from slavery to the full rights of citizenship is the most important political change we have known since the adoption of the constitution of 1787. No thoughtful man can fail to appreciate its beneficent effect upon our institutions and people. It has freed us from the perpetual danger of war and dissolution. It has added immensely to the moral and industrial forces of our people. It has liberated the master as well as the slave from the relation which wronged and enfeebled both. It has surrendered to their own guardianship the manhood of more than 5,000,000 people, and has opened to each one of them a career of freedom and usefulness; it has given new inspiration to the power of self-help in both races, by making labor more honorable to one, and more necessary to the other. The influence of this force will grow greater and bear richer fruit with coming years. No doubt the great change has caused serious disturbance to our southern community. This is to be deplored, though it was unavoidable; but those who resisted the change should remember that, under our institutions, there was no middle ground for the negro race between slavery and equal citizenship. There can be no permanent disfranchised peasantry in the United States. Freedom can never yield its fulness of blessings as long as law, or its administration, places the smallest obstacle in the pathway of any virtuous citizen. The emancipated race has already made remarkable progress. With unquestioning devotion to the Union, with a patience and gentleness not born of fear, they have " followed the light as God gave them to see the light." They are rapidly laying the material foundations for self-support, widening the circle of intelligence, and beginning to enjoy the blessings that gather around the homes of the industrious poor. They deserve the generous encouragement of all good men. So far as my authority can lawfully extend, they shall enjoy the full and equal protection of the constitution and laws.

The free enjoyment of equal suffrage is still in question, and a frank statement of the issue may aid its solution. It is alleged that in many communities negro citizens are practically denied the freedom of the ballot. In so far as the truth of this allegation is admitted, it is answered that in many places honest local government is impossible, if the mass of uneducated negroes are allowed to vote. These are grave allegations. So far as the latter is true, it is the only palliation that can be offered for opposing the freedom of the ballot. A bad local government is certainly a great evil which ought to be prevented, but to violate the freedom and sanctity of suffrage is more than an evil; it is a crime, which, if persisted in, will destroy the government itself. Suicide is not a remedy. If in other lands it be high treason to compass the death of the king, it should be counted no less a crime here to strangle our sovereign power and stifle its voice. It has been said that unsettled questions have no pity for the repose of nations; it should be said, with the utmost emphasis, that this question of suffrage will never give repose or safety to the States or to the nation until each, within its own jurisdiction, makes and keeps the ballot free and pure by the strong sanctions of law.

But the danger which arises from ignorance in the voter cannot be denied. It covers a field far wider than that of negro suffrage, and the present condition of that race. It is a danger that lurks and hides in the courses and fountains of power in every State. We have no standard by which to measure the disaster that may be brought upon us by ignorance and vice in citizens when joined to corruption and fraud in suffrage. The voters of the Union, who make and unmake constitutions, and upon whose will hangs the destiny of our governments, can transmit their supreme authority to no successor, save the coming generation of voters, who are sole heirs of our sovereign powers. If that generation comes to its inheritance blinded by ignorance and corrupted by vice, the fall of the Republic will be certain and remediless. The census has already sounded the alarm in appalling figures, which mark how dangerously high the tide of illiteracy has risen among our voters and their children. To the South the question is of supreme importance, but the responsibility for the existence of slavery did not rest on the South alone. The nation itself is responsible for the extension of suffrage, and is under special obligations to aid in removing the illiteracy which it has added to the voting population of the North and South alike. There is but one remedy. All the constitutional power of the nation and of the States and all the volunteer forces of the people should be summoned to meet this danger by the saving influence of universal education.

It is a high privilege and sacred duty of those now living to educate their successors, and fit them by intelligence and virtue for the inheritance which awaits them in this beneficent work. Sections and races should be forgotten, and partisanship should be unknown. Let our people find a new meaning in the divine oracle which declares that " a little child shall lead them." For our little children will soon control the destinies of the Republic.

My countrymen, we do not now differ in our judgment concerning the controversies of past generations, and fifty years hence our children will not be divided in their opinions concerning our controversies. They will surely bless their fathers and their fathers' God that the Union was preserved, that slavery was overthrown, and that both races were made equal before the law. We may hasten or we may retard, but we cannot prevent the final reconciliation. Is it not possible for us now to make a truce with time, by anticipating and accepting its inevitable verdicts? Enterprises of the highest importance to our moral and material well-being invite us, and offer ample scope for the employment of our best powers. Let all our people, leaving behind them the battle-fields of dead issues, move forward, and, in the strength of liberty and a restored Union, win the grander victories of peace.

The prosperity which now prevails is without parallel in our history. Fruitful seasons have done much to secure it, but they have not done all.

The preservation of the public credit, and the resumption of specie payments, so successfully attained by the administration of my predecessors, has enabled our people to secure the blessings which the seasons brought. By the experience of commercial nations in all ages, it has been found that gold and silver afford the only safe foundation for a monetary system. Confusion has recently been created by variations in the relative value of the two metals, but I confidently believe that arrangements can be made between the leading commercial nations which will secure the general use of both metals. Congress should provide that compulsory coinage of silver now required by law may not disturb our monetary system by driving either metal out of circulation. If possible, such adjustment should be made that the purchasing power of every coined dollar will be exactly equal to its debt-paying power in the markets of the world. The chief duty of the national government, in connection with the currency of the country, is to coin and declare its value. Grave doubts have been entertained whether Congress is authorized, by the constitution, to make any form of paper money legal tender. The present issue of United States notes has been sustained by the necessities of war, but such paper should depend for its value and currency upon its convenience in use and its prompt redemption in coin at the will of a holder, and not upon its compulsory circulation. These notes are not money, but promises to pay money. If holders demand it, the promise should be kept.

The refunding of the national debt, at a lower rate of interest, should be accomplished without compelling the withdrawal of the national bank notes, and thus disturbing the business of the country. I venture to refer to the position I have occupied on financial questions, during my long service in Congress, and to say that time and experience have strengthened the opinions I have so often expressed on these subjects. The finances of the government shall suffer no detriment which it may be possible for my administration to prevent.

The interests of agriculture deserve more attention from the government than they have yet received. The farms of the United States afford homes and employment for more than one-half the people, and furnish much the largest part of all our exports. As the government lights our coasts for the protection of mariners and for the benefit of commerce, so it should give to the tillers of the soil the lights of practical science and experience.

Our manufactures are rapidly making us industrially independent, and are opening to capital and labor new and profitable fields of employment. This steady and healthy growth should still be maintained.

Our facilities for transportation should be promoted by the continued improvement of our harbors and great interior water-ways, and by the increase of our tonnage on the ocean. The development of the world's commerce has led to an urgent demand for shortening

13

the great sea-voyage around Cape Horn, by constructing ship canals or railways across the isthmus which
unites the two continents. Various plans to this end
have been suggested, but none of them have been sufficiently matured to warrant the United States extending pecuniary aid. The subject is one which will
immediately engage the attention of the government
with a view to thorough protection to American interests. We will urge no narrow policy, nor seek
peculiar or exclusive privileges in any commercial
route; but, in the language of my predecessors, I believe it is to be " the right and duty of the United
States to assert and maintain such supervision and authority over any inter-oceanic canal across the isthmus
that connects North and South America as will protect
our national interests."

The constitution guarantees absolute religious freedom. Congress is also prohibited from making any
law respecting the establishment of religion or prohibiting the free exercise thereof. The Territories of
the United States are subject to the direct legislative
authority of Congress, and hence the general government is responsible for any violation of the constitution in any of them. It is, therefore, a reproach to
the government that in the most populous of the
Territories the constitutional guarantee is not enjoyed
by the people, and the authority of Congress is set at
naught. The Mormon church not only offends the
moral sense of mankind by sanctioning polygamy, but
prevents the administration of justice through the
ordinary instrumentalities of law. In my judgment
it is the duty of Congress, while respecting to the

JAMES A. GARFIELD.

utmost the conscientious convictions and religious scruples of every citizen, to prohibit, within its jurisdiction, all criminal practices, especially of that class which destroy family relations and endanger social order; nor can any ecclesiastical organization be safely permitted to usurp in the smallest degree the functions and powers of the national government.

The civil service can never be placed on a satisfactory basis until it is regulated by law. For the good of the service itself, for the protection of those who are intrusted with the appointing power, against the waste of time and the obstruction to public business caused by inordinate pressure for place, and for the protection of incumbents against intrigue and wrong, I shall, at the proper time, ask Congress to fix the tenure of minor offices of the several executive departments, and prescribe the grounds upon which removals shall be made during the terms for which the incumbents have been appointed.

Finally, acting always within the authority and limitations of the constitution, invading neither the rights of States nor the reserved rights of the people, it will be the purpose of my administration to maintain authority, and in all places within its jurisdiction to enforce obedience to all the laws of the Union; in the interest of the people, to demand a rigid economy in all the expenditures of the government, and to require honest and faithful services of all the executive officers, remembering that offices were created not for the benefit of incumbents or their supporters but for the service of the government.

And, now, fellow citizens, I am about to assume the

great trust which you have committed to my hands. I appeal to you for that earnest and thoughtful support which makes this government—in fact as it is in law—a government of the people. I shall greatly rely upon the wisdom and patriotism of Congress, and of those who may share with me the responsibilities and duties of the administration; and, above all, upon our efforts to promote the welfare of this great people and their government I reverently invoke the support and blessing of Almighty God.

Donnelly, Ignatius, an American politician and prose writer, born in Philadelphia, November 3, 1831; died January 1, 1901. He studied law, was admitted to the bar in 1852, removed to Minnesota in 1856, and established himself in practice there. Engaging in politics, he was elected lieutenant-governor in 1859, and was re-elected in 1861. As representative from Minnesota he sat in the 38th, 39th and 40th Congresses, and was a member of the lower house of the State Legislature, 1886–87, and again in 1897. He was also state senator, 1874–78, and again in 1890. In 1900 he was the candidate of the People's Party for vice-president. He was the author of two fanciful archæological works, and in " The Great Cryptogram " ardently championed the theory of the Baconian authorship of Shakespeare.

RECONSTRUCTION.

IN THE HOUSE OF REPRESENTATIVES, JANUARY 18, 1866.

[The House having under consideration House bill No. 543, to provide for restoring to the States lately in insurrection their full political rights, Mr. Donnelly said :]

MR. SPEAKER,—I desire to express myself in favor of the main purposes of the bill now under consideration. [To provide for restoring to the States lately in insurrection their full political rights.]

Through the clouds of a great war and the confusion of a vast mass of uncertain legislation we are at length reaching something tangible; we have passed the " Serbonian bog," and are approaching good dry land.

This is the logical conclusion of the war. The war

was simply the expression of the determination of the
nation to subordinate the almost unanimous will of
the white people of the rebellious States to the unity
and prosperity of the whole country. Having gone
thus far we cannot pause. We must still subordinate
their wishes to our welfare.

This bill proposes to commence at the very foundation and build upward.

We have the assurance of President Johnson that
"the rebellion has in its revolutionary progress deprived the rebellious States of all civil government,"
and that their State institutions have been "prostrated
and paid out upon the ground."

In such a state of anarchy and disorganization the
very foundations of society are laid bare; and we
reach, as it were, the primary rocks, the everlasting
granite of justice and right which underlies all human
government.

In the language of the great Edmund Burke:

"When men break up the original compact or
agreement which gives its corporate form and capacity
to a State they are no longer a people; they have no
longer a corporate existence; they have no longer a
legal coactive force to bind within nor a claim to be
recognized abroad. They are a number of vague,
loose individuals, and nothing more; with them all
is to begin again. Alas! they little know how many a
weary step is to be taken before they can form themselves into a mass which has a true political personality." *

* Burke's Works, vol. iii, p, 82.

I shall not stop to consider the objection made to the second section of the bill by the gentleman from Wisconsin [Mr. Paine]. With the purpose and intent of his remarks I thoroughly concur. I conclude, however, that the object of the gentleman from Pennsylvania [Mr. Stevens], in providing for such a partial and temporary recognition of the rebel governments, was to protect society from the evils of a total abrogation of all law and order. But it seems to me that whatever binding force those governments can have, founded as they are upon revolution and by the hands of revolutionary agents, is to be derived solely from such recognition as Congress may give them. It may be possible in this and other particulars to perfect the bill. I desire to speak rather to its general scope and purpose.

Government having, by the acknowledgment of the President, ceased to exist, law being swept aside, and chaos having come again in those rebellious States, by what principle shall the law-making power of the nation—the Congress—govern itself? Shall it bend its energies to renew old injustice? Shall it receive to its fraternal embrace only that portion of the population which circumstance or accident or century-old oppression may have brought to the surface? Shall it—having broken up the armies and crushed the hopes of the rebels—pander to their bigotries and cringe to their prejudices? Shall it hesitate to do it right out of deference to the sentiments of those who but a short time since were mowed down at the mouth of its cannon?

It is to my mind most clear that slavery having ceased

to exist the slaves became citizens; being citizens they are a part of the people; and being a part of the people no organization deserves a moment's consideration at our hands which attempts to ignore them. If they were white people whom it was thus sought to disfranchise and outlaw not a man in the nation would dare to say nay to this proposition; every impulse of our hearts would rise up in indignant remonstrance against their oppressors. But it has pleased Almighty God, who takes counsel of no man, not even of the founders of the rebellion, to paint them of a different complexion, and that variation in the *pigmentum mucum* is to rise up as a perpetual barrier in our pathway toward equal justice and equal rights.

For one, with the help of God, I propose to do what I know to be right in the face of all prejudices and all obstructions; and so long as I have a seat in this body I shall never vote to reconstruct any rebellious State on any such basis of cruelty and injustice as that proposed by the Opposition here.

Take the case of South Carolina. She has 300,000 whites and 400,000 blacks; and we are asked to hand over the 400,000 blacks to the unrestrained custody and control of the 300,000 whites. We are to know no one but the whites; to communicate with no one but the whites; this floor is to recognize no one but white representatives of the whites. The whites are to make the laws, execute the laws, interpret the laws, and write the history of their own deeds; but below them, under them, there is to be a vast population—a majority of the whole people—seething and writhing in a condition of suffering, darkness, and wretchedness unparalleled in the world.

And this is to be an American State! This is to be a component part of the great, humane, Christian Republic of the world. This is to be the protection the mighty Republic is to deal out to its poor black friends who were faithful to it in its hour of trial; this is the punishment it is to inflict upon its perfidious enemies.

No, sir, no sophistry, no special pleading, can lead the American people to this result. Through us or over us it will reconstruct those States on a basis of impartial and eternal justice. Such a mongrel, patchwork, bastard reconstruction as some gentlemen propose, even if put into shape, would not hold together a twelvemonth. Four million human beings consigned to the uncontrolled brutality of 7,000,000 of human beings! The very thought is monstrous. The instinct of justice which God has implanted in every soul revolts at it. The voice of lamentation would swell up from that wretched land and fill the ears of mankind. Leaders and avengers would spring up on every hilltop of the north. The intellect, the morality, the soul of the age would fight in behalf of the oppressed, and the structure of so-called reconstruction would go down in blood.

Does any man think that it is in the American people, who rose at the cry of the slave under the lash of his master, to abide in quiet the carnival of arson, rapine, and murder now raging over the south? Sir, a government which would perpetuate such a state of things would be a monstrous barbarism; the legislative body which would seek to weave such things into the warp and woof of the national life would deserve the vengeance of Almighty God.

A senator from Pennsylvania [Mr. Cowan] the other day in the United States Senate said:

" I have no doubt but there are large numbers of the American people who are exceedingly anxious to compel negro suffrage through the southern States. But has any one of them ever made an argument to show that the southern States would be better governed; that there would be more peace and more quiet in consequence of it? I have never heard those arguments if they have been made, and I do not know how anybody could make them."

I will give the honorable senator an argument most potent and convincing as to the kind of " peace and quiet" which now reign in the south without negro suffrage and which will reign there so long as negro suffrage is denied. General Ord has just made a report upon the condition of things in Arkansas. He sums up matters as follows:

" Outrages, assaults, and murders committed on the persons of freed men and women are being continually reported from all sections of the State, and a decided want of disposition to punish offenders apparently exists with the local civil officers and in the minds of the people. There have been reported fifty-two murders of freed persons by white men in this State in the past three or four months, and no reports have been received that the murderers have been imprisoned or punished. In some parts of the State, particularly in the southwest and southeast, freedmens' lives are threatened if they report their wrongs to the agent of the bureau, and in many instances the parties making reports are missed and never heard of afterward. " It is believed that the number of murders reported is not half the number committed during the time mentioned."

Or if this is not sufficient, I would answer the distinguished senator still further by quoting from the report of the officers of the Freedmen's Bureau as to the state of affairs in Tennessee as a further testimony to the condition of southern society without impartial suffrage:

" Captain Kendrick reports in substance that having proceeded to Union City, he conversed with many of the citizens, who told him that but few freedmen were left about there, as they were driving them away as rapidly as possible. There seems to be a fixed determination that the freedmen shall not reside there, and the citizens force them to fly by ravishing the females, shooting, beating, whipping, and cheating them. The superintendent of the bureau there, while investigating a case of assault upon a negro, was compelled to desist by threats upon his life. The magistrate of the town states that he is powerless to administer justice, owing to the feeling in the community.

" Captain Kendrick mentions the case of a freed-woman named Emeline, living in Union City, who, during the absence of her husband, was brutally vio-

lated by a party of whites. She appealed to the justice
of the peace, who informed her that nothing could be
done for her on account of the feeling in the town.
The next day two men, named Goodlow and Avons,
of Union City, took her into a field and whipped her.
A freedman named Callum was whipped by a man
named Stanley for saying that he had fought in the
Union army. A Mr. Roscol, county trustee, has been
persistently persecuted by a gang of desperadoes because he was prominent in defending the Union, and
has been shot at several times while sitting in his house.
About a dozen bullet holes may be seen in his door.
At Troy the freedmen are getting on prosperously and
have no complaints to make. The feeling of hostility
toward northern men at this place, the captain reports,
is more bitter even than at Union City. Loyal citizens are waylaid and shot and the ruffians escape punishment.

"A man named Hancock was called out of church,
where he had just experienced religion, by a Dr. Mar-
shall, who told him two persons outside wished to see
him. When he had gone a short distance two men
named Carruthers attacked and severely beat him with
clubs because Hancock wore a federal uniform coat.
Several other cases of outrage of an aggravated character and even murder are reported by Captain Kendrick, and those who are thus maltreated dare not
utter a word of complaint through fear of the desperadoes. He recommends that a detachment of troops be
permanently stationed in this county, and says that
matters will grow worse instead of better until it is
done."

I find in the morning papers the following letter, which explains itself:

HEADQUARTERS, DEPARTMENT OF THE SOUTH,
CHARLESTOWN, S. C., Jan. 10, 1867.

GENERAL,—According to an article in the Charleston "Daily News" of this morning, it appears that the jail at Kingstree, South Carolina, has been destroyed by fire, and twenty-two colored prisoners smothered or burned to death, while the only white prisoner was permitted to escape. The article states that the jailer, who had the keys, refused to open the doors without the authority of the sheriff, and the sheriff refused to act without the orders of the lieutenant commanding the troops at Kingstree. This statement presents a degree of barbarity that would appear incredible except in a community where no value is placed upon the lives of colored citizens. The general commanding directs that you cause an immediate and thorough investigation of this affair; that in the meantime you arrest the sheriff and jailer, and if the facts prove to be as stated, that you hold them in military confinement under the charge of murder until the civil authorities shall be ready and willing to try them.

Very respectfully, your obedient servant,

J. W. CLOUS,
Brev. Capt. and First Lieut. Sixth Infantry,
A.A.A.G.

Brev. Maj. Gen. H. K. SCOTT,
Com. Mil. Com., S. C.

I might fill pages with similar testimony, but it is not required.

It is too evident that when you strip a man of all means of self-defence, either through the courts or the laws, deprive him of education and leave him to the mercy of his fellow men, he must suffer all the pangs which our unworthy human nature is capable of inflicting. Who is there believes that man can safely intrust himself solely and alone to the mercy of his fellow man? Let such a one step forward and select his master! Let him in the wide circle of the world choose out that man—pure, just, and humane—upon whose vast, all-embracing charity he can throw the burden of his life. Alas! there is no such man.

Life is a perpetual struggle even under the most favorable circumstances; an unending fight of man against man,

" For some slight plank whose weight will bear but one."

And occasionally how monstrous and horrible are the giant selfishnesses which start up under our feet like ghouls and affrights!

History is the record of the gradual amelioration of deep-rooted, ancient injustice. What a hard, long, bloody, terrible fight it has been! But for the fact that our national organization rests upon a basis of new colonizations we would not possess the large measure of liberty we now enjoy; we would be as are the old lands of the world, still weighed down by the burdens of feudality and barbarism. But being peopled by the overflowings of the poor laboring people of

Europe, who left the errors and prejudices of the Old World in mid-ocean, we have started upon our career of national greatness on the grand basis of the perfect political equality of all men.

We cannot fail to recognize the all-fashioning hand of God as clearly in this sublime declaration as in the geologic eras, the configuration of the continents, or the creation of man himself. What a world of growth has already budded and flowered and borne fruit from this seed! What an incalculable world of growth is to arise from it in the future!

Now, then, comes the question to each of us, by what rule shall we reconstruct these prostrated and well nigh desolated States? Shall it be by the august rule of the Declaration of Independence; or shall we bend our energies to perpetuate injustice, cruelty, and oppression; and make of this fair government a monstrosity, with golden words of promise upon its banners, a fair seeming upon its surface, but a hideous and inhuman despotism within it; the Christianity and civilization of the nineteenth century crystallized into a nation with Dahomey and Timbuctoo in its bowels! A living lie, a rotten pretense, a mockery, and a sham, with death in its heart.

There are but two forms of government in the world; injustice, armed and powerful and taking to itself the shape of king or aristocracy; and, on the other hand, absolute human justice, resting upon the broad and enduring basis of equal rights to all. Give this and give intelligence and education to understand it and you have a structure which will stand while the world stands. Anything else than this is mere repression, the piling of rocks into the mouth of the volcano, which sooner or later will fling them to the skies.

What is this equality of rights? Is it the prescribing of a limit to human selfishness? It is the hospital measure which gives so many feet of breathing space to each man in the struggle for life. I must not intrude upon my neighbor's limit nor he upon mine. It is universal selfishness regulated by a sentiment of universal justice; fair play recognized as a common necessity. Break down this barrier and the great waves sweep in and all is anarchy. Hear Motley's description of society in the ancient time, ere this principle arose " to curb the great and raise the lowly: "

" The sword is the only symbol of the law, the cross is a weapon of offence, the bishop a consecrated pirate, and every petty baron a burglar; while the people alternately the prey of duke, prelate, and seignior, shorn and butchered like sheep, esteem it happiness to sell themselves into slavery or to huddle beneath the castle walls of some little potentate for the sake of his wolfish protection." *

Sir, all history teaches us that man would be safer in the claws of wild beasts than in the uncontrollable custody of his fellow men. And can any man doubt that he who lives in a community and has no share in the making of the laws which govern him is in the uncontrolled custody of those who make the laws? The courts simply interpret the laws, and what will it avail a man to appeal to the courts if the laws under every interpretation are against him?

* Rise of the Dutch Republic, p. 14.

Set a man down in the midst of a community, place the mark of Cain upon his brow, declare him an outlaw, take from him every protection, and you at once invite everything base, sordid, and abominable in human nature to rise up and assail him. Is there any man within the sound of my voice who thinks so highly of our common humanity that he would dare trust himself in such a position for a day or for an hour?

But if to this you superadd the fact that the poor wretch so stripped of all protection was but the other day a bondman, and was forcibly wrested from the hands of his master, and that to the common sordidness of our nature must be added the inflamed feelings growing out of a long civil war and the wrath and bitterness begotten of disappointed cupidity, you have a condition of things at which the very soul shudders.

But this is not all; you must go a step farther and remember that the poor wretch who thus stands helpless, chained, and naked in the midst of his mortal foes was our true, loyal, and faithful friend in the day of our darkness and calamity; and that those who now flock around him like vultures gathering to the carnage were but the other day our deadly enemies and sought our destruction and degradation by bloody and terrible means.

Sir, I say to you that if, in the face of every prompting of self-interest and self-protection, and humanity and gratitude, and Christianity and statesmanship, we abandon these poor wretches to their fate the wrath of an offended God cannot fail to fall upon the nation.

41

There never was in the history of the world an instance wherein right and wrong met so squarely face to face and looked each other so squarely in the eyes as in this matter. Never did truth array herself in such shining and glorious habiliments; never did the dark face of error look so hideous and forbidding as in this hour. And yet in the minds of some we find hesitation and doubt.

I cannot but recur to a famous parallel in history.

On the 22d of January, 1689, the English Parliament assembled to decide upon the most momentous question ever submitted to that body. The king, James II, had fled the realm; the great seal of royalty had been thrown into the Thames; William had landed; the nation was revolutionized.

The great debate commenced. On the one side was the party of human liberty striving to cast down forever a dynasty strangely devoted to tyranny and absolutism; striving to make plainer the doctrine that the king reigned by virtue of the consent of his subjects. On the other hand were arrayed all the evil forces of the time and all the restraints of conservatism.

In precisely the same temper in which it is now argued that a State can do no wrong and that under no circumstances can it cease to be a State, it was then argued that, although the king had fled the land and was at the court of France, nevertheless the magistrate was still present, that the throne, by the maxim of English law, could not be vacant for a moment; and that any government organized to act during the king's absence must act in the king's name.

It was most plain that the liberty, the prosperity of England could only be secured by the deposition of James; and yet those who sought by direct measures to reach that end were encountered at every step by a mass of technical objections. The musty precedents of the law, a thousand years old, were raked up; and texts of the Holy Book were called into the defence of royalty as liberally as we have seen them in our own day paraded in defence of slavery. St. Paul's injunction to the Romans to obey the civil power played as important a part in those debates as the texts of Ham and Onesimus have played upon the floor of this House.

Either the liberty of England must have perished, encumbered in this mass of precedents and technicalities, or the common sense of England must reach its own safety over the whole mass of rubbish. The common sense of England triumphed. James having fled, he was declared to have abdicated the throne, and the throne being vacant, Parliament asserted the right to fill it.

Now, in like manner at this day the resolute common sense of the American people must find its way out of the entanglements that surround it and go straight forward to its own safety.

The purpose of government is the happiness of the people, therefore of the whole people. A government cannot be half a republic and half a despotism—a republic just and equable to one class of its citizens, a despotism cruel and destructive to another class; it must become either all despotism or all republic.

If you make it all republic the future is plain. All

evils will correct themselves. Temporary disorders
will subside, the path will lie wide open before every
man and every step and every hour will take him farther away from error and darkness. Give the right
to vote and you give the right to aid in making the
laws; the laws being made by all will be for the benefit
of all; the improvement and advancement of each
member of the community will be the improvement
and advancement of the whole community.

Dealing with men, with all the attributes of men,
with the souls, hearts, and minds of men, it is con-
temptible to attempt to turn justice aside by appeals
to the color of the skin. At what precise point of the
mingling of complexions shall these statesmen drive
the stake and say, Thus far is man and beyond is
brute; here human rights begin and there they ter-
minate! What chemist shall analyze the mixture of
man and beast and tell us what fraction of an immortal
soul is possessed by such a one? Or how many mulat-
toes go as component parts to make up one soul in
heaven?

Sir, such a doctrine is too monstrous for consideration! The earth is God's and all the children of God
have an equal right upon its surface; and human legislation which would seek to subvert this truth merely
legislates injustice into law; and he who believes that
injustice conserves the peace, order, or welfare of society has read history to little purpose.

Let us then go straight forward to our duty, taking
heed of nothing but the right. In this wise shall we
build a work in accord with the will of him who is
daily fashioning the world to a higher destiny; a work

resting at no point upon wrong or injustice, but every-where reposing upon truth and justice; a work which all mankind will be interested in preserving in every age, since it will insure the increasing glory and well-being of mankind through all ages.

Choate, Joseph H., an eminent American lawyer and orator, born at Salem, Mass., January 24, 1832. He removed to New York city in 1856, having been admitted to the bar in 1855, and quickly attained to eminence in his profession. In the political campaign of 1856 he made numerous addresses in support of the Free Soil candidate, and has since been conspicuous as a Republican. While president of the American Bar Association he made in 1898 a noteworthy address before it in behalf of trial by jury. Until 1898 he had filled no political office, but at the close of that year he was appointed ambassador to England, in which capacity he has been very popular, his public addresses having been much admired by the English people. Choate's oration upon Rufus Choate is an excellent instance of his oratorical ability. He is a polished speaker, exceptionally happy in his occasional speeches, which are enlivened by the play of a delicate humor.

ORATION ON RUFUS CHOATE.

DELIVERED AT THE UNVEILING OF THE STATUE OF RUFUS CHOATE IN THE COURT HOUSE OF BOSTON, OCTOBER 15, 1898.

MANY a noted orator, many a great lawyer, has been lost in oblivion in forty years after the grave closed over him, but I venture to believe that the bar of Suffolk, aye, the whole bar of America, and the people of Massachusetts, have kept the memory of no other man alive and green so long, so vividly and so lovingly as that of Rufus Choate. Many of his characteristic utterances have become proverbial and the flashes of his wit, the play of his fancy, and the gorgeous pictures of his imagination are the constant themes of reminiscence wherever American lawyers assemble for social converse. What Mr. Dana so well said over his bier is still true to-day: " When as lawyers we meet together in tedious hours and seek to entertain ourselves, we find we do better with anecdotes of Mr. Choate than on our own original resources." The admirable biography of Professor Brown and his arguments, so far as they have been preserved, are text-books in the profession—and so the influence of his genius, character, and conduct is still potent and far-reaching in the land.

You will not expect me, upon such an occasion, to enter upon any narrative of his illustrious career, so familiar to you all, or to undertake any analysis of those remarkable powers which made it possible. All that has been done already by many appreciative admirers and has become a part of American literature. I can only attempt, in a most imperfect manner, to present a few of the leading traits of that marvellous personality which we hope that this striking statue will help to transmit to the students, lawyers and citizens who, in the coming years, shall throng these portals.

How it was that such an exotic nature, so ardent and tropical in all its manifestations, so truly southern and Italian in its impulses, and at the same time so robust and sturdy in its strength, could have been produced upon the bleak and barren soil of our northern cape and nurtured under the chilling blasts of its east winds is a mystery insoluble. Truly " this is the Lord's doing, and it is marvellous in our eyes."

In one of his speeches in the Senate he draws the

distinction between "the cool and slow New England men and the mercurial children of the sun who sat down side by side in the presence of Washington to form our more perfect union."

If ever there was a mercurial child of the sun, it was himself most happily described. I am one of those who believe that the stuff that a man is made of has more to do with his career than any education or environment. The greatness that is achieved, or is thrust upon some men, dwindles before that of him who is born great. His horoscope was propitious. The stars in their courses fought for him. The birthmark of genius, distinct and ineffaceable, was on his brow. He came of a long line of pious and devout ancestors, whose living was as plain as their thinking was high. It was from father and mother that he derived the flame of intellect, the glow of spirit, and the beauty of temperament that were so unique.

And his nurture to manhood was worthy of the child. It was "the nurture and admonition of the Lord." From that rough pine cradle, which is still preserved in the room where he was born, to his premature grave at the age of fifty-nine, it was one long course of training and discipline of mind and character, without pause or rest. It began with that well-thumbed and dog's-eared Bible from Hog Island, its leaves actually worn away by the pious hands that had turned them, read daily in the family from January to December, in at Genesis and out at Revelations every two years; and when a new child was born in the household the only celebration, the only festivity, was to turn back to the first chapter and read once more how "in the beginning God created the heaven and the earth" and all that in them is.

This book, so early absorbed and never forgotten, saturated his mind and spirit more than any other, more than all other books combined. It was at his tongue's end, at his fingers' ends—always close at hand until those last languid hours at Halifax, when it solaced his dying meditations. You can heardly find speech, argument or lecture of his, from first to last, that is not sprinkled and studded with biblical ideas and pictures and biblical words and phrases. To him the book of Job was a sublime poem. He knew the Psalms by heart and dearly loved the prophets, and above all Isaiah, upon whose gorgeous imagery he made copious drafts. He pondered every word, read with most subtle keenness, and applied with happiest effect. One day, coming into the Crawford House, cold and shivering—and you remember how he could shiver—he caught sight of the blaze in the great fireplace and was instantly warm before the rays could reach him, exclaiming "Do you remember that verse in Isaiah, 'Aha! I am warm. I have seen the fire?'" and so his daily conversation was marked.

And upon this solid rock of the Scriptures he built a magnificent structure of knowledge and acquirement, to which few men in America have ever attained. History, philosophy, poetry, fiction, all came as grist to his mental mill. But with him time was too precious to read any trash; he could winnow the wheat from the chaff at sight, almost by touch. He sought knowledge, ideas, for their own sake and for the language in which they were conveyed.

I have heard a most learned jurist gloat over the purchase of the last sensational novel, and have seen a most distinguished bishop greedily devouring the stories of Gaboriau one after another, but Mr. Choate seemed to need no such counter-irritant or blister to draw the pain from his hurt mind. Business, company, family, sickness—nothing could rob him of his one hour each day in the company of illustrious writers of all ages. How his whole course of thought was tinged and embellished with the reflected light of the great Greek orators, historians and poets; how Roman history, fresh in the mind as the events of yesterday, supplied him with illustrations and supports for his own glowing thoughts and arguments, all of you who have either heard him or read him know.

But it was to the great domain of English literature that he daily turned for fireside companions and really kindred spirits. As he said in a letter to Sumner, with whom his literary fraternity was at one time very close: " Mind that Burke is the fourth Englishman,— Shakespeare, Bacon, Milton, Burke;" and then in one of those dashing outbursts of playful extravagance which were so characteristic of him, fearing that Sumner in his proposed review might fail to do full justice to the great ideal of both, he adds: "Out of Burke might be cut 50 Mackintoshes 175 Macaulays, 40 Jeffreys, and 250 Sir Robert Peels, and leave him greater than Pitt and Fox together."

In the constant company of these great thinkers and writers he revelled and made their thoughts his own; and his insatiable memory seemed to store up all things committed to it, as the books not in daily use are stacked away in your public library, so that at that moment, with notice or without, he could lay his hand straightway upon them. What was once imbedded in the gray matter of his brain did not lie buried there, as with most of us, but grew and flourished and bore fruit. What he once read he seemed never to forget.

This love of study became a ruling passion in his earliest youth. To it he sacrificed all that the youth of our day—even the best of them—consider indispensable, and especially the culture and training of the body; and when we recall his pale face, worn and lined as it was in his later years, one of his most pathetic utterances is found in a letter to his son at school: "I hope that you are well and studious and among the best scholars. If this is so, I am willing you should play every day till the blood is ready to burst from your cheeks. Love the studies that will make you wise, useful, and happy when there shall be no blood at all to be seen in your cheeks or lips."

He never rested from his delightful labors—and that is the pity of it—he took no vacations. Except for one short trip to Europe, when warned of a possible breakdown in 1850, an occasional day at Essex, a three days' journey to the White Mountains, was all that he allowed himself. Returning from such an outing in the summer of 1854, on which it was my great privilege to accompany him, he said, " That is my entire holiday for this year."

So that when he told Judge Warren so playfully that " The lawyer's vacation is the space between the question put to a witness and his answer," it was of himself almost literally true. Would that he had realized his constant dream of an ideal cottage in the old walnut grove in Essex, where he might spend whole summers with his books, his children, and his thoughts.

His splendid and blazing intellect, fed and enriched by constant study of the best thoughts of the great minds of the race; his all-persuasive eloquence, his teeming and radiant imagination, whirling his hearers along with it and sometimes overpowering himself, his brilliant and sportive fancy, lighting up the most arid subjects with the glow of sunrise, his prodigious and never-failing memory, and his playful wit, always bursting forth with irresistible impulse, have been the subject of scores of essays and criticisms, all struggling with the vain effort to describe and crystallize the fascinating and magical charm of his speech and his influence.

And now, in conclusion, let me speak of his patriotism. I have always believed that Mr. Webster, more than any other man, was entitled to the credit of that grand and universal outburst of devotion with which the whole north sprang to arms in defence of the constitution and the Union many years after his death, when the first shot at Fort Sumter, like a fire-bell in the night, roused them from their slumber and convinced them that the great citadel of their liberties was in actual danger.

Differ as we may and must as to his final course in his declining years, the one great fact can never be blotted out, that the great work of his grand and noble life was the defence of the constitution—so that he came to be known of all men as its one defender—

that for thirty years he preached to the listening nation the crusade of nationality and fired New England and the whole north with its spirit. He inspired them to believe that to uphold and preserve the Union against every foe was the first duty of the citizen; that if the Union was saved, all was saved; that if that was lost, all was lost. He molded better even than he knew. It was his great brain that designed, his flaming heart that forged, his sublime eloquence that welded the sword which was at last, when he was dust, to consummate his life's work and make liberty and union one and inseparable forever.

And so, in large measure, it was with Mr. Choate. His glowing heart went out to his country with the passionate ardor of a lover. He believed that the first duty of the lawyer, orator, scholar was to her. His best thoughts, his noblest words were always for her. Seven of the best years of his life, in the Senate and House of Representatives, at the greatest personal sacrifice he gave absolutely to her service.

On every important question that arose he made, with infinite study and research, one of the great speeches of the debate. He commanded the affectionate regard of his fellows and of the watchful and listening nation. He was a profound and constant student of her history and revelled in tracing her growth and progress from Plymouth Rock and Salem Harbor until she filled the continent from sea to sea. He loved to trace the advance of the Puritan spirit, with which he was himself deeply imbued, from Winthrop and Endicott, and Carver and Standish, through all the heroic periods and events of colonial and revolutionary and national life, until in his own last years it dominated and guided all of free America.

He knew full well and displayed in his many splendid speeches and addresses that one unerring purpose of freedom and of union ran through her whole history; that there was no accident in it all; that all the generations, from the "Mayflower" down, marched to one measure and followed one flag: that all the struggles, all the self-sacrifice, all the prayers and the tears, all the fear of God, all the soul-trials, all the yearnings for national life, of more than two centuries, had contributed to make the country that he served and loved. He, too, preached, in season and out of season, the gospel of Nationality.

He was the faithful disciple of Webster while that great master lived, and after his death he bore aloft the same standard and maintained the same cause. Mr. Everett spoke nothing more than the truth when he said in Faneuil Hall, while all the bells were tolling, at the moment when the vessel bringing home the dead body of his life-long friend cast anchor in Boston harbor: "If ever there was a truly disinterested patriot, Rufus Choate was that man. In his political career there was no share of selfishness. Had he been willing to purchase advancement at the price often paid for it, there was never a moment from the time he first made himself felt and known that he could not have commanded anything that any party had to bestow. But he desired none of the rewards or honors of success."

He foresaw clearly that the division of the country into geographical parties must end in civil war. What

he could not see was, that there was no other way—
that only by cutting out slavery by the sword could
America secure liberty and union too; but to the last
drop of his blood and the last fibre of his being he
prayed and pleaded for the life of the nation, according
to his light. Neither of these great patriots lived to
see the fearful spectacle which they had so eloquently
deprecated.

But when at last the dread day came, and our young
heroes marched forth to bleed and die for their country—their own sons among the foremost—they carried in their hearts the lessons which both had taught;
and all Massachusetts, all New England, from the beginning, marched behind them, "carrying the flag and
keeping step to the music of the Union," as he had
bade them; and so, I say, let us award to them both
their due share of the glory.

Thus to-day we consign this noble statue to the
keeping of posterity, to remind them of "the patriot,
jurist, orator, scholar, citizen, and friend," whom we
are proud to have known and loved.

Harrison, Benjamin, a distinguished American politician, twenty-second President of the United States, born at North Bend, Ohio, August 20, 1833; died in Indianapolis, Ind., February   , 1901.   He was a grandson of President William Henry Harrison, and after completing his college education in 1862, practised law in Indianapolis until the opening of the Civil War.   He served in the Federal army, 1862–65, and rose to the rank of brigadier-general.   He sat in the United States Senate, 1881–87, and in 1888 was the successful candidate of the Republican Party for the Presidency.   He was renominated in 1892, but was defeated. Upon his retirement from the White House he resumed his legal practice, in which he displayed signal ability, and he was one of the members of the Peace Conference at The Hague.   In his latest years he became distinguished as an orator, his public addresses being as strong in substance as they were eloquent in delivery.   A volume issued shortly before his death, entitled "Views of an Ex-President," contains several of his latest public utterances.

INAUGURAL ADDRESS.

DELIVERED MARCH 4, 1889.

Fellow Citizens:

There is no constitutional or legal requirement that the President shall take the oath of office in the presence of the people, but there is so manifest an appropriateness in the public induction to office of the Chief Executive officer of the nation that from the beginning of the government the people, to whose service the official oath consecrates the officer, have been called to witness the solemn ceremonial.   The oath taken in the presence of the people becomes a mutual covenant. The officer covenants to serve the whole body of the people by a faithful execution of the laws, so that they may be the unfailing defence and security of those who respect and observe them, and that neither wealth, station, nor the power of combinations shall be able to evade their just penalties or to wrest them from a beneficent public purpose to serve the ends of cruelty or selfishness.

My promise is spoken; yours unspoken, but not the less real and solemn. The people of every State have here their representatives. Surely I do not misinterpret the spirit of the occasion when I assume that the whole body of the people covenant with me and with each other to-day to support and defend the Constitution and the Union of the States, to yield willing obedience to all the laws and each to every other citizen his equal civil and political rights. Entering thus solemnly into covenant with each other, we may reverently invoke and confidently expect the favor and help of Almighty God—that he will give to me wisdom, strength, and fidelity, and to our people a spirit of fraternity and a love of righteousness and peace.

This occasion derives peculiar interest from the fact that the Presidential term, which begins this day, is the twenty-sixth under our Constitution. The first inauguration of President Washington took place in New York, where Congress was then sitting, on the thirtieth day of April, 1789, having been deferred by reason of delays attending the organization of Congress and the canvass of the electoral vote. Our people have already worthily observed the centennials of the

15

Declaration of Independence, of the battle of Yorktown, and of the adoption of the Constitution, and will
shortly celebrate in New York the institution of the
second great department of our constitutional scheme
of government. When the centennial of the institution of the judicial department, by the organization of
the Supreme Court, shall have been suitably observed,
as I trust it will be, our nation will have fully entered
its second century.

I will not attempt to note the marvellous and, in
great part, happy contrasts between our country as it
steps over the threshold into its second century of organized existence under the Constitution and that
weak but wisely ordered young nation that looked un-
dauntedly down the first century, when all its years
stretched out before it.

Our people will not fail at this time to recall the incidents which accompanied the institution of government under the Constitution, or to find inspiration and
guidance in the teachings and example of Washington
and his great associates, and hope and courage in the
contrast which thirty-eight populous and prosperous
States offer to the thirteen States, weak in everything
except courage and the love of liberty, that then
fringed our Atlantic seaboard.

The Territory of Dakota has now a population
greater than any of the original States (except Virginia), and greater than the aggregate of five of the
smaller States in 1790. The centre of population when
our national capital was located was east of Baltimore, and it was argued by many well-informed persons that it would move eastward rather than west-

ward; yet in 1880 it was found to be near Cincinnati, and the new census about to be taken will show another stride to the westward. That which was the body has come to be only the rich fringe of the nation's robe. But our growth has not been limited to territory, population, and aggregate wealth, marvellous as it has been in each of those directions. The masses of our people are better fed, clothed, and housed than their fathers were. The facilities for popular education have been vastly enlarged and more generally diffused.

The virtues of courage and patriotism have given recent proof of their continued presence and increasing power in the hearts and over the lives of our people. The influences of religion have been multiplied and strengthened. The sweet offices of charity have greatly increased. The virtue of temperance is held in higher estimation. We have not attained an ideal condition. Not all of our people are happy and prosperous; not all of them are virtuous and law-abiding. But on the whole, the opportunities offered to the individual to secure the comforts of life are better than are found elsewhere, and largely better than they were here one hundred years ago.

The surrender of a large measure of sovereignty to the general government, effected by the adoption of the Constitution, was not accomplished until the suggestions of reason were strongly reinforced by the more imperative voice of experience. The divergent interests of peace speedily demanded a "more perfect Union." The merchant, the ship-master, and the manufacturer discovered and disclosed to our statesmen and to the people that commercial emancipation must be added to the political freedom which had been so bravely won. The commercial policy of the mother country had not relaxed any of its hard and oppressive features. To hold in check the development of our commercial marine, to prevent or retard the establishment and growth of manufactures in the States, and so to secure the American market for their shops and the carrying trade for their ships, was the policy of European statesmen, and was pursued with the most selfish vigor.

Petitions poured in upon Congress urging the imposition of discriminating duties that should encourage the production of needed things at home. The patriotism of the people, which no longer found a field of exercise in war, was energetically directed to the duty of equipping the young Republic for the defence of its independence by making its people self-dependent. Societies for the promotion of home manufactures and for encouraging the use of domestics in the dress of the people were organized in many of the States. The revival at the end of the century of the same patriotic interest in the preservation and development of domestic industries and the defence of our working people against injurious foreign competition is an incident worthy of attention. It is not a departure but a return that we have witnessed. The protective policy had then its opponents. The argument was made, as now, that its benefits inured to particular classes or sections.

If the question became in any sense or at any time sectional, it was only because slavery existed in some of the States. But for this there was no reason why the cotton-producing States should not have led or walked abreast with the New England States in the production of cotton fabrics. There was this reason only why the States that divide with Pennsylvania the mineral treasures of the great southeastern and central mountain ranges should have been so tardy in bringing to the smelting furnace and to the mill the coal and iron from their near opposing hillsides. Mill fires were lighted at the funeral pile of slavery. The Emancipation Proclamation was heard in the depths of the earth as well as in the sky; men were made free, and material things became our better servants.

The sectional element has happily been eliminated from the tariff discussion. We have no longer States that are necessarily only planting States. None is excluded from achieving that diversification of pursuits among the people which brings wealth and contentment. The cotton plantation will not be less valuable when the product is spun in the country town by operatives whose necessities call for diversified crops and create a home demand for garden and agricultural products. Every new mine, furnace and factory is an extension of the productive capacity of the State, more real and valuable than added territory.

Shall the prejudices and paralysis of slavery continue to hang upon the skirts of progress? How long will those who rejoice that slavery no longer exists cherish or tolerate the incapacities it put upon their communities? I look hopefully to the continuance of our protective system and to the consequent development of manufacturing and mining enterprises in the

States hitherto wholly given to agriculture as a potent influence in the perfect unification of our people. The men who have invested their capital in these enterprises, the farmers who have felt the benefit of their neighborhood, and the men who work in shop or field, will not fail to find and to defend a community of interest.

Is it not quite possible that the farmers and the promoters of the great mining and manufacturing enterprises which have recently been established in the South may yet find that the free ballot of the workingman, without distinction of race, is needed for their defence as well as for his own? I do not doubt that if those men in the South who now accept the tariff views of Clay and the constitutional expositions of Webster would courageously avow and defend their real convictions, they would not find it difficult, by friendly instruction and co-operation, to make the black man their efficient and safe ally, not only in establishing correct principles in our national administration, but in preserving for their local communities the benefits of social order and economical and honest government. At least until the good offices of kindness and education have been fairly tried, the contrary conclusion cannot be plausibly urged.

I have altogether rejected the suggestion of a special Executive policy for any section of our country. It is the duty of the Executive to administer and enforce in the methods and by the instrumentalities pointed out and provided by the Constitution all the laws enacted by Congress. These laws are general, and their administration should be uniform and equal. As a citizen may not elect what laws he will obey, neither may the Executive elect which he will enforce. The duty to obey and to execute embraces the Constitution in its entirety and the whole code of laws enacted under it. The evil example of permitting individuals, corporations, or communities to nullify the laws because they cross some selfish or local interest or prejudice is full of danger, not only to the nation at large, but much more to those who use this pernicious expedient to escape their just obligations or to obtain an unjust advantage over others. They will presently themselves be compelled to appeal to the law for protection, and those who would use the law as a defence must not deny that use of it to others.

If our great corporations would more scrupulously observe their legal limitations and duties, they would have less cause to complain of the unlawful limitations of their rights or of violent interference with their operations. The community that by concert, open or secret, among its citizens, denies to a portion of its members their plain rights under the law, has severed the only safe bond of social order and prosperity. The evil works from a bad centre both ways. It demoralizes those who practice it, and destroys the faith of those who suffer by it in the efficiency of the law as a safe protector. The man in whose breast that faith has been darkened is naturally the subject of dangerous and uncanny suggestions. Those who use unlawful methods, if moved by no higher motive than the selfishness that prompted them, may well stop and inquire what is to be the end of this.

An unlawful expedient cannot become a permanent

condition of government. If the educated and influential classes in a community either practice or connive at the systematic violation of laws that seem to them to cross their convenience, what can they expect when the lesson that convenience or a supposed class interest is a sufficient cause for lawlessness has been well learned by the ignorant classes? A community where law is the rule of conduct and where courts, not mobs, execute its penalties, is the only attractive field for business investments and honest labor.

Our naturalization laws should be so amended as to make the inquiry into the character and good disposition of persons applying for citizenship more careful and searching. Our existing laws have been in their administration an unimpressive and often an unintelligible form. We accept the man as a citizen without any knowledge of his fitness, and he assumes the duties of citizenship without any knowledge as to what they are. The privileges of American citizenship are so great and its duties so grave that we may well insist upon a good knowledge of every person applying for citizenship and a good knowledge by him of our institutions. We should not cease to be hospitable to immigration, but we should cease to be careless as to the character of it. There are men of all races, even the best, whose coming is necessarily a burden upon our public revenues or a threat to social order. These should be identified and excluded.

We have happily maintained a policy of avoiding all interference with European affairs. We have been only interested spectators of their contentions in diplomacy and in war, ready to use our friendly offices to promote peace, but never obtruding our advice and never attempting unfairly to coin the distresses of other powers into commercial advantage to ourselves. We have a just right to expect that our European policy will be the American policy of European courts.

It is so manifestly incompatible with those precautions for our peace and safety, which all the great powers habitually observe and enforce in matters affecting them, that a shorter waterway between our eastern and western seaboards should be dominated by any European government, that we may confidently expect that such a purpose will not be entertained by any friendly power.

We shall in the future, as in the past, use every endeavor to maintain and enlarge our friendly relations with all the great powers, but they will not expect us to look kindly upon any project that would leave us subject to the dangers of a hostile observation or environment. We have not sought to dominate or to absorb any of our weaker neighbors, but rather to aid and encourage them to establish free and stable governments resting upon the consent of their own people. We have a clear right to expect, therefore, that no European government will seek to establish colonial dependencies upon the territory of these independent American States. That which a sense of justice restrains us from seeking, they may be reasonably expected willingly to forego.

It must be assumed, however, that our interests are so exclusively American that our entire inattention to any events that may transpire elsewhere can be taken for granted. Our citizens, domiciled for purposes of

trade in all countries and in many of the islands of
the sea, demand and will have our adequate care in
their personal and commercial rights. The necessities of our navy require convenient coaling stations
and dock and harbor privileges. These and other trad-
ing privileges we will feel free to obtain only by means
that do not in any degree partake of coercion, however
feeble the government from which we ask such concessions. But having fairly obtained them by methods and for purposes entirely consistent with the most
friendly disposition toward all other powers, our consent will be necessary to any modification or impair-
ment of the concession.

We shall neither fail to respect the flag of any
friendly nation, or the just rights of its citizens, nor
to exact the like treatment for our own. Calmness,
justice, and consideration should characterize our diplomacy. The offices of an intelligent diplomacy or of
friendly arbitration in proper cases should be adequate
to the peaceful adjustment of all international difficulties. By such methods we will make our contribution
to the world's peace, which no nation values more
highly, and avoid the opprobrium which must fall
upon the nation that ruthlessly breaks it.

The duty devolved by law upon the President to
nominate, and by and with the advice and consent of
the Senate to appoint, all public officers whose appointment is not otherwise provided for in the Constitution
or by act of Congress, has become very burdensome,
and its wise and efficient discharge full of difficulty.
The civil list is so large that a personal knowledge of
any large number of the applicants is impossible. The

President must rely upon the representation of others, and these are often made inconsiderately and without any just sense of responsibility. I have a right, I think, to insist that those who volunteer or are invited to give advice as to appointments shall exercise consideration and fidelity. A high sense of duty and an ' ambition to improve the service should characterize all public officers.

There are many ways in which the convenience and comfort of those who have business with our public offices may be promoted by a thoughtful and obliging officer, and I shall expect those whom I may appoint to justify their selection by a conspicuous efficiency in the discharge of their duties. Honorable party service will certainly not be esteemed by me a disqualification for public office, but it will in no case be allowed to serve as a shield of official negligence, incompetency, or delinquency. It is entirely creditable to seek public office by proper methods and with proper motives, and all applicants will be treated with consideration; but I shall need, and the heads of departments will need, time for enquiry and deliberation. Persistent importunity will not, therefore, be the best support of an application for office. Heads of departments, bureaus, and all other public officers having any duty connected therewith, will be expected to enforce the Civil Service law fully and without evasion. Beyond this obvious duty I hope to do something more to advance the reform of the civil service. The ideal, or even my own ideal, I shall probably not attain. Retrospect will be a safer basis of judgment than promises. We shall not, however, I am sure, be able to put our civil

service upon a non-partisan basis until we have secured
an incumbency that fair-minded men of the opposition
will approve for impartiality and integrity.   As the
number of such in the civil list is increased, removals
from office will diminish.

While a Treasury surplus is not the greatest evil,
it is a serious evil.   Our revenue should be ample
to meet the ordinary annual demands upon our Treasury, with a sufficient margin for those extraordinary
but scarcely less imperative, demands which arise now
and then.   Expenditure should always be made with
economy, and only upon public necessity.   Wasteful-
ness, profligacy, or favoritism in public expenditure is
criminal.   But there is nothing in the condition of our
country or of our people to suggest that anything
presently necessary to the public prosperity, security,
or honor, should be unduly postponed.

It will be the duty of Congress wisely to forecast
and estimate these extraordinary demands, and, having
added them to our ordinary expenditures, to so adjust
our revenue laws that no considerable annual surplus
will remain.   We will fortunately be able to apply to
the redemption of the public debt any small and unfore-
seen excess of revenue.   This is better than to reduce
our income below our necessary expenditures, with
the resulting choice between another change of our
revenue laws and an increase of the public debt.   It
is quite possible, I am sure, to effect the necessary reduction in our revenues without breaking down our
protective tariff or seriously injuring any domestic industry.

The construction of a sufficient number of modern

warships and of their necessary armament should progress as rapidly as is consistent with care and perfection in plans and workmanship. The spirit, courage, and skill of our naval officers and seamen have many times in our history given to weak ships and inefficient guns a rating greatly beyond that of the naval list. That they will again do so upon occasion, I do not doubt; but they ought not, by premeditation or neglect, to be left to the risks and exigencies of an unequal combat. We should encourage the establishment of American steamship lines. The exchanges of commerce demand stated, reliable, and rapid means of communication; and until these are provided, the development of our trade with the States lying south of us is impossible.

Our pension laws should give more adequate and discriminating relief to the Union soldiers and sailors and to their widows and orphans. Such occasions as this should remind us that we owe everything to their valor and sacrifice.

It is a subject of congratulation that there is a near prospect of the admission into the Union of the Dakotas and Montana and Washington Territories. This act of justice has been unreasonably delayed in the case of some of them. The people who have settled these Territories are intelligent, enterprising, and patriotic, and the accession of these new States will add strength to the nation. It is due to the settlers in the Territories who have availed themselves of the invitations of our land laws to make homes upon the public domain that their titles should be speedily adjusted and their honest entries confirmed by patent.

It is very gratifying to observe the general interest now being manifested in the reform of our election laws. Those who have been for years calling attention to the pressing necessity of throwing about the bailot-box and about the elector further safeguards, in order that our elections might not only be free and pure, but might clearly appear to be so, will welcome the accession of any who did not so soon discover the need of reform. The National Congress has not as yet taken control of elections in that case over which the Constitution gives it jurisdiction, but has accepted and adopted the election laws of the several States, provided penalties for their violation and a method of supervision. Only the inefficiency of the State laws or an unfair partisan administration of them could suggest a departure from this policy.

It was clear, however, in the contemplation of the framers of the Constitution, that such an exigency might arise, and provision was wisely made for it. The freedom of the ballot is a condition of our national life, and no power vested in Congress or in the Executive to secure or perpetuate it should remain unused upon occasion. The people of all the congressional districts have an equal interest that the election in each shall truly express the views and wishes of a majority of the qualified electors residing within it. The results of such elections are not local, and the insistence of electors residing in other districts that they shall be pure and free does not savor at all of impertinence.

If in any of the States the public security is thought to be threatened by ignorance among the electors, the obvious remedy is education. The sympathy and help of our people will not be withheld from any community struggling with special embarrassments or difficulties connected with the suffrage, if the remedies proposed proceed upon lawful lines and are promoted by just and honorable methods. How shall those who practice election frauds recover that respect for the sanctity of the ballot which is the first condition and obligation of good citizenship? The man who has come to regard the ballot-box as a juggler's hat has renounced his allegiance.

Let us exalt patriotism and moderate our party contentions. Let those who would die for the flag on the field of battle give a better proof of their patriotism and a higher glory to their country by promoting fraternity and justice. A party success that is achieved by unfair methods or by practices that partake of revolution is hurtful and evanescent, even from a party standpoint. We should hold our differing opinions in mutual respect, and, having submitted them to the arbitrament of the ballot, should accept an adverse judgment with the same respect that we would have demanded of our opponents if the decision had been in our favor.

No other people have a government more worthy of their respect and love, or a land so magnificent in extent, so pleasant to look upon, and so full of generous suggestion to enterprise and labor. God has placed upon our head a diadem, and has laid at our feet power and wealth beyond definition or calculation. But we must not forget that we take these gifts upon the condition that justice and mercy shall hold the reins of power, and that the upward avenues of hope shall be free to all the people.

I do not mistrust the future. Dangers have been in frequent ambush along our path, but we have uncovered and vanquished them all. Passion has swept some of our communities, but only to give us a new demonstration that the great body of our people are stable, patriotic, and law-abiding. No political party can long pursue advantage at the expense of public honor or by rude and indecent methods, without protest and fatal disaffection in its own body. The peaceful agencies of commerce are more fully revealing the necessary unity of all our communities, and the increasing intercourse of our people is promoting mutual respect. We shall find unalloyed pleasure in the revelation which our next census will make of the swift development of the great resources of some of the States. Each State will bring its generous contribution to the great aggregate of the nation's increase. And when the harvests from the fields, the cattle from the hills, and the ores of the earth shall have been weighed, counted, and valued, we will turn from them all to crown with the highest honor the State that has most promoted education, virtue, justice and patriotism among its people.

Ingalls, John J., an American politician and orator, born at Middleton, Mass., December 29, 1833 ; died at Las Vegas, N. M., August 16, 1900. He studied law upon leaving college, and after admittance to the bar in 1857 removed to Atchison, Kan., the following year. In 1862 he entered the Kansas Senate, and was the unsuccessful candidate for the Lieutenant-Governorship the same year, as also in 1864. After editing the " Atchison Champion " for a few years, he entered the United States Senate in 1873, retaining his seat there until he retired from political life in 1891. His latest years were devoted to lecturing and journalism. Ingalls was a ready and eloquent debator, but his political ideals were not high, and he did not possess the entire confidence of his listeners. His style was glittering rather than polished.

ON THE POLITICAL SITUATION.

SPEECH IN THE SENATE OF THE UNITED STATES, JAN-
UARY 14, 1891.

MR. PRESIDENT,—Two portentous perils threaten the safety if they do not endanger the existence of the republic.

The first of these is ignorant, debased, degraded, spurious, and sophisticated suffrage; suffrage contaminated by the feculent sewage of decaying nations; suffrage intimidated and suppressed in the South; suffrage impure and corrupt, apathetic and indifferent, in the great cities of the North, so that it is doubtful whether there has been for half a century a presidential election in this country that expressed the deliberate and intelligent judgment of the whole body of the American people.

In a newspaper interview a few months ago, in which I commented upon these conditions and alluded to the efforts of the bacilli doctors of politics, the bacteriologists of our system, who endeavor to cure the ills under which we suffer by their hypodermic injections of the lymph of independent non-partisanship and the Brown-Séquard elixir of civil-service reform, I said that "the purification of politics" by such methods as these was an "iridescent dream." Remembering the cipher dispatches of 1877 and the attempted purchase of the electoral votes of many southern States in that campaign, the forgery of the Morey letter in 1880, by which Garfield lost the votes of three States in the North, and the characterization and portraiture of Blaine and Cleveland and Harrison by their political adversaries, I added that " the Golden Rule and the Decalogue had no place in American political campaigns."

It seems superfluous to explain, Mr. President, that in those utterances I was not inculcating a doctrine, but describing a condition. My statement was a statement of facts as I understood them, and not the announcement of an article of faith. But many reverend and eminent divines, many disinterested editors, many ingenuous orators, perverted those utterances into the personal advocacy of impurity in politics.

I do not complain, Mr. President. It was, as the world goes, legitimate political warfare; but it was an illustration of the truth that there ought to be purification in our politics, and that the Golden Rule and the Decalogue ought to have a place in political campaigns. "Do unto others as ye would that others should do unto you" is the supreme injunction, obligatory upon all. "If thine enemy smite thee upon one cheek turn to him the other" is a sublime and lofty precept. But I take this occasion to observe that until it is more generally regarded than it has been or appears likely to be in the immediate future, if my political enemy smites me upon one cheek, instead of turning to him the other I shall smite him under the butt end of his left ear if I can. If this be political immorality, I am to be included among the unregenerated.

The election bill that was under consideration a few days ago is intended to deal with one part of the great evil to which I have alluded, but it is an imperfect, a partial, and an incomplete remedy. Violence is bad; but fraud is no better; and it is more dangerous because it is more insidious.

Burke said in one of those immortal orations that emptied the House of Commons, but which will be read with admiration so long as the English tongue shall endure, that when the laws of Great Britain were not strong enough to protect the humblest Hindoo upon the shores of the Ganges the nobleman was not safe in his castle upon the banks of the Thames. Sir, that lofty sentence is pregnant with admonition for us. There can be no repose, there can be no stable and permanent peace in this country under this government until it is just as safe for the black Republican to vote in Mississippi as it is for the white Democrat to vote in Kansas.

The other evil, Mr. President, the second to which

I adverted as threatening the safety if it does not endanger the existence of the republic, is the tyranny of combined, concentrated, centralized, and incorporated capital. And the people are considering this great problem now. The conscience of the nation is shocked at the injustice of modern society. The moral sentiment of mankind has been aroused at the unequal distribution of wealth, at the unequal diffusion of the burdens, the benefits, and the privileges of society.

At the beginning of our second century the American people have become profoundly conscious that the ballot is not the panacea for all the evils that afflict humanity; that it has not abolished poverty nor prevented injustice. They have discovered that political equality does not result in social fraternity; that under a democracy the concentration of greater political power in fewer hands, the accumulation and aggregation of greater amounts of wealth in individuals, are more possible than under a monarchy, and that there is a tyranny which is more fatal than the tyranny of kings.

George Washington, the first President of the Republic, at the close of his life in 1799 had the largest private fortune in the United States of America. Much of this came by inheritance, but the Father of his Country, in addition to his other virtues, shining and illustrious, was a very prudent, sagacious, thrifty, and forehanded man. He knew a good thing when he saw it a great way off. He had a keen eye for the main chance. As a surveyor in his youth he obtained knowledge that enabled him to make exceedingly valuable locations upon the public domain. The establishment of the national capital in the immediate vicinity of his patrimonial possessions did not diminish their value. He was a just debtor, but he was an exact if not an exacting creditor. And so it came to pass that when he died he was, to use the expressive phraseology of the day, the richest man in the country.

At this time, ninety years afterward, it is not without interest to know that the entire aggregate and sum of his earthly possessions, his estate, real, personal, and mixed, Mount Vernon and his lands along the Kanawha and the Ohio, slaves, securities, all of his belongings, reached the sum total of between $800,000 and $900,000. This was less than a century ago, and it is within bounds to say that at this time there are many scores of men, of estates, and of corporations in this country whose annual income exceed, and there has been one man whose monthly revenue since that period exceeded, the entire accumulations of the wealthiest citizen of the United States at the end of the last century.

At that period the social condition of the United States was one of practical equality. The statistics of the census of 1800 are incomplete and fragmentary, but the population of the Union was about 5,300,000, and the estimated wealth of the country was between $3,000,000,000 and $4,000,000,000. There was not a millionaire, and there was not a tramp nor a pauper, so far as we know, in the country, except such as had been made so by infirmity, or disease, or inevitable calamity. A multitude of small farmers contentedly tilled the soil. Upon the coast a race of fishermen and sailors, owning the craft that they sailed, wrested their substance from the stormy seas. Labor was the rule and luxury the exception. The great mass of the people lived upon the products of the farms that they cultivated. They spun and wove and manufactured their clothing from flax and from wool. Commerce and handicrafts afforded honorable competence. The prayer of Agur was apparently realized. There was neither poverty nor riches. Wealth was uniformly diffused, and none were condemned to hopeless penury and dependence. Less than four per cent. of the entire population lived in towns, and there were but four cities whose population exceeded 10,000 persons. Westward to the Pacific lay the fertile solitudes of an unexplored continent, its resources undeveloped and unsuspected. The dreams of Utopia seemed about to be fulfilled—the wide, the universal diffusion of civil, political, and personal rights among the great body of the people, accompanied by efficient and vigorous guaranties for the safety of life, the protection of property, and the preservation of liberty.

Since that time, Mr. President, the growth in wealth and numbers in this country has had no precedent in the building of nations. The genius of the people, stimulated to prodigious activity by freedom, by individualism, by universal education, has subjugated the desert and abolished the frontier. The laboring capacity of every inhabitant of this planet has been duplicated by machinery. In Massachusetts alone we are told that its engines are equivalent to the labor of one hundred million men. We now perform one-third of the world's mining, one-quarter of its manufacturing, one-fifth of its farming, and we possess one-sixth part of its entire accumulated wealth.

The Anglo-Saxon, Mr. President, is not by nature or instinct an anarchist, a socialist, a nihilist, or a communist. He does not desire the repudiation of debts, public or private, and he does not favor the forcible redistribution of property. He came to this continent, as he has gone everywhere else on the face of the earth, with a purpose. The 40,000 English colonists who came to this country between 1620 and 1650 formed the most significant, the most formidable migration that has ever occurred upon this globe since time began. They brought with them social and political ideas, novel in their application, of inconceivable energy and power, the home, the family, the State, individualism, the right of personal effort, freedom of conscience, an indomitable love of liberty and justice, a genius for self-government, an unrivalled capacity for conquest, but preferring charters to the sword, and they have been inexorable and relentless in the accomplishment of their designs. They were fatigued with caste and privilege and prerogative. They were tired of monarchs, and so, upon the bleak and inhospitable shores of New England they decreed the sovereignty of the people, and there they builded " a church without a bishop, and a state without a king."

The result of that experiment, Mr. President, has been ostensibly successful. Under the operation of those great forces, after two hundred and seventy years, this country exhibits a peaceful triumph over many subdued nationalities, through a government automatic in its functions and sustained by no power but the invisible majesty of law. With swift and constant communication by lines of steam transportation by land and lake and sea, with telegraphs extending their nervous reticulations from State to State, the remotest members of this gigantic republic are animated by a vitality as vigorous as that which throbs at its mighty heart, and it is through the quickened intelligence that has been communicated by those ideas that these conditions, which have been fatal to other nations, have become the pillars of our strength and the bulwarks of our safety.

Mr. President, if time and space signified now what they did when independence was declared, the United States could not exist under one government. It would not be possible to secure unity of purpose or identity of interest between communities separated by such barriers and obstacles as Maine and California. But time and distance are relative terms, and, under the operations of these forces, this continent has dwindled to a span. It is not as far from Boston to San Francisco to-day as it was from Boston to Baltimore in 1791; and as the world has shrunk, life has expanded. For all the purposes for which existence is valuable in this world—for comfort, for convenience, for opportunity, for intelligence, for power of locomotion, and superiority to the accidents and the fatalities of nature—the fewest in years among us, Mr. President, has lived longer and has lived more worthily than Methuselah in all his stagnant centuries.

When the Atlantic cable was completed, it was not merely that a wire, finer by comparison than the gossamer of morning, had sunk to its path along the peaks and the plateaus of the deep, but the earth instantaneously grew smaller by the breadth of the Atlantic.

'A new volume in the history of the world was opened. The to-morrow of Europe flashed upon the yesterday of America. Time, up to the period when this experiment commenced on this continent, yielded its treasures grudgingly and with reluctance. The centuries crept from improvement to improvement with tardy and sluggish steps, as if nature were unwilling to acknowledge the mastery of man. The great inventions of glass, of gunpowder, of printing, and the mariner's compass consumed a thousand years, but as the great experiment upon this continent has proceeded, the ancient law of progress has been disregarded, and the mind is bewildered by the stupendous results of its marvellous achievements.

The application of steam to locomotion on land and sea, the cotton-gin, electric illumination and telegraphy, the cylinder printing press, the sewing machine, the photographic art, tubular and suspension bridges, the telephone, the spectroscope, and the myriad forms of new applications of science to health and domestic comfort, to the arts of peace and war, have alone rendered democracy possible. The steam-engine emancipated millions from the slavery of daily toil and left them at liberty to pursue a higher range of effort; labor has become more remunerative, and the flood of wealth has raised the poor to comfort and the middle classes to affluence. With prosperity has attended leisure, books, travel; the masses have been provided with schools, and the range of mental inquiry has become wider and more daring. The sewing-machine does the work of a hundred hands, and gives rest and hope to weary lives. Farming, as my distinguished friend from New York (Mr. Evarts) once said, has become a "sedentary occupation." The reaper no longer swings his sickle in midsummer fields through the yellowish grain, followed by those who gather the wheat and the tares, but he rides in a vehicle, protected from the meridian sun, accomplishing in comfort in a single hour the former labors of a day.

By these and other emancipating devices of society the laborer and the artisan acquire the means of study and recreation. They provide their children with better opportunities than they possessed. Emerging from the obscure degradation to which they have been consigned by monarchies, they have assumed the leadership in politics and society. The governed have become the governors; the subjects have become the kings. They have formed States; they have invented political systems; they have made laws; they have established literatures; and it is not true, Mr. President, in one sense, that during this extraordinary period the rich have grown richer and the poor have grown poorer. There has never been a time, since the angel stood with the flaming sword before the gates of Eden, when the dollar of invested capital paid as low a return in interest as it does to-day; nor has there been an hour when the dollar that is earned by the laboring man would buy so much of everything that is essential for the welfare of himself and his family as it will to-day.

Mr. President, monopolies and corporations, however strong they may be, cannot permanently enslave such a people. They have given too many convincing proofs of their capacity for self-government. They have made too many incredible sacrifices for this great system, which has been builded and established here, to allow it to be overthrown. They will submit to no dictation.

We have become, Mr. President, the wealthiest nation upon the face of this earth, and the greater part of these enormous accumulations has been piled up during the past fifty years. From 1860 to 1880, notwithstanding the losses incurred by the most destructive war of modern times, the emancipation of four billions of slave property, the expenses of feeding the best fed, of clothing the best clothed, and of sheltering the best-sheltered people in the world, notwithstanding all the losses by fire and flood during that period of twenty years, the wealth of the country increased at the rate of $250,000 for every hour. Every time that the clock ticked above the portal of this Chamber the aggregated, accumulated permanent wealth of this country increased more than $70.

Sir, it rivals, it exceeds the fictions of the "Arabian Nights." There is nothing in the story of the lamp of Aladdin that surpasses it. It is without parallel or precedent; and the national ledger now shows a balance to our credit, after all that has been wasted and squandered and expended and lost and thrown away, of between $60,000,000,000 and $70,000,000,000. I believe myself that, upon a fair cash market valuation, the aggregate wealth of this country to-day is not less than $100,000,000,000. This is enough, Mr. President, to make every man and every woman and every child beneath the flag comfortable; to keep the wolf away from the door. It is enough to give to every family a competence, and yet we are told that there are thousands of people who never have enough to eat in any one day in the year. We are told by the statisticians of the Department of Labor of the United States that, notwithstanding this stupendous aggregation, there are a million American citizens, able-bodied and willing to work, who tramp the streets of our cities and the country highways and byways, in search of labor with which to buy their daily bread, in vain.

Mr. President, is it any wonder that this condition of things can exist without exciting profound apprehension? I heard, or saw rather, for I did not hear it —I saw in the morning papers that, in his speech yesterday, the senator from Ohio (Mr. Sherman) devoted a considerable part of his remarks to the defense of millionaires; that he declared that they were the froth upon the beer of our political system.

(Mr. Sherman: I said speculators.)

Speculators. They are very nearly the same, for the millionaires of this country, Mr. President, are not the producers and the laborers. They are arrayed like Solomon in all his glory, but "they toil not, neither do they spin"—yes, they do spin. This class, Mr. President, I am glad to say, is not confined to this country alone. These gigantic accumulations have not been the result of industry and economy. There would be no protest against them if they were. There is an anecdote floating around the papers, speaking about beer, that some gentleman said to the keeper of a saloon that he would give him a recipe for selling more beer, and when he inquired what it was, he said, "Sell less froth." If the millionaires and speculators of this country are the froth upon the beer of our system, the time has come when we should sell more beer by selling less froth.

The people are beginning to inquire whether, under "a government of the people by the people for the people," under a system in which the bounty of nature is supplemented by the labor of all, any citizen can show a moral, yes, or a legal, title to $200,000,000. Some have the temerity to ask whether or not any man can show a clear title to $100,000,000. There have been men rash enough to doubt whether, under a system so constituted and established, by speculation or otherwise, any citizen can show a fair title to $10,000,000 when the distribution of wealth per capita would be less than $1,000. If I were put upon my *voir dire* I should hesitate before admitting that, in the sense of giving just compensation and equivalent, any man in this country or any other country ever absolutely earned a million dollars. I do not believe he ever did.

What is the condition to-day, Mr. President, by the statistics? I said that at the beginning of this century there was a condition of practical social equality; wealth was uniformly diffused among the great mass of the people. I repeat that the people are not anarchists; they are not socialists; they are not communists; but they have suddenly awaked to the conception of the fact that the bulk of the property of the country is passing into the hands of what the senator from Ohio, by a euphemism, calls the "speculators" of the world, not of America alone. They infest the financial and social system of every country upon the face of the earth. They are the men of no politics—neither Democrat nor Republican. They are the men of all nationalities and of no nationality; with no politics but plunder, and with no principle but the spoliation of the human race.

A table has been compiled for the purpose of showing how wealth in this country is distributed, and it is full of the most startling admonition. It has appeared in the magazines; it has been commented upon in this Chamber; it has been the theme of editorial discussion. It appears from this compendium that there are in the United States two hundred persons who have an aggregate of more than $20,000,000 each; and there has been one man—the Midas of the century—at whose touch everything seemed to turn to gold, who acquired within less than the lifetime of a single individual, out of the aggregate of the national wealth that was earned by the labor of all applied to the common bounty of nature, an aggregate that exceeded the assessed valuation of four of the smallest States in this Union.

(Mr. Hoar: And more than the whole country had when the constitution was formed.)

Yes, and, as the senator from Massachusetts well observes,—and I thank him for the suggestion,—much more, many times more than the entire wealth of the country when it was established and founded. Four hundred persons possess $10,000,000 each, 1,000 persons $5,000,000 each, 2,000 persons $2,500,000 each, 6,000 persons $1,000,000 each, and 15,000 persons $500,000 each, making a total of 31,100 people who possess $36,250,000,000.

Mr. President, it is the most appalling statement that ever fell upon moral ears. It is, so far as the results of democracy as a social and political experiment are concerned, the most terrible commentary that ever was recorded in the book of time; and Nero fiddles while Rome burns. It is thrown off with a laugh and a sneer as the "froth upon the beer" of our political and social system. As I said, the assessed valuation recorded in the great national ledger standing to our credit is about $65,000,000,000.

Our population is 62,500,000, and by some means, some device, some machination, some incantation, honest or otherwise, some process that cannot be defined, less than a two-thousandth part of our population have obtained possession, and have kept out of the penitentiary in spite of the means they have adopted to acquire it, of more than one-half of the entire accumulated wealth of the country.

That is not the worst, Mr. President. It has been chiefly acquired by men who have contributed little to the material welfare of the country, and by processes that I do not care in appropriate terms to describe; by the wrecking of the fortunes of innocent men, women, and children; by jugglery, by book-keeping, by financiering, by what the senator from Ohio calls "speculation,"—and this process is going on with frightful and constantly accelerating rapidity.

The entire industry of this country is passing under the control of organized and confederated capital. More than fifty of the necessaries of life to-day, without which the cabin of the farmer and the miner cannot be lighted, or his children fed or clothed, have passed absolutely under the control of syndicates and trusts and corporations composed of speculators, and, by means of these combinations and confederations, competition is destroyed; small dealings are rendered impossible; competence can no longer be acquired, for it is superfluous and unnecessary to say that if, under a system where the accumulations distributed per capita would be less than a thousand dollars, 31,000 obtained possession of more than half of the accumulated wealth of the country, it is impossible that others should have a competence or an independence.

So it happens, Mr. President, that our society is becoming rapidly stratified—almost hopelessly stratified —into the condition of superfluously rich and helplessly poor. We are accustomed to speak of this as the land of the free and the home of the brave. It will soon be the home of the rich and the land of the slave.

We point to Great Britain and we denounce aristocracy and privileged and titled classes and landed estates. We thought, when we had abolished primogeniture and entail, that we had forever forbidden and prevented these enormous and dangerous accumulations; but, sir, we had forgotten that capital could combine; we were unaware of the yet undeveloped capacity of corporations; and so, as I say, it happens upon the threshold and in the vestibule of our second century, with all its magnificent record behind us, with this tremendous achievement in the way of wealth, population, invention, opportunity for happiness, we are in a condition compared with which the accumulated fortunes of Great Britain are puerile and insignificant.

It is no wonder, Mr. President, that the laboring, industrial, and agricultural classes, who have been made intelligent under the impulse of universal education, have at last awakened to this tremendous condition and are inquiring whether or not this experiment has been successful. And, sir, the speculators must beware. They have forgotten that the conditions, political and social, here are not a reproduction of the conditions under which these circumstances exist in other lands. Here is no dynasty; here is no privilege or caste or prerogative; here are no standing armies; here are no hereditary bondsmen, but every atom in our political system is quick, instinct, and endowed with life and power.

His ballot at the box is the equivalent of the ballot of the richest speculator. Thomas Jefferson, the great apostle of modern democracy, taught the lesson to his followers—and they have profited well by his instruction—that under a popular democratic representative government wealth, culture, intelligence were ultimately no match for numbers.

The numbers in this country, Mr. President, have learned at last the power of combination, and the speculators should not forget that, while the people of this country are generous and just, they are jealous also, and that, when discontent changes to resentment, and resentment passes into exasperation, one volume of a nation's history is closed and another will be opened.

The speculators, Mr. President! The cotton product of this country, I believe, is about 6,000,000 bales.

(Mr. Butler: Seven million bales.)

Seven million bales, I am told. The transactions of the New York Cotton Exchange are 40,000,000 bales, representing transactions speculative, profitable, re-

17

munerative, by which some of these great accumulations have been piled up, an inconceivable burden upon the energies and industries of the country.

The production of coal oil, I believe, in this country has averaged something like 20,000,000 barrels a year. The transactions of the New York Petroleum Exchange year by year average 2,000,000,000 barrels, fictitious, simulated, the instruments of the gambler and the speculator, by means of which, through an impost upon the toil and labor and industry of every laborer engaged in the production of petroleum, additional difficulties are imposed.

It is reported that the coal alone that is mined in Pennsylvania, indispensable to the comfort of millions of men, amounts in its annual product to about $40,-000,000 of which one-third is profit over and above the cost of production and a fair return for the capital invested.

That is "speculation," Mr. President, and every dollar over and above the cost of production, with a fair return upon the capital invested, every dollar of that fifteen or sixteen millions is filched, robbed, violently plundered out of the earnings of the laborers and operatives and farmers who are compelled to buy it; and yet it goes by the euphemistic name of "speculation," and is declared to be legitimate; it is eulogized and defended as one of those practices that is entitled to respect and approbation.

Nor is this all, Mr. President. The hostility between the employers and the employed in this country is becoming vindictive and permanently malevolent. Labor and capital are in two hostile camps to-day.

Lockouts and strikes and labor difficulties have become practically the normal condition of our system, and it is estimated that during the year that has just closed, in consequence of these disorders, in consequence of this hostility and this warfare, the actual loss in labor, in wages, in the destruction of perishable commodities by the interruption of railway traffic, has not been less than $300,000,000.

Mr. President, this is a serious problem. It may well engage the attention of the representatives of the States and of the American people. I have no sympathy with that school of political economists which teaches that there is an irreconcilable conflict between labor and capital, and which demands indiscriminate, hostile, and repressive legislation against men because they are rich, and corporations because they are strong. Labor and capital should not be antagonists, but allies rather. They should not be opponents and enemies, but colleagues and auxiliaries whose co-operating rivalry is essential to national prosperity. But I cannot forbear to affirm that a political system under which such despotic power can be wrested from the people and vested in a few is a democracy only in name.

A financial system under which more than half of the enormous wealth of the country, derived from the bounty of nature and the labor of all, is owned by a little more than thirty thousand people, while one million American citizens able and willing to toil are homeless tramps, starving for bread, requires readjustment.

A social system which offers to tender, virtuous and dependent women the alternative between prostitution and suicide as an escape from beggary is organized crime for which some day unrelenting justice will demand atonement and expiation.

Mr. President, the man who loves his country and the man who studies her history will search in vain for any natural cause for this appalling condition. The earth has not forgotten to yield her increase. There has been no general failure of harvests. We have had benignant skies and the early and the latter rain. Neither famine nor pestilence has decimated our population or wasted its energies. Immigration is flowing in from every land, and we are in the lusty prime of national youth and strength, with unexampled resources and every stimulus to their development; but, sir, the great body of the American people are engaged to-day in studying these problems that I have suggested in this morning hour. They are disheartened with misfortunes. They are weary with unrequited toil. They are tired of the exactions of the speculators. They desire peace and rest. They are turning their attention to the great industrial questions which underlie their material prosperity. They are indifferent to party. They care nothing for Republicanism nor for Democracy as such. They are ready to say, "A plague on both your houses," and they are ready also, Mr. President, to hail and to welcome any organization, any measure, any leader that promises them relief from the profitless strife of politicians and this turbulent and distracting agitation which has already culminated in violence and may end in blood.

Such, sir, is the verdict which I read in the elections from which we have just emerged, a verdict that was unexpected by the leaders of both parties, and which surprised alike the victors and the vanquished. It was a spontaneous, unpremeditated protest of the people against existing conditions. It was a revolt of the national conscience against injustice, a movement that is full of pathos and also full of danger, because such movements sometimes make victims of those who are guiltless. It was not a Republican defeat. It was not a Democratic victory. It was a great upheaval and uprising, independent of and superior to both. It was a crisis that may become a catastrophe, filled with terrible admonition, but not without encouragement to those who understand and are ready to cooperate with it. It was a peaceful revolution, an attempt to resume rights that seemed to have been infringed.

It is many years, Mr. President, since I predicted this inevitable result. In a speech delivered in this Chamber on the 15th of February, 1878, from the seat that is now adorned by my honorable friend from Texas who sits before me [Mr. Reagan] I said:

"We can not disguise the truth that we are on the verge of an impending revolution. The old issues are dead. The people are arraying themselves upon one side or the other of a portentous contest. On one side is capital, formidably intrenched in privilege, arrogant from continued triumph, conservative, tenacious of old theories, demanding new concessions, enriched by domestic levy and foreign commerce, and struggling to adjust all values to its own standard. On the other is labor, asking for employment, striving to develop domestic industries, battling with the forces of nature, and subduing the wilderness; labor, starving and sullen in cities, resolutely determined to overthrow a system under which the rich are growing richer and the poor are growing poorer; a system which gives to a Vanderbilt the possession of wealth beyond the dreams of avarice and condemns the poor to a poverty which has no refuge from starvation but the prison or the grave.

"Our demands for relief, for justice, have been met with indifference or disdain.

"The laborers of the country asking for employment are treated like impudent mendicants begging for bread."

Mr. President, it may be cause, it may be coincidence, it may be effect, it may be *post hoc* or it may be *propter hoc,* but it is historically true that this great blight that has fallen upon our industries, this paralysis that has overtaken our financial system, coincided in point of time with the diminution of the circulating medium of the country. The public debt was declared to be payable in coin, and then the money power of silver was destroyed. The value of property diminished in proportion, wages fell, and the value of everything was depreciated except debts and gold. The mortgage, the bond, the coupon, and the tax have retained immortal youth and vigor. They have not depreciated. The debt remains, but the capacity to pay has been destroyed. The accumulation of years disappears under the hammer of the sheriff, and the debtor is homeless, while the creditor obtains the security for his debt for a fraction of what it was actually worth when the debt was contracted.

There is, Mr. President, a deep-seated conviction among the people, which I fully share, that the demonetization of silver in 1873 was one element of a great conspiracy to deliver the fiscal system of this country over to those by whom it has, in my opinion, finally been captured. I see no proof of the assertion that the Demonetization Act of 1873 was fraudulently or corruptly procured, but from the statements that have been made it is impossible to avoid the conviction that it was part of a deliberate plan and conspiracy formed by those who have been called speculators to still further increase the value of the standard by which their accumulations were to be measured. The attention of the people was not called to the subject. It is one of the anomalies and phenomena of legislation.

That bill was pending in its various stages for four years in both Houses of Congress. It passed both bodies by decided majorities. It was read and re-read and reprinted thirteen times, as appears by the records. It was commented upon in newspapers; it was the subject of discussion in financial bodies all over the country; and yet we have the concurrent testimony of every senator and every member of the House of Representatives who was present during the time that the legislation was pending and proceeding that he knew nothing whatever about the demonetization of silver and the destruction of the coinage of the silver dollar. The senator from Nevada [Mr. Stewart], who knows so many things, felt called upon to make a speech of an hour's duration to show that he knew nothing whatever about it. I have heard other members declaim and with one consent make excuse that they knew nothing about it.

As I say, it is one of the phenomena and anomalies of legislation, and I have no other explanation to make than this: I believe that both Houses of Congress and the President of the United States must have been hypnotized. So great was the power of capital, so profound was the impulse, so persistent was the determination, that the promoters of this scheme succeeded, by the operation of mind power and will force, in capturing and bewildering the intelligence of men of all parties, of members of both Houses of Congress, and the members of the Cabinet, and the President of the United States.

And yet, Mr. President, it cannot be doubted that the statements that these gentlemen make are true. There is no doubt of the sincerity or the candor of those who have testified upon this matter; and it is incredible (I am glad it occurred before I was a member of this body) that a change in our financial system, that deprived one of the money metals of its debt-paying power, that changed the whole financial system of the country, and, to a certain extent, the entire fiscal methods of the world, could have been engineered through the Senate and the House of Representatives and the Cabinet of the President, and secured Executive approval without a single human being knowing anything whatever about it. In an age of miracles, Mr. President, wonders never cease.

It is true, that this marvel was accomplished when

the subject was not one of public discussion. It was done at a time when, although the public mind was intensely interested in financial subjects, and methods of relief from existing conditions were assiduously sought, the suggestion had never proceeded from any quarter that this could be accomplished by the demonetization of silver, or ceasing to coin the silver dollar. It was improvidently done, but it would not be more surprising, it would not be more of a strain upon human credulity, if fifteen years from now we were to be informed that no one was aware that in the bill that is now pending the proposition was made for the free coinage of silver.

Mr. President, there is not a State west of the Alleghany Mountains and south of the Potomac and Ohio rivers that is not in favor of the free coinage of silver. There is not a State in which, if that proposition were to be submitted to a popular vote, it would not be adopted by an overwhelming majority. I do not mean by that inclusion to say that in those States east of the Alleghanies and north of the Ohio and Potomac rivers there is any hostility or indisposition to receive the benefits that would result from the remonetization of silver. On the contrary, in the great commonwealths that lie to the northeast upon the Atlantic seaboard, New York, Pennsylvania, and the manufacturing and commercial States, I am inclined to believe, from the tone of the press, from the declarations of many assemblies, that if the proposition were to be submitted there it would also receive a majority of the votes.

If the proposition were to be submitted to the votes of the people of this country at large whether the silver dollar should be recoined and silver remonetized, notwithstanding the prophecies, the predictions, the animadversions of those who are opposed to it, I have not the slightest doubt that the great majority of the people, irrespective of party, would be in favor of it, and would so record themselves. They have declared in favor of it for the past fifteen years, and they have been juggled with, they have been thwarted, they have been paltered with and dealt with in a double sense. The word of promise that was made to their ear in the platforms of political parties has been broken to their hope. There was a majority in this body at the last session of Congress in favor of the free coinage of silver. The compromise that was made was not what the people expected, nor what they had a right to demand. They felt they had been trifled with, and that is one cause of the exasperation expressed in the verdict of November 4th.

I feel impelled to make one further observation. Warnings and admonitions have been plenty in this debate. We have been admonished of the danger that would follow; we have been notified of what would occur if the free coinage of silver were supported by a majority of this body, or if it were to be adopted as a part of our financial system. I am not a prophet, nor the son of a prophet, but I say to those who are now arraying themselves against the deliberately expressed judgment of the American people,—a judgment that they know has been declared and recorded,—I say to the members of this body,—I say, so far as I may do so with propriety, to the members of the co-ordinate branch of Congress,—and I say, if without impropriety I may do so, to the Executive of the nation, that there will come a time when the people will be trifled with no longer on this subject.

Once, twice, thrice by Executive intervention, Democratic and Republican, by parliamentary proceedings that I need not characterize, by various methods of legislative jugglery, the deliberate purpose of the American people, irrespective of party, has been thwarted, it has been defied, it has been contumeliously trodden under foot; and I repeat to those who have been the instruments and the implements,—no matter what the impulse or the motive or the intention may have been,—at some time the people will elect a House of Representatives, they will elect a Senate of the United States, they will elect a President of the United States, who will carry out their pledges and execute the popular will.

Mr. President, by the readjustment of the political forces of the nation under the eleventh census, the seat of power has at last been transferred from the circumference of this country to its center. It has been transformed from the seaboard to that great intramontane region between the Alleghanies and the Sierras, extending from the British possessions to the Gulf of Mexico, a region whose growth is one of the wonders and marvels of modern civilization. It seems as if the column of migration had paused in its westward march to build upon those tranquil plains and in those fertile valleys a fabric of society that should be the wonder and admiration of the world; rich in every element of present prosperity, but richer in every prophecy of future greatness and renown.

When I went west, Mr. President, as a carpet-bagger, in 1858, St. Louis was an outpost of civilization, Jefferson City was the farthest point reached by a railroad, and in all that great wilderness, extending from the sparse settlements along the Missouri to the summits of the Sierra Nevada, and from the Yellowstone to the cañons of the Rio Grande, a vast solitude from which I have myself, since that time, voted to admit seven States into the American Union, there was neither harvest nor husbandry, neither habitation nor home, save the hut of the hunter and the wigwam of the savage. Mr. President, we have now within those limits, extending southward from the British possessions and embracing the States of the Mississippi Valley, the Gulf, and the southeastern Atlantic, a vast productive region, the granary of the world, a majority of the members of this body, of the House of Representatives, and of the Electoral College.

We talk with admiration of Egypt. For many centuries the ruins of its cities, its art, its religions, have been the marvel of mankind. The Pyramids have survived the memory of their builders, and the Sphinx still questions, with solemn gaze, the vague mystery of the desert.

The great fabric of Egyptian civilization, with its wealth and power, the riches of its art, its creeds and faiths and philosophies, was reared, from the labors of a few million slaves under the lash of despots, upon a narrow margin 450 miles long and 10 miles wide, comprising in all, with the delta of the Nile, no more than 10,000 square miles of fertile land.

Who, sir, can foretell the future of that region to

which I have adverted, with its 20,000 miles of navigable water-courses, with its hundreds of thousands of square miles of soil excelling in fecundity all that of the Nile, when the labor of centuries of freemen under the impulse of our institutions shall have brought forth their perfect results?

Mr. President, it is to that region, with that population and with such a future, that the political power of this country has at last been transferred, and they are now unanimously demanding the free coinage of silver. It is for that reason that I shall cordially support the amendment proposed by the senator from Nevada. In doing so I not only follow the dictates of my own judgment, but I carry out the wishes of a great majority of my constituents irrespective of party or of political affiliation. I have been for the free coinage of silver from the outset, and I am free to say that after having observed the operations of the act of 1878 I am more than ever convinced of the wisdom of that legislation and the futility of the accusations by which it was assailed.

The people of the country that I represent have lost their reverence for gold. They have no longer any superstition about coin. Notwithstanding the declarations of the monometallists, notwithstanding the assaults that have been made by those who are in favor of still further increasing the value of the standard by which their possessions are measured, they know that money is neither wealth, nor capital, nor value, and that it is merely the creation of the law by which all these are estimated and measured.

We speak, sir, about the volume of money, and

about its relation to the wealth and capital of the country. Let me ask you, sir, for a moment, what would occur if the circulating medium were to be destroyed? Suppose that the gold and silver were to be withdrawn suddenly from circulation and melted up into bars and ingots and buried in the earth from which they were taken. Suppose that all the paper money, silver certificates, gold certificates, national-bank notes, treasury notes, were stacked in one mass at the end of the treasury building and the torch applied to them, and they were to be destroyed by fire, and their ashes scattered, like the ashes of Wickliffe, upon the Potomac, to be spread abroad, wide as its waters be.

What would be the effect? Would not this country be worth exactly as much as it is to-day? Would there not be just as many acres of land, as many houses, as many farms, as many days of labor, as much improved and unimproved merchandise, and as much property as there is to-day? The result would be that commerce would languish, the sails of the ships would be furled in the harbors, the great trains would cease to run to and fro on their errands, trade would be reduced to barter, and, the people finding their energies languishing, civilization itself would droop, and we should be reduced to the condition of the nomadic wanderers upon the primeval plains.

Suppose, on the other hand, that instead of being destroyed, all the money in this country were to be put in the possession of a single man—gold, and paper, and silver—and he were to be moored in mid-Atlantic upon a raft with his great hoard, or to be stationed in the middle of Sahara's desert without food to nourish, or shelter to cover, or the means of transportation to get away. Who would be the richest man, the possessor of the gigantic treasure or the humblest settler upon the plains of the west, with a dugout to shelter him, and with corn meal and water enough for his daily bread?

Doubtless, Mr. President, you search the Scriptures daily, and are therefore familiar with the story of those depraved politicians of Judea who sought to entangle the Master in his talk, by asking him if it were lawful to pay tribute to Cæsar or not. He perceiving the purpose that they had in view, said unto them, " Show me the tribute money; " and they brought him a penny. He said, " Whose is this image and superscription? " and they replied, " Cæsar's; " and he said, " Render unto Cæsar the things that are Cæsar's, and unto God the things that are God's."

I hold, Mr. President, between my thumb and finger, a silver denarius, or " penny," of that ancient time— perhaps the identical coin that was brought by the hypocritical Herodian—bearing the image and superscription of Cæsar. It has been money for more than twenty centuries. It was money when Jesus walked the waves and in the tragic hour at Gethsemane. Imperial Cæsar is " dead and turned to clay." He has yielded to a mightier conqueror, and his eagles, his ensigns, and his trophies are indistinguishable dust. His triumphs and his victories are a schoolboy's tale. Rome herself is but a memory. Her marble porticoes and temples and palaces are in ruins. The sluggish monk and the lazy Roman *lazzaroni* haunt the Senate House and the Coliseum, and the derisive owl wakes

the echoes of the voiceless Forum. But this little con-
temporary disk of silver is money still, because it
bears the image and superscripture of Cæsar. And,
sir, it will continue to be money for twenty centuries
more, should it resist so long the corroding canker and
the gnawing tooth of time. But if one of these pages
should take this coin to the railway track, as boys
sometimes do, and allow the train to pass over it, in
one single instant its function would be destroyed.
It would contain as many grains of silver as before,
but it would be money no longer, because the image
and superscription of Cæsar had disappeared.

Mr. President, money is the creation of law, and
the American people have learned that lesson, and
they are indifferent to the assaults, they are indifferent
to the arguments, they are indifferent to the as-
persions which are cast upon them for demanding that the law of the United States shall place the
image and superscription of Cæsar upon silver enough
and gold enough and paper enough to enable them to
transact without embarrassment, without hindrance,
without delay, and without impoverishment their daily
business affairs, and that shall give them a measure of
values that will not make their earnings and their belongings the sport and the prey of speculators.

Mr. President, this contest can have but one issue.
The experiment that has begun will not fail. It is useless to deny that many irregularities have been toler-
ated here; that many crimes have been committed in
the sacred name of liberty; that our public affairs have
been scandalous episodes to which every patriotic heart
reverts with distress; that there have been envy and

jealousy in high places; that there have been treacherous and lying platforms; that there have been shallow compromises and degrading concessions to popular errors; but, amid all these disturbances, amid all these contests, amid all these inexplicable aberrations, the path of the nation has been steadily onward.

At the beginning of our second century we have entered upon a new social and political movement whose results cannot be predicted, but which are certain to be infinitely momentous. That the progress will be upward I have no doubt. Through the long and desolate tract of history, through the seemingly aimless struggles, the random gropings of humanity, the turbulent chaos of wrong, injustice, crime, doubt, want, and wretchedness, the dungeon and the block, the inquisition and the stake, the trepidations of the oppressed, the bloody exultations and triumphs of tyrants,—

> The unlifted ax, the agonizing wheel,
> Luke's iron crown and Damien's bed of steel,—

the tendency has been toward the light. Out of every conflict some man or sect or nation has emerged with higher privileges, greater opportunities, purer religion and greater capacity for happiness and out of the conflict in which we are now engaged, I am confident there will arise liberty, justice, equality; the continental unity of the American republic, the social fraternity and the indubitable independence of the American people.

17

Eliot, Charles W., a distinguished American scholar, born in Boston, Mass., March 20, 1834. He was professor of mathematics and chemistry at Harvard University, 1858–63, and professor of chemistry at the Massachusetts Institute of Technology, 1865–69. In 1869 he became president of Harvard University, which position he still holds. He has been a frequent speaker at educational and civic functions, and has written much upon educational and other important topics of the time. He is an impressive, scholarly orator, whose grasp of the subject at hand is always adequate and sure. Many of his addresses have been published. His speech at the New England banquet represents him fairly as a public speaker.

INAUGURAL ADDRESS AS PRESIDENT OF HARVARD UNIVERSITY.

DELIVERED OCTOBER 19, 1869.

MR. PRESIDENT,—I hear in your voice the voice of the Alumni, welcoming me to high honors and arduous labors, and charging me to be faithful to the duties of this consecrated office. I take up this weighty charge with a deep sense of insufficiency, but yet with youthful hope and a good courage. High examples will lighten the way. Deep prayers of devoted living and sainted dead will further every right effort, every good intention. The University is strong in the ardor and self-sacrifice of its teachers, in the vigor and wisdom of the Corporation and Overseers, and in the public spirit of the community. Above all, I devote myself to this sacred work in the firm faith that the God of the fathers will be also with the children.

The endless controversies whether language, philosophy, mathematics, or science supply the best mental training, whether general education should be chiefly literary or chiefly scientific, have no practical lesson for us to-day. This University recognizes no real antagonism between literature and science, and consents to no such narrow alternatives as mathematics or classics, science or metaphysics. We would have them all, and at their best. To observe keenly, to reason soundly, and to imagine vividly are operations as essential as that of clear and forcible expression; and to develop one of these faculties it is not necessary to repress and dwarf the others.

A university is not closely concerned with the applications of knowledge until its general education branches into professional. Poetry and philosophy and science do indeed conspire to promote the material welfare of mankind; but science no more than poetry finds its best warrant in its utility. Truth and right are above utility in all realms of thought and action.

It were a bitter mockery to suggest that any subject whatever should be taught less than it now is in American colleges. The only conceivable aim of a college government in our day is to broaden, deepen, and invigorate American teaching in all branches of learning. It will be generations before the best of American institutions of education will get growth enough to bear pruning. The descendants of the Pilgrim Fathers are still very thankful for the parched corn of learning.

Recent discussions have added pitifully little to the world's stock of wisdom about the staple of education. Who blows to-day such a ringing trumpet-call to the study of language as Luther blew? Hardly a significant word has been added in two centuries to Milton's description of the unprofitable way to study languages. Would any young American learn how to profit by travel, that foolish beginning but excellent sequel to education, he can find no apter advice than Bacon's.

The practice of England and America is literally centuries behind the precept of the best thinkers upon education. A striking illustration may be found in the prevailing neglect of the systematic study of the English language. How lamentably true to-day are these words of Locke: "If any one among us have a facility or purity more than ordinary in his mother tongue, it is owing to chance, or his genius, or anything rather than to his education or any care of his teacher."

The best result of the discussion which has raged so long about the relative educational value of the main branches of learning is the conviction that there is room for them all in a sound scheme, provided that right methods of teaching be employed. It is not because of the limitation of their faculties that boys of eighteen come to college, having mastered nothing but a few score pages of Latin and Greek and the bare elements of mathematics.

Not nature, but an unintelligent system of instruction from the primary school through the college, is responsible for the fact that many college graduates have so inadequate a conception of what is meant by scientific observation, reasoning, and proof. It is possible for the young to get actual experience of all the principal methods of thought. There is a method of thought in language, and a method in mathematics, and another of natural and physical science, and another of faith. With wise direction even a child would drink at all these springs.

The actual próblem to be solved is not what to teach, but how to teach. The revolutions accomplished in other fields of labor have a lesson for teachers. New England could not cut her hay with scythes, nor the West her wheat with sickles. When millions are to be fed where formerly there were but scores, the single fish-line must be replaced by seines and trawls, the human shoulders by steam elevators, and the wooden-axled ox-cart on a corduroy road by the smooth-running freight train.

In education there is a great hungry multitude to be fed. The great well at Orvieto, up whose spiral paths files of donkeys painfully brought the sweet water in kegs, was an admirable construction in its day; but now we tap Fresh Pond in our chambers. The Orvieto well might remind some persons of educational methods not yet extinct. With good methods we may confidently hope to give young men of twenty or twenty-five an accurate general knowledge of all the main subjects of human interest, besides a minute and thorough knowledge of the one subject which each may select as his principal occupation in life. To think this impossible is to despair of mankind; for unless a general acquaintance with many branches of knowledge—good as far as it goes—be attainable by great numbers of men, there can be no such thing as an intelligent public opinion; and in the modern world the intelligence of public opinion is the one condition of social progress.

What has been said of needed reformation in methods of teaching the subjects which have already been nominally admitted to the American curriculum applies not only to the university, but to the preparatory schools of every grade down to the primary. The American college is obliged to supplement the American school. Whatever elementary instruction the schools fail to give, the college must supply. The improvement of the schools has of late years permitted the college to advance the grade of its teaching and adapt the methods of its later years to men instead of boys.

This improvement of the college reacts upon the schools to their advantage; and this action and reaction will be continuous. A university is not built in the air, but on social and literary foundations which preceding generations have bequeathed. If the whole structure needs rebuilding, it must be rebuilt from the foundation. Hence sudden reconstruction is impossible in our high places of education. Such inducements as the College can offer for enriching and enlarging the course of study pursued in preparatory schools, the Faculty has recently decided to give. The requirements in Latin and Greek grammar are to be set at a thorough knowledge of forms and general principles; the lists of classical authors accepted as equivalents for the regular standards are to be enlarged; an accquaintance with physical geography is to be required; the study of elementary mechanics is to be recommended; and prizes are to be offered for reading aloud and for the critical analysis of passages from English authors. At the same time the university will take to heart the counsel which it gives to others.

In every department of learning the university would search out by trial and reflection the best methods of instruction. The university believes in the thorough study of language. It contends for all languages,—Oriental, Greek, Latin, Romance, German, and especially for the mother tongue; seeing in them all one institution, one history, one means of discipline, one department of learning. In teaching languages it is for this American generation to invent, or to accept from abroad, better tools than the old; to devise, or to transplant from Europe, prompter and more comprehensive methods than the prevailing; and to command more intelligent labor, in order to gather rapidly and surely the best fruit of that culture and have time for other harvests.

The University recognizes the natural and physical sciences as indispensable branches of education, and has long acted upon this opinion; but it would have science taught in a rational way, objects and instruments in hand,—not from books merely, not through the memory chiefly, but by the seeing eye and the informing fingers. Some of the scientific scoffers at gerund-grinding and nonsense verses might well look at home; the prevailing methods of teaching science, the world over, are, on the whole, less intelligent than the methods of teaching language.

The University would have scientific studies in school and college and professional school develop and discipline those powers of the mind by which science has been created and is daily nourished,—the powers of observation, the inductive faculty, the sober imagination, the sincere and proportionate judgment. A student in the elements gets no such training by studying even a good text-book, though he really master it, nor yet by sitting at the feet of the most admirable lecturer.

If there be any subject which seems fixed and settled in its educational aspects, it is the mathematics; yet there is no department of the University which has been, during the last fifteen years, in such a state of vigorous experiment upon methods and appliances of teaching as the mathematical department. It would be well if the primary schools had as much faith in the possibility of improving their way of teaching multiplication.

The important place which history, and mental, moral, and political philosophy, should hold in any broad scheme of education is recognized of all; but none know so well how crude are the prevailing methods of teaching these subjects as those who teach them best. They cannot be taught from books alone; but must be vivified and illustrated by teachers of active, comprehensive, and judicial mind. To learn by rote a list of dates is not to study history.

Mr. Emerson says that history is biography. In a deep sense this is true. Certainly the best way to impart the facts of history to the young is through the quick interest they take in the lives of the men and

THEODORE ROOSEVELT.

women who fill great historical scenes or epitomize epochs. From the centres so established their interest may be spread over great areas. For the young especially it is better to enter with intense sympathy into the great moments of history than to stretch a thin attention through its weary centuries.

Philosophical subjects should never be taught with authority. They are not established sciences; they are full of disputed matters, and open questions, and bottomless speculations. It is not the function of the teacher to settle philosophical and political controversies for the pupil, or even to recommend to him any one set of opinions as better than another. Exposition, not imposition, of opinions is the professor's part. The student should be made acquainted with all sides of these controversies, with the salient points of each system; he should be shown what is still in force of institutions or philosophies mainly outgrown, and what is new in those now in vogue. The very word "education" is a standing protest against dogmatic teaching. The notion that education consists in the authoritative inculcation of what the teacher deems true may be logical and appropriate in a convent, or a seminary for priests, but it is intolerable in universities and public schools, from primary to professional. The worthy fruit of academic culture is an open mind, trained to careful thinking, instructed in the methods of philosophic investigation, acquainted in a general way with the accumulated thought of past generations, and penetrated with humility. It is thus that the University in our day serves Christ and the Church.

The increasing weight, range, and thoroughness of

the examination for admission to college may strike some observers with dismay. The increase of real requisitions is hardly perceptible from year to year; but on looking back ten or twenty years the changes are marked and all in one direction. The dignity and importance of this examination has been steadily rising, and this rise measures the improvement of the preparatory schools.

When the gradual improvement of American schools has lifted them to a level with the German gymnasia we may expect to see the American college bearing a nearer resemblance to the German Faculties of Philosophy than it now does. The actual admission examination may best be compared with the first examination of the University of France. This examination, which comes at the end of a French boy's school life, is for the degree of Bachelor of Arts or of Sciences. The degree is given to young men who come fresh from school and have never been under university teachers: a large part of the recipients never enter the university. The young men who come to our examination for admission to college are older than the average of French Bachelors of Arts. The examination tests not only the capacity of the candidates, but also the quality of their school instruction; it is a great event in their lives, though not, as in France, marked by any degree. The examination is conducted by college professors and tutors who have never had any relations whatever with those examined. It would be a great gain if all subsequent college examinations could be as impartially conducted by competent examiners brought from without the college and paid for their services.

When the teacher examines his class, there is no effective examination of the teacher. If the examinations for the scientific, theological, medical, and dental degrees were conducted by independent boards of examiners appointed by professional bodies of dignity and influence, the significance of these degrees would be greatly enhanced. The same might be said of the degree of Bachelor of Laws were it not that this degree is at present earned by attendance alone, and not by attendance and examination. The American practice of allowing the teaching body to examine for degrees has been partly dictated by the scarcity of men outside the Faculties who are at once thoroughly acquainted with the subjects of examination and sufficiently versed in teaching to know what may fairly be expected both of students and instructors.

This difficulty could now be overcome. The chief reason, however, for the existence of this practice is that the Faculties were the only bodies that could confer degrees intelligently when degrees were obtained by passing through a prescribed course of study without serious checks, and completing a certain term of residence without disgrace. The change in the manner of earning the university degrees ought, by right, to have brought into being an examining body distinct from the teaching body. So far as the college proper is concerned, the Board of Overseers have, during the past year, taken a step which tends in this direction.

The rigorous examination for admission has one good effect throughout the college course; it prevents a waste of instruction upon incompetent persons. A school with a low standard for admission and a high standard of graduation, like West Point, is obliged to dismiss a large proportion of its students by the way. Hence much individual distress, and a great waste of resources, both public and private. But, on the other hand, it must not be supposed that every student who enters Harvard College necessarily graduates. Strict annual examinations are to be passed. More than a fourth of those who enter the college fail to take their degrees.

Only a few years ago all students who graduated at this college passed through one uniform curriculum. Every man studied the same subjects in the same proportions, without regard to his natural bent or preference. The individual student had no choice either of subjects or teachers. This system is still the prevailing system among American colleges and finds vigorous defenders. It has the merit of simplicity. So had the school methods of our grandfathers,—one primer, one catechism, one rod for all children. On the whole, a single common course of studies, tolerably well selected to meet the average needs, seems to most Americans a very proper and natural thing, even for grown men.

As a people we do not apply to mental activities the principle of division of labor; and we have but a halting faith in special training for high professional employments. The vulgar conceit that a Yankee can turn his hand to anything we insensibly carry into high places, where it is preposterous and criminal. We are accustomed to seeing men leap from farm or shop to court-room or pulpit, and we half believe that common men can safely use the seven-league boots of genius.

What amount of knowledge and experience do we habitually demand of our lawgivers? What special training do we ordinarily think necessary for our diplomatists? In great emergencies, indeed, the nation has known where to turn. Only after years of the bitterest experience did we come to believe the professional training of a soldier to be of value in war. This lack of faith in the prophecy of a natural bent, and in the value of a discipline concentrated upon a single object, amounts to a national danger.

In education the individual traits of different minds have not been sufficiently attended to. Through all the period of boyhood the school studies should be representative; all the main fields of knowledge should be entered upon. But the young man of nineteen or twenty ought to know what he likes best and is most fit for. If his previous training has been sufficiently wide, he will know by that time whether he is most apt at language, or philosophy, or natural science, or mathematics. If he feels no loves he will at least have his hates. At that age the teacher may wisely abandon hates. At that age the teacher may wisely abandon the school-dame's practice of giving a copy of nothing but zeros to the child who alleges that he cannot make that figure.

When the revelation of his own peculiar taste and capacity comes to a young man, let him reverently give it welcome, thank God, and take courage. Thereafter he knows his way to happy, enthusiastic work, and, God willing, to usefulness and success. The civilization of a people may be inferred from the variety of its tools. There are thousands of years between the stone hatchet and the machine-shop. As tools multiply, each is more ingeniously adapted to its own exclusive purpose. So with the men that make the State. For the individual, concentration, and the highest development of his own peculiar faculty, is the only prudence. But for the State it is variety not uniformity, of intellectual product, which is needful.

These principles are the justification of the system of elective studies which has been gradually developed in this college during the past twenty years. At present the Freshman year is the only one in which there is a fixed course prescribed for all. In the other three years more than half the time allotted to study is filled with subjects chosen by each student from lists which comprise six studies in the Sophomore year, nine in the Junior year, and eleven in the Senior year. The range of elective studies is large, though there are some striking deficiencies. The liberty of choice of subject is wide, but yet has very rigid limits. There is a certain framework which must be filled; and about half the material of the filling is prescribed. The choice offered to the student does not lie between liberal studies and the professional or utilitarian studies. All the studies which are open to him are liberal and disciplinary, not narrow or special. Under this system the College does not demand, it is true, one invariable set of studies of every candidate for the first degree in Arts; but its requisitions for this degree are nevertheless high and inflexible, being nothing less than four years devoted to liberal culture.

It has been alleged that the elective system must weaken the bond which unites members of the same class. This is true; but, in view of another much more efficient cause of the diminution of class intimacy, the point is not very significant. The increased size of the college classes inevitably works a great change in this respect. One hundred and fifty young men cannot be so intimate with each other as fifty used to be. This increase is progressive. Taken in connection with the rising average age of the students, it would compel the adoption of methods of instruction different from the old, if there were no better motive for such change.

The elective system fosters scholarship, because it gives free play to natural preferences and inborn aptitudes, makes possible enthusiasm for a chosen work, relieves the professor and the ardent disciple of the presence of a body of students who are compelled to an unwelcome task, and enlarges instruction by substituting many and various lessons given to small, lively classes, for a few lessons many times repeated to different sections of a numerous class. The College therefore proposes to persevere in its efforts to establish, improve, and extend the elective system. Its administrative difficulties, which seem formidable at first, banish before a brief experience.

There has been much discussion about the comparative merits of lectures and recitations. Both are useful: lectures, for inspiration, guidance, and the comprehensive methodizing which only one who has a view of the whole field can rightly contrive; recitations, for securing and testifying a thorough mastery, on the part of the pupil, of the treatise or author in hand, for conversational comment and amplification, for emulation and competition. Recitations alone readily degenerate into dusty repetitions, and lectures alone are too often a useless expenditure of force. The lecturer pumps laboriously into sieves. The water may be wholesome, but it runs through. A mind must work to grow.

Just as far, however, as the student can be relied on to master and appreciate his author without the aid of frequent questioning and repetitions, so far is it possible to dispense with recitations. Accordingly in the later college years there is a decided tendency to diminish the number of recitations, the faithfulness of the student being tested by periodical examinations. This tendency is in a right direction if prudently controlled.

The discussion about lectures and recitations has brought out some strong opinions about text-books and their use. Impatience with text-books and manuals is very natural in both teachers and taught. These books are indeed, for the most part, very imperfect, and stand in constant need of correction by the well-informed teacher. Stereotyping, in its present undeveloped condition, is in part to blame for their most exasperating defects. To make the metal plates keep pace with the progress of learning is costly. The manifest deficiencies of text-books must not, however, drive us into a too-sweeping condemnation of their use.

It is a rare teacher who is superior to all manuals in his subject. Scientific manuals are, as a rule, much worse than those upon language, literature, or philosophy; yet the main improvement in medical education in this country during the last twenty years has been the addition of systematic recitations from text books to the lectures which were formerly the principal means of theoretical instruction. The training of a medical student, inadequate as it is, offers the best example we have of the methods and fruits of an education mainly scientific. The transformation which the average student of a good medical school undergoes in three years is strong testimony to the efficiency of the training he receives.

There are certain common misapprehensions about colleges in general, and this college in particular, to which I wish to devote a few moments' attention. And, first, in spite of the familiar picture of the moral dangers which environ the student, there is no place so safe as a good college during the critical passage from boyhood to manhood.

The security of the college commonwealth is largely due to its exuberant activity. Its public opinion, though easily led astray, is still high in the main. Its scholarly tastes and habits, its eager friendships and quick hatreds, its keen debates, its frank discussions of character and of deep political and religious questions,—all are safeguards against sloth, vulgarity, and depravity. Its society and not less its solitudes are full of teaching. Shams, conceit, and fictitious distinctions get no mercy. There is nothing but ridicule for bombast and sentimentality. Repression of genuine sentiment and emotion is indeed, in this college, carried too far. Reserve is more respectable than any undiscerning communicativeness.

But neither Yankee shamefacedness nor English
19

stolidity is admirable. This point especially touches you, young men, who are still undergraduates. When you feel a true admiration for a teacher, a glow of enthusiasm for work, a thrill of pleasure at some excellent saying, give it expression. Do not be ashamed of these emotions. Cherish the natural sentiment of personal devotion to the teacher who calls out your better powers. It is a great delight to serve an intellectual master. We Americans are but too apt to lose this happiness. German and French students get it. If ever, in after years, you come to smile at the youthful reverence you paid, believe me, it will be with tears in your eyes.

Many excellent persons see great offence in any system of college rank; but why should we expect more of young men than we do of their elders? How many men and women perform their daily tasks from the highest motives alone,—for the glory of God and the relief of man's estate? Most people work for bare bread, a few for cake. The college rank-list reinforces higher motives. In the campaign for character no auxiliaries are to be refused. Next to despising the enemy, it is dangerous to reject allies. To devise a suitable method of estimating the fidelity and attainments of college students is, however, a problem which has long been under discussion and has not yet received a satisfactory solution. The worst of rank as a stimulus is the self-reference it implies in the aspirants. The less a young man thinks about the cultivation of his mind, about his own mental progress,—about himself, in short,—the better.

The petty discipline of colleges attracts altogether

too much attention both from friends and foes. It is to be remembered that the rules concerning decorum, however necessary to maintain the high standard of manners and conduct which characterizes this college, are nevertheless justly described as petty. What is technically called a quiet term cannot be accepted as the acme of university success. This success is not to be measured by the frequency or rarity of college punishments. The criteria of success or failure in a high place of learning are not the boyish escapades of an insignificant minority, nor the exceptional cases of ruinous vice. Each year must be judged by the added opportunities of instruction, by the prevailing enthusiasm in learning, and by the gathered wealth of culture and character. The best way to put boyishness to shame is to foster scholarship and manliness. The manners of a community cannot be improved by main force any more than its morals. The statutes of the University need some amendment and reduction in the chapters on crimes and misdemeanors. But let us render to our fathers the justice we shall need from our sons.

What is too minute or precise for our use was doubtless wise and proper, in its day. It was to inculcate a reverent bearing and due consideration for things sacred that the regulations prescribed a black dress on Sunday. Black is not the only decorous wear in these days; but we must not seem, in ceasing from this particular mode of good manners, to think less of the gentle breeding of which only the outward signs, and not the substance, have been changed.

Harvard College has always attracted and still attracts students in all conditions of life. From the city

trader or professional man who may be careless how
much his son spends at Cambridge, to the farmer or
mechanic who finds it a hard sacrifice to give his boy
his time early enough to enable him to prepare for
college, all sorts and conditions of men have wished
and still wish to send their sons hither. There are always scores of young men in this university who earn
or borrow every dollar they spend here. Every year
many young men enter this college without any resources whatever. If they prove themselves men of
capacity and character they never go away for lack of
money. More than twenty thousand dollars a year is
now devoted to aiding students of narrow means to
compass their education, beside all the remitted fees
and the numerous private benefactions. These latter
are unfailing. Taken in connection with the proceeds
of the funds applicable to the aid of poor students, they
enable the Corporation to say that no good student
need ever stay away from Cambridge or leave college
simply because he is poor.

There is one uniform condition, however, on which
help is given,—the recipient must be of promising ability and the best character. The community does not
owe superior education to all children, but only to
the *élite*,—to those who, having the capacity, prove
by hard work that they have also the necessary perseverance and endurance. The process of preparing to
enter college under the difficulties which poverty en-
tails is just such a test of worthiness as is needed.
At this moment there is no college in the country more
eligible for a poor student than Harvard on the mere
ground of economy. The scholarship funds are

mainly the fruit of the last fifteen years. The future will take care of itself; for it is to be expected that the men who in this generation have had the benefit of these funds, and who succeed in after-life, will pay many-fold to their successors in need the debt which they owe, not to the college, but to benefactors whom they cannot even thank save in heaven.

No wonder that scholarships are founded. What greater privilege than this of giving young men of promise the coveted means of intellectual growth and freedom? The angels of heaven might envy mortals so fine a luxury. The happiness which the winning of a scholarship gives is not the recipient's alone; it flashes back to the home whence he came and gladdens anxious hearts there. The good which it does is not his alone, but descends, multiplying at every step, through generations. Thanks to the beneficent mysteries of hereditary transmission, no capital earns such interest as personal culture. The poorest and the richest students are equally welcome here, provided that with their poverty or their wealth they bring capacity, ambition, and purity.

The poverty of scholars is of inestimable worth in this money-getting nation. It maintains the true standards of virtue and honor. The poor friars, not the bishops, saved the Church. The poor scholars and preachers of duty defend the modern community against its own material prosperity. Luxury and learning are ill bed-fellows. Nevertheless, this college owes much of its distinctive character to those who, bringing hither from refined homes good breeding, gentle tastes, and a manly delicacy, add to them openness and activity of mind, intellectual interests, and a sense of public duty. It is as high a privilege for a rich man's son as for a poor man's to resort to these academic halls and so to take his proper place among cultivated and intellectual men. To lose altogether the presence of those who in early life have enjoyed the domestic and social advantages of wealth would be as great a blow to the College as to lose the sons of the poor. The interests of the college and the country are identical in this regard. The country suffers when the rich are ignorant and unrefined. Inherited wealth is an unmitigated curse when divorced from culture.

Harvard College is sometimes reproached with being aristocratic. If by "aristocracy" be meant a stupid and pretentious caste, founded on wealth and birth and an affectation of European manners, no charge could be more preposterous: the College is intensely American in affection and intensely democratic in temper. But there is an aristocracy to which the sons of Harvard have belonged, and let us hope will ever aspire to belong,—the aristocracy which excels in manly sports, carries off the honors and prizes of the learned professions, and bears itself with distinction in all fields of intellectual labor and combat; the aristocracy which in peace stands firmest for the public honor and renown, and in war rides first into the murderous thickets.

The attitude of the University in the prevailing discussions touching the education and fit employments of women demands brief explanation. America is the natural arena for these debates; for here the female sex has a better past and a better present than else-where. Americans, as a rule, hate disabilities of all sorts, whether religious, political or social. Equality between the sexes, without privilege or oppression on either side, is the happy custom of American homes. While this great discussion is going on, it is the duty of the University to maintain a cautious and expectant policy. The Corporation will not receive women as students into the College proper, nor into any school whose discipline requires residence near the school. The difficulties involved in a common residence of hundreds of young men and women of immature char-acter and marriageable age are very grave. The ne-cessary police regulations are exceedingly burden-some.

The Corporation are not influenced to this decision, however, by any crude notions about the innate capa-cities of women. The world knows next to nothing about the natural mental capacities of the female sex. Only after generations of civil freedom and social equality will it be possible to obtain the data necessary for an adequate discussion of woman's natural tenden-cies, tastes, and capabilities.

Again, the Corporation do not find it necessary to entertain a confident opinion upon the fitness or un-fitness of women for professional pursuits. It is not the business of the University to decide this mooted point. In this country the University does not under-take to protect the community against incompetent lawyers, ministers, or doctors. The community must protect itself by refusing to employ such. Practical, not theoretical, considerations determine the policy of the University. Upon a matter concerning which prejudices are deep, and opinion inflammable, and experience scanty, only one course is prudent or justifiable when such great interests are at stake,—that of cautious and well-considered experiment.

The practical problem is to devise a safe, promising, and instructive experiment. Such an experiment the Corporation have meant to try in opening the newly established University Courses of Instruction to competent women. In these courses the University offers to young women who have been to good schools, as many years as they wish of liberal culture in studies which have no direct professional value, to be sure, but which enrich and enlarge both intellect and character. The University hopes thus to contribute to the intellectual emancipation of women. It hopes to prepare some women better than they would otherwise have been prepared for the profession of teaching, the one learned profession to which women have already acquired a clear title. It hopes that the proffer of this higher instruction will have some reflex influence upon schools for girls,—to discourage superficiality and to promote substantial education.

The governing bodies of the University are the Faculties, the Board of Overseers, and the Corporation. The University as a place of study and instruction is, at any moment, what the Faculties make it. The professors, lecturers, and tutors of the University are the living sources of learning and enthusiasm. They personally represent the possibilities of instruction. They are united in several distinct bodies, the academic and professional Faculties, each of which practically determines its own processes and rules. The discussion of methods of instruction is the principal business of these bodies.

As a fact, progress comes mainly from the Faculties. This has been conspicuously the case with the Academic and Medical Faculties during the last fifteen or twenty years. The undergraduates used to have a notion that the time of the Academic Faculty was mainly devoted to petty discipline. Nothing could be farther from the truth. The Academic Faculty is the most active, vigilant, and devoted body connected with the University. It, indeed, is constantly obliged to discuss minute details which might appear trivial to an inexperienced observer.

But in education technical details tell. Whether German be studied by the Juniors once a week as an extra study, or twice a week as an elective, seems, perhaps, an unimportant matter; but, twenty years hence, it makes all the difference between a generation of Alumni who know German and a generation who do not. The Faculty renews its youth, through the frequent appointments of tutors and assistant professors, better and oftener than any other organization within the University.

Two kinds of men make good teachers,—young men, and men who never grow old. The incessant discussions of the Academic Faculty have borne much fruit; witness the transformation of the University since the beginning of President Walker's administration. And it never tires. New men take up the old debates, and one year's progress is not less than another's. The divisions within the Faculty are never between the old and the young officers. There are always old radicals and young conservatives.

The Medical Faculty affords another illustration of the same principle,—that for real university progress we must look principally to the teaching bodies. The Medical School to-day is almost three times as strong as it was fifteen years ago. Its teaching power is greatly increased, and its methods have been much improved. This gain is the work of the Faculty of the School.

If, then, the Faculties be so important, it is a vital question how the quality of these bodies can be maintained and improved. It is very hard to find competent professors for the University. Very few Americans of eminent ability are attracted to this profession. The pay has been too low, and there has been no gradual rise out of drudgery, such as may reasonably be expected in other learned callings. The law of supply and demand, or the commercial principle that the quality as well as the price of goods is best regulated by the natural contest between producers and consumers, never has worked well in the province of high education. And in spite of the high standing of some of its advocates it is well-nigh certain that the so-called law never can work well in such a field.

The reason is that the demand for instructors of the highest class on the part of parents and trustees is an ignorant demand, and the supply of highly educated teachers is so limited that the consumer has not sufficient opportunities of informing himself concerning the real qualities of the article he seeks. Originally a bad judge, he remains a bad judge, because the supply is not sufficiently abundant and various to instruct him. Moreover a need is not necessarily a demand. Everybody knows that the supposed law affords a very imperfect protection against short weight, adulteration, and sham, even in the case of those commodities which are most abundant in the market and most familiar to buyers. The most intelligent community is defenceless enough in buying clothes and groceries. When it comes to hiring learning and inspiration and personal weight, the law of supply and demand breaks down altogether. A university cannot be managed like a railroad or a cotton-mill.

There are, however, two practicable improvements in the position of college professors which will be of very good effect. Their regular stipend must and will be increased, and the repetitions which now harass them must be diminished in number. It is a strong point of the elective system that by reducing the size of classes or divisions and increasing the variety of subjects it makes the professors' labors more agreeable.

Experience teaches that the strongest and most devoted professors will contribute something to the patrimony of knowledge, or if they invent little themselves, they will do something toward defending, interpreting, or diffusing the contributions of others. Nevertheless, the prime business of American professors in this generation must be regular and assiduous class teaching. With the exception of the endowments of the Observatory, the University does not hold a single fund primarily intended to secure to men of learning the leisure and means to prosecute original researches.

The organization and functions of the Board of

Overseers deserve the serious attention of all men who are interested in the American method of providing the community with high education through the agency of private corporations. Since 1866 the Overseers have been elected by the Alumni. Five men are chosen each year to serve six years. The body has therefore a large and very intelligent constituency and is rapidly renewed. The ingenious method of nominating to the electors twice as many candidates as there are places to be filled in any year is worthy of careful study as a device of possible application in politics. The real function of the Board of Overseers is to stimulate and watch the President and Fellows. Without the Overseers the President and Fellows would be a board of private trustees, self-perpetuated and self-controlled.

Provided as it is with two governing boards, the University enjoys that principal safeguard of all American governments,—the natural antagonism between two bodies of different constitution, powers, and privileges. While having with the Corporation a common interest of the deepest kind in the welfare of the University and the advancement of learning, the Overseers should always hold toward the Corporation an attitude of suspicious vigilance. They ought always to be pushing and prying. It would be hard to overstate the importance of the public supervision exercised by the Board of Overseers. Experience proves that our main hope for the permanence and ever-widening usefulness of the University must rest upon this double-headed organization.

The English practice of setting up a single body of

private trustees to carry on a school or charity according to the personal instructions of some founder or founders has certainly proved a lamentably bad one; and when we count by generations the institutions thus established have proved short-lived. The same causes which have brought about the decline of English endowed schools would threaten the life of this University were it not for the existence of the Board of Overseers. These schools were generally managed by close corporations, self-elected, self-controlled, without motive for activity, and destitute of external stimulus and aid. Such bodies are too irresponsible for human nature. At the time of life at which men generally come to such places of trust, rest is sweet, and the easiest way is apt to seem the best way; and the responsibility of inaction, though really heavier, seems lighter than the responsibility of action.

These corporations were often hampered by founders' wills and statutory provisions which could not be executed and yet stood in the way of organic improvements. There was no systematic provision for thorough inspections and public reports thereupon. We cannot flatter ourselves that under like circumstances we should always be secure against like dangers. Provoked by crying abuses, some of the best friends of education in England have gone the length of maintaining that all these school endowments ought to be destroyed and the future creation of such trusts rendered impossible. French law practically prohibits the creation of such trusts by private persons.

Incident to the Overseers' power of inspecting the University and publicly reporting upon its condition is the important function of suggesting and urging improvements. The inertia of a massive university is formidable. A good past is positively dangerous if it make us content with the present and so unprepared for the future. The present constitution of our Board of Overseers has already stimulated the Alumni of several other New England colleges to demand a similar control over the property-holding Board of Trustees which has heretofore been the single source of all authority.

We come now to the heart of the University,—the Corporation. This board holds the funds, makes appointments, fixes salaries, and has, by right, the initiative in all changes of the organic law of the University. Such an executive board must be small to be efficient. It must always contain men of sound judgment in finance; and literature and the learned professions should be adequately represented in it. The Corporation should also be but slowly renewed; for it is of the utmost consequence to the University that the Government should have a steady aim, and a prevailing spirit which is independent of individuals and transmissible from generation to generation.

And what should this spirit be?

First, it should be a catholic spirit. A university must be indigenous; it must be rich; but, above all, it must be free. The winnowing breeze of freedom must blow through all its chambers. It takes a hurricane to blow wheat away. An atmosphere of intellectual freedom is the native air of literature and science. This University aspires to serve the nation by training men to intellectual honesty and independence of mind. The

Corporation demands of all its teachers that they be grave, reverent, and high-minded; but it leaves them, like their pupils, free. A university is built, not by a sect, but by a nation.

Secondly, the actuating spirit of the Corporation must be a spirit of fidelity,—fidelity to the many and various trusts reposed in them by the hundreds of persons who out of their penury or their abundance have given money to the President and Fellows of Harvard College in the beautiful hope of doing some perpetual good upon this earth. The Corporation has constantly done its utmost to make this hope a living fact. One hundred and ninety-nine years ago William Pennoyer gave the rents of certain estates in the county of Norfolk, England, that "two fellows and two scholars for ever should be educated, brought up, and maintained" in this College. The income from this bequest has never failed; and to-day one of the four Pennoyer scholarships is held by a lineal descendant of William Pennoyer's brother Robert. So a lineal descendant of Governor Danforth takes this year the income of the property which Danforth bequeathed to the College in 1699.

The Corporation have been as faithful in the greater things as in the less. They have been greatly blessed in one respect: in the whole life of the Corporation— seven generations of men—nothing has ever been lost by malfeasance of officers or servants. A reputation for scrupulous fidelity to all trusts is the most precious possession of the Corporation. That safe, the College might lose everything else and yet survive: that lost beyond repair, and the days of the College would be

numbered. Testators look first to the trustworthiness
and permanence of the body which is to dispense their
benefactions.

The Corporation thankfully receive all gifts which
may advance learning; but they believe that the interests of the University may be most effectually promoted by not restricting too narrowly the use to which
a gift may be applied. Whenever the giver desires it,
the Corporation will agree to keep any fund separately
invested under the name of the giver, and to apply the
whole proceeds of such investment to any object the
giver may designate. By such special investment,
however, the insurance which results from the absorp-
tion of a specific gift in the general funds is lost. A
fund invested by itself may be impaired or lost by
a single error of judgment in investing. The chance of
such loss is small in any one generation, but appreciable
in centuries. Such general designations as salaries,
books, dormitories, public buildings, scholarships
(graduate or undergraduate), scientific collections,
and expenses of experimental laboratories, are of permanent significance and effect; while experience proves
that too specific and minute directions concerning the
application of funds must often fail of fulfilment simply in consequence of the changing needs and habits
of successive generations.

Again, the Corporation should always be filled with
the spirit of enterprise. An institution like this College is getting decrepit when it sits down contentedly
on its mortgages. On its invested funds the Corporation should be always seeking how safely to make a
quarter of a per cent. more. A quarter of one per cent.

means a new professorship. It should be always pushing after more professorships, better professors, more land and buildings, and better apparatus. It should be eager, sleepless, and untiring, never wasting a moment in counting laurels won, ever prompt to welcome and apply the liberality of the community, and liking no prospect so well as that of difficulties to be overcome and labors to be done in the cause of learning and public virtue.

You recognize, gentlemen, the picture which I have drawn in thus delineating the true spirit of the Corporation of this College. I have described the noble quintessence of the New England character,—that character which has made us a free and enlightened people,—that character which, please God, shall yet do a great work in the world for the lifting up of humanity.

Apart from the responsibility which rests upon the Corporation, its actual labors are far heavier than the community imagines. The business of the University has greatly increased in volume and complexity during the past twenty years, and the drafts made upon the time and thought of every member of the Corporation are heavy indeed. The high honors of the function are in these days most generously earned.

The President of the University is primarily an executive officer; but, being a member of both governing boards and of all the Faculties, he has also the influence in their debates to which his more or less perfect intimacy with the University and greater or less personal weight may happen to entitle him. An administrative officer who undertakes to do everything himself will

20

do but little and that little ill. The President's first duty is that of supervision. He should know what each officer's and servant's work is, and how it is done. But the days are past in which the President could be be called on to decide everything from the purchase of a door-mat to the appointment of a professor. The principle of divided and subordinate responsibilities whcih rules in government bureaus, in manufactories, and all great companies, which makes a modern army a possibility, must be applied in the University.

The President should be able to discern the practical essence of complicated and long-drawn discussions. He must often pick out that promising part of theory which ought to be tested by experiment, and must decide how many of things desirable are also attainable and what one of many projects is ripest for execution. He must watch and look before,—watch, to seize opportunities to get money, to secure eminent teachers and scholars, and to influence public opinion toward the advancement of learning; and look before, to anticipate the due effect on the University of the fluctuations of public opinion on educational problems; of the progress of the institutions which feed the University; of the changing condition of the professions which the University supplies; of the rise of new professions; of the gradual alteration of social and religious habits in the community. The University must accommodate itself promptly to significant changes in the character of the people for whom it exists. The institutions of higher education in any nation are always a faithful mirror in which are sharply reflected the national history and character. In this mobile nation the action and reaction between the University and society at large are more sensitive and rapid' than in stiffer communities. The President, therefore, must not need to see a house built before he can comprehend the plan of it. He can profit by a wide intercourse with all sorts of men, and by every real discussion on education, legislation, and sociology.

The most important function of the President is that of advising the Corporation concerning appointments, particularly about appointments of young men who have not had time and opportunity to approve themselves to the public. It is in discharging this duty that the President holds the future of the University in his hands. He cannot do it well unless he have insight, unless he be able to recognize, at times beneath some crusts, the real gentleman and the natural teacher. This is the one oppressive responsibility of the President: all other cares are light beside it. To see every day the evil fruit of a bad appointment must be the cruelest of official torments. Fortunately the good effect of a judicious appointment is also inestimable; and here, as everywhere, good is more penetrating and diffusive than evil.

It is imperative that the statutes which define the President's duties should be recast, and the customs of the College be somewhat modified, in order that lesser duties may not crowd out the greater. But, however important the functions of the President, it must not be forgotten that he is emphatically a constitutional executive. It is his character and his judgment which are of importance, not his opinions. He is the executive officer of deliberative bodies in which decisions are reached after discussion by a majority vote. These decisions bind him. He cannot force his own opinions upon anybody. A university is the last place in the world for a dictator. Learning is always republican. It has idols, but not masters.

What can the community do for the University? It can love, honor, and cherish it. Love it and honor it. The University is upheld by this public affection and respect. In the loyalty of her children she finds strength and courage. The Corporation, the Overseers, and the several Faculties need to feel that the leaders of public opinion, and especially the sons of the College, are at their back, always ready to give them a generous and intelligent support. Therefore we welcome the Chief Magistrate of the Commonwealth, the senators, judges, and other dignitaries of the State, who by their presence at this ancient ceremonial bear witness to the pride which Massachusetts feels in her eldest University. Therefore we rejoice in the presence of this throng of the Alumni, testifying their devotion to the College which, though all changes, is still their home. Cherish it. This University, though rich among American colleges, is very poor in comparison with the great universities of Europe. The wants of the American community have far outgrown the capacity of the University to supply them. We must try to satisfy the cravings of the select few as well as the needs of the average many. We cannot afford to neglect the Fine Arts. We need groves and meadows as well as barracks, and soon there will be no chance to get them in this expanding city. But, above all, we need professorships, books, and apparatus, that teaching and scholarship may abound.

And what will the University do for the community? First, it will make a rich return of learning, poetry, and piety. Secondly, it will foster the sense of public duty,—that great virtue which makes republics possible. The founding of Harvard College was an heroic act of public spirit. For more than a century the breath of life was kept in it by the public spirit of the Province and of its private benefactors. In the last fifty years the public spirit of the friends of the College has quadrupled its endowments. And how have the young men nurtured here in successive generations repaid the founders for their pious care? Have they honored freedom and loved their country? For answer we appeal to the records of the national service; to the lists of the senate, the cabinet, and the diplomatic service, and to the rolls of the army and navy.

Honored men, here present, illustrate before the world the public quality of the graduates of this College. Theirs is no mercenary service. Other fields of labor attract them more and would reward them better; but they are filled with the noble ambition to deserve well of the republic. There have been doubts, in times yet recent, whether culture were not selfish; where men of refined tastes and manners could really love Liberty and be ready to endure hardness for her sake; whether, in short, gentlemen would in this century prove as loyal to noble ideas as in other times they had been to kings. In yonder old playground, fit spot whereon to commemorate the manliness which there was nurtured, shall soon rise a noble monument which for generations will give convincing answer to such shallow doubts; for over its gates will be written, "In memory of the sons of Harvard who died for their country." The future of the University will not be unworthy of its past.

Depew, Chauncey M., an American lawyer, well known as an after-dinner orator, born at Peekskill, N. Y., April 23, 1834. He studied law, and was admitted to the bar in 1858. His interest in politics resulted in his entrance into the lower house of the State Legislature in 1861, and during 1863 he was the Secretary of State of New York. In 1869 he became attorney for the New York Central railway and from 1885 to 1898 was president of the entire Vander-bilt railway system. For many years he has declined all political appointments, and his many public addresses have been delivered on civic occasions. He is a ready, fluent speaker, whose addresses are often enlivened by humorous touches. His witty after-dinner speeches have been especially admired.

SPEECH AT THE DINNER TO CELEBRATE THE ANNIVERSARY OF THE BIRTH OF GENERAL GRANT.

DELIVERED AT DELMONICO'S, APRIL 27, 1888.

I DO not propose, as has been announced, to deliver a formal oration upon General Grant, but, as one of the many gentlemen who are to speak here to-night, to express the judgment of a busy man of affairs upon his character and career. We are not yet far enough from this striking personality to read accurately the verdict of posterity, and we are so near that we still feel the force of the mighty passions in the midst of which he moved and lived.

The hundred years of our national existence are crowded with an unusual number of men eminent in arms and in statesmanship; but of all the illustrious list one only has his birthday a legal holiday—George Washington.

Of the heroes and patriots who filled the niches in our temple of fame for the first century, the birthdays of only two of them are of such significance that they receive wide celebrations—Lincoln and Grant.

When the historian of the future calmly and impartially writes the story of this momentous period, these two names will be inseparably linked together. The President supplemented the General, and the General the President, and without them the great battle of human rights and American unity might have been lost.

Reticent as to his plans, secretive as to his movements, repelling inquiry, and disdaining criticism, General Grant invited the deepest hostility from the country at large. Three years of war, which had carried grief to every household, and in which the failures had been greater than the successes, had made the people dispirited, impatient, and irritable. The conditions were such that the demand for the removal of Grant many times would have been irresistible, and the call for recruits to fill his depleted ranks unanswered, except for the peculiar hold the President had upon the country.

Lincoln was not an accidental or experimental President. As a member of Congress he became familiar with the details of government, and in the debate with Douglas had demonstrated a familiarity with the questions before the people, and a genius for their solution, unequaled among his contemporaries.

No one of the statesman of the time who might

possibly have been President could have held the country up to the high-water mark of the continuous struggle of hope against defeat, of fighting not only against a solid enemy, but an almost equal division in his own camps. His humble origin, his homely ways, his quaint humor, his constant touch and sympathy with the people, inspired the confidence which enabled him to command and wield all the forces of the Republic. He alone could stand between the demand for Grant's removal, the criticism upon his plans, the fierce outcries against his losses, and satisfy the country of the infallibility of his own trust in the ultimate success of the command.

On the other hand, the aspiration of Lincoln for the defeat of the rebellion and the reunion of the States could not have been realized except for Grant. Until he appeared upon the scene the war had been a bloody and magnificent failure. The cumulative and concentrated passions of the Confederacy had fused the whole people into an army of aggression and defence. The North, without passion or vindictiveness, fought with gloved hands, at the expense of thousands of lives and fatal blows to prestige and credit. The lesson was learned that a good brigadier, an able general of division, a successful corps commander, might be paralyzed under the burden of supreme responsibility. Victories were fruitless, defeats disastrous, delays demoralizing, until the spirit of war entered the camp in the person of Ulysses S. Grant. Without sentiment or passion, he believed that every reverse could be retrieved and victory should be followed with the annihilation of the enemy's forces. "My terms are unconditional surrender; I move immediately upon your works," was the legend of Donelson which proclaimed the new method of warfare. He hurled his legions against the ramparts of Vicksburg, sacrificing thousands of lives which might have been saved by delay, but saved the loss of tens of thousands by malarial fever and camp diseases, and possibly at the expense of defeat. He believed that the river of blood shed to-day, and followed by immediate results, was infinitely more merciful to friend and foe than the slower disasters of war which make the hecatombs of the dead.

From the surrender of Vicksburg rose the sun of national unity to ascend to the zenith at Appomattox, and never to set. Where all others had failed in the capture of Richmond, he succeeded by processes which aroused the protest and horror of the country and the criticism of posterity—but it triumphed. For thirty nights in succession he gave to the battle-torn and decimated army the famous order, "By the left flank, forward"; and for thirty days hurled them upon the ever-succeeding breastworks and ramparts of the enemy. But it was with the same inexorable and indomitable idea that, with practically inexhaustible resources behind him, the rebellion could be hammered to death.

As Grant fought without vindictiveness or feeling of revenge, in the supreme moment of victory the soldier disappeared and the patriot and statesman took his place. He knew that the exultation of the hour would turn to ashes in the future unless the surrendered rebel soldier became a loyal citizen. He knew that the Republic could not hold vassal provinces by the power of the bayonet and live. He returned arms, gave food, transportation, horses, stock, and said, "Cultivate your farms and patriotism." And they did. Whatever others may have done, the Confederate soldier has never violated the letter or the spirit of that parole.

All other conquerors have felt that the triumphal entry into the enemy's capital should be the crowning event of the war. The Army of the Potomac had been seeking to capture Richmond for four years, and when the hour arrived for the victorious procession Grant halted it, that no memory of humiliation should stand in the way of the rebel capital becoming once more the capital of a loyal State.

The curse of power is flattery; the almost inevitable concomitant of greatness, jealousy; and yet no man ever lived who so rejoiced in the triumph of others as General Grant.

This imperturbable man hailed the victories of his generals with wild delight. Sheridan, riding down the Valley, reversing the tide of battle, falling with resistless blows upon the enemy until they surrendered, drew from his admiring commander the exulting remark to the country: "Behold one of the greatest generals of this or any other age." His companion and steadfast friend through all his campaigns, the only man who rivaled him in genius and the affections of his countrymen, the most accomplished soldier and superb tactician, who broke the source of supply and struck the deadliest blow in the march from Atlanta to the sea, received at every step of his career the most generous recognition of his services and abilities. He knew and was glad that the march of Xenophon and the Ten Thousand Greeks, which had been the inspiration of armies for over two thousand years, would be replaced, for the next two thousand, by the resistless tramp of Sherman and his army.

Grant was always famous among his soldiers for the rare quality of courage in the presence of danger. But the country is indebted to him for a higher faculty, which met and averted a peril of the gravest character.

One of the most extraordinary and singular men who ever filled a great place was Andrew Johnson. He was a human paradox of conflicting qualities, great and small, generous and mean, bigoted and broad, patriotic and partisan. He loved his country with a passionate devotion, but would have destroyed it to rebuild it upon his own model. Born a "poor white," hating with the intensity of wounded pride the better and dominant class, in a delirium of revenge and vindictiveness he shouted, "Treason is odious and must be punished," and by drumhead court-martial or summary process at law would have executed every one of the Confederate generals and left behind a vendetta to disturb the peace of uncounted generations.

Between their execution and this madman appears the calm and conquering force of General Grant, with the declaration: "My parole is the honor of the nation." When, swinging to the other extreme, and in the exercise of doubtful power, the President would have reversed the results of the war by reorganizing a government upon the lines which he thought best, he was again met by this same determined purpose, exclaiming: "My bayonets will again be the salvation of the nation."

General Grant will live in history as the greatest soldier of his time, but it will never be claimed for him that he was the best of Presidents. No man, however remarkable his endowments, could fill that position with supreme ability unless trained and educated for the task. He said to a well-known publicist in the last days of his second term: "You have criticised severely my administration in your newspaper; in some cases you were right, in others wrong. I ask this of you, in fairness and justice, that in summing up the results of my presidency you will only say that General Grant, having had no preparation for civil office, performed its duties conscientiously and according to the best of his ability."

The times of Reconstruction presented problems which required the highest qualities of statesmanship and business. In the unfamiliarity with the business of a great commercial nation General Grant did not, however, differ much from most of the men who have been successful or defeated candidates for the presidency of the United States. It is a notable fact that though we are the only purely industrial nation in the world, we have never selected our rulers from among the great business men of the country. And the conditions and prejudices of success present insuperable obstacles to such a choice.

Yet Grant's administration will live in history for two acts of supreme importance. When the delirium of fiat money would have involved the nation in bankruptcy, his great name and fame alone served to win

the victory for honest money and to save the credit
and prosperity of the Republic. He, the first soldier
of his time, gave the seal of his great authority to the
settlement of international disputes by arbitration.

The quality of his greatness was never so conspicuous as in the election of General Garfield. He carried
with him around the world the power and majesty
of the American nation—he had been the companion
of kings and counsellor of cabinets. His triumphal
march had belted the globe, and through the Golden
Gate of the Pacific he entered once more his own
land, expecting to receive the nomination of his party
for a third term for the presidency. In the disappointment of defeat and the passions it involved, the election of the nominee of that Convention depended entirely upon him. Had he remained in his tent, Garfield would never have been President of the United
States; but, gathering all the chieftains, and commanding them, when they would sulk or retire, to accompany him to the front, his appearance in the canvass
won the victory.

He was at West Point only to be a poor scholar and
to graduate with little promise and less expectancy
from his instructors. In the barter and trade of his
Western home he was invariably cheated. As a
subaltern officer in the Mexican War, which he de-
tested, he simply did his duty and made no impress
upon his companions or superiors. As a wood-seller
he was beaten by all the wood-choppers of Missouri.
As a merchant he could not compete with his rivals.
As a clerk he was a listless dreamer, and yet the moment supreme command devolved upon him the dross

disappeared, dullness and indifference gave way to a clarified intellect which grasped the situation with the power of inspiration. The larger the field, the greater the peril, the more mighty the results dependent upon the issue, the more superbly he rose to all the requirements of the emergency. From serene heights unclouded by passion, jealousy, or fear, he surveyed the whole boundless field of operations, and with unerring skill forced each part to work in harmony with the general plan. The only commander who never lost a battle, his victories were not luck, but came from genius and pluck.

Cæsar surpassed him because he was both a great soldier and a great statesman; but he was immeasurably inferior to Grant because his ambition was superior to his patriotism. Frederick the Great and Napoleon I. revelled in war for its triumphs and its glory, but General Grant, reviewing that most superb of armies beside the Emperor and Von Moltke and Bismarck, electrified the military nations of Europe by proclaiming his utter detestation of war. The motto which appeared in the sky at the consummation of his victories, and was as distinct as the Cross of Constantine, was, " Let us have peace." Under its inspiration he returned to Lee his sword. He stood between the Confederate leaders and the passions of the hour, and with his last breath repeated it as a solemn injunction and legacy to his countrymen. As his spirit hovers over us to-night, let the sentiment be the active principle of our faith. He meant that political divisions of our country, inevitable and necessary for its freedom and prosperity, should not be upon sectional lines. A Solid North has been broken. The Solid South must disappear. On these broad lines, supplemented from time to time with the immediate questions of the hour, partisanship is always within patriotic limits, and the successful party is the best judgment of the people.

We leave this hall to carry into the Presidential canvass our best efforts for the success of the principles in which we severally believe, the parties which we severally love, and the candidates we honor; but let us labor to bring about such conditions all over this country that we may fight our political battles under the common banner of patriotism and peace.

Clemens, Samuel L., "Mark Twain," a celebrated American humorist, born at Florida, Mo., November 30, 1835. He worked in a printing office in early youth, and from 1857 to 1861 was a pilot on the Mississippi River steamboats. During a portion of the Civil War period he served in the Confederate army, and subsequently came into notice as a humorous lecturer. He quickly acquired popularity, his book entitled "The Innocents Abroad" making him widely known, and for thirty years has been the most popular humorist of his time, his fame being almost as great in England as at home. He has published many books, mainly, though not entirely, of a humorous nature.

NEW ENGLAND WEATHER.

ADDRESS DELIVERED BEFORE THE NEW ENGLAND
SOCIETY, DECEMBER 22, 1876.

GENTLEMEN,—I reverently believe that the Maker who makes us all makes everything in New England but the weather.

I don't know who makes that, but I think it must be raw apprentices in the Weather Clerk's factory, who experiment and learn how in New England for board and clothes, and then are promoted to make weather for countries that require a good article and will take their custom elsewhere if they don't get it.

There is a sumptuous variety about the New England weather that compels the stranger's admiration—and regret.

The weather is always doing something there; always attending strictly to business; always getting up new designs and trying them on the people to see how they will go.

But it gets through more business in spring than in any other season. In the spring I have counted one hundred and thirty-six different kinds of weather inside of four and twenty hours.

It was I that made the fame and fortune of that man that had that marvellous collection of weather on exhibition at the Centennial that so astonished the foreigners. He was going to travel all over the world and get specimens from all the climes. I said, "Don't you do it; you come to New England on a favorable spring day." I told him what we could do in the way of style, variety, and quantity.

Well, he came, and he made his collection in four days.

As to variety—why, he confessed that he got hundreds of kinds of weather that he had never heard of before. And as to quantity—well, after he had picked out and discarded all that was blemished in any way, he not only had weather enough, but weather to spare; weather to hire out; weather to sell; to deposit; weather to invest; weather to give to the poor.

The people of New England are by nature patient and forbearing; but there are some things which they will not stand. Every year they kill a lot of poets for writing about "Beautiful Spring."

These are generally casual visitors, who bring their notions of spring from somewhere else, and cannot, of course, know how the natives feel about spring. And so, the first thing they know, the opportunity to inquire how they feel has permanently gone by .

Old Probabilities has a mighty reputation for accurate prophecy and thoroughly well deserves it. You take up the papers and observe how crisply and confidently he checks off what to-day's weather is going to be on the Pacific, down South, in the Middle States, in the Wisconsin region; see him sail along in the joy and pride of his power till he gets to New England, and then,—see his tail drop.

He doesn't know what the weather is going to be in New England. He can't any more tell than he can tell how many Presidents of the United States there's going to be next year. Well, he mulls over it, and by and by he gets out something about like this: Probable nor'-east to sou'-west winds, varying to the southard and westard and eastard and points between; high and low barometer, sweeping around from place to place; probable areas of rain, snow, hail, and drought, succeeded or preceded by earthquakes, with thunder and lightning.

Then he jots down this postscript from his wandering mind to cover accidents: " But it is possible that the program may be wholly changed in the meantime."

Yes, one of the brightest gems in the New England weather is the dazzling uncertainty of it. There is only one thing certain about it, you are certain there is going to be plenty of weather—a perfect grand review; but you never can tell which end of the procession is going to move first. You fix up for the drought; you leave your umbrella in the house and sally out with your sprinkling-pot, and ten to one you get drowned.

You make up your mind that the earthquake is due;

you stand from under and take hold of something to steady yourself, and, the first thing you know, you get struck by lightning.

These are great disappointments. But they can't be helped. The lightning there is peculiar; it is so convincing! When it strikes a thing it doesn't leave enough of that thing behind for you to tell whether— well, you'd think it was something valuable, and a Congressman had been there.

And the thunder. When the thunder commences to merely tune up, and scrape, and saw, and key up the instruments for the performance, strangers say, "Why, what awful thunder you have here!" But when the baton is raised and the real concert begins, you'll find that stranger down in the cellar, with his head in the ash-barrel.

Now, as to the size of the weather in New England—lengthways, I mean. It is utterly disproportioned to the size of that little country. Half the time, when it is packed as full as it can stick, you will see that New England weather sticking out beyond the edges and projecting around hundreds and hundreds of miles over the neighboring States. She can't hold a tenth part of her weather. You can see cracks all about, where she has strained herself trying to do it.

I could speak volumes about the inhuman perversity of the New England weather, but I will give but a single specimen. I like to hear rain on a tin roof, so I covered part of my roof with tin, with an eye to that luxury. Well, sir, do you think it ever rains on the tin? No, sir; skips it every time.

Mind, in this speech I have been trying merely to

do honor to the New England weather; no language could do it justice.

But, after all, there are at least one or two things about that weather (or, if you please, effects produced by it) which we residents would not like to part with.

If we had not our bewitching autumn foliage, we should still have to credit the weather with one feature which compensates for all its bullying vagaries—the ice-storm—when a leafless tree is clothed with ice from the bottom to the top—ice that is as bright and clear as crystal; every bough and twig is strung with ice-beads, frozen dew-drops, and the whole tree sparkles, cold and white, like the Shah of Persia's diamond plume.

Then the wind waves the branches, and the sun comes out and turns all those myriads of beads and drops to prisms that glow and hum and flash with all manner of colored fires, which change and change again, with inconceivable rapidity, from blue to red, from red to green, and green to gold; the tree becomes a sparkling fountain, a very explosion of dazzling jewels; and it stands there the acme, the climax, the supremest possibility in art or nature of bewildering, intoxicating, intolerable magnificence! One cannot make the words too strong.

Month after month I lay up hate and grudge against the New England weather; but when the ice-storm comes at last I say, " There, I forgive you now; the books are square between us; you don't owe me a cent; go and sin some more; your little faults and foibles count for nothing; you are the most enchanting weather in the world! "

Evarts, William M., an eminent American lawyer and orator, born in Boston, Mass., February 6, 1818 ; died in New York City, February 28, 1901. After leaving college he studied law, and began practice in New York City, soon rising to eminence in his profession, and becoming conspicuous for his legal acquirements. Actively interested in politics, he was an early member of the Republican party, and in the impeachment trial in 1868 was counsel for the President. He was District Attorney of New York City, 1849–53 ; Attorney-General of the United States, 1868–69 ; United States counsel in the Geneva arbitration tribunal and counsel in many cases of importance. He held the office of Secretary of State under President Hayes, and sat in the National Senate, 1885–91. He was a conspicuously brilliant orator on social occasions and a very eloquent orator on more important ones. The centennial oration delivered by him at Philadelphia on July 4, 1876 is a notable example of his oratory.

————

THE DAY WE CELEBRATE.

ADDRESS AT THE BANQUET OF THE NEW ENGLAND
SOCIETY, DECEMBER 22, 1876.

EVER since I have been a member of this Society, which is ever since I have been a resident of the city of New York, it has been the same day that is celebrated, the same people that celebrated it, and they have celebrated it in the same way. It must have been a great day that would bear so much celebration. They must have been a great people that could celebrate it even to their own satisfaction so often, and they must have had a very good way of celebrating it when it could have maintained its freshness so many successive years. I have taken part myself in a good many of these celebrations and have furnished my share of the gratification or amusement of the occasion. I have laughed with you year after year at your favorite President Choate's efforts here. My labors in this behalf, full of fidelity to the memory of our Pilgrim Fathers, have earned for me, let me say here in advance, some respect and regard for my present position, and a little of the indulgence that I have extended to others is all I ask for myself.

Now, there are several considerations about a New England dinner speech which relieve it from embarrassments. In the first place our New England ancestors and their descendants for the most part have always held that it was what a man did, and not what he said, that was of any account. Besides it was always understood that whatever was said in this room never went any further; and thirdly, that no man ever was to be called into question elsewhere for what he said. A New England dinner is favorably known, no doubt, in the luxury of your accustomed celebrations, regarded only as a dinner of courses; but it is as a dinner of discourses that it has its greatest fame. All opinions, provided they concur in praising ourselves and our ancestors; all criticism upon others, provided they do not disparage our own superiority; all homage to the rest of the country, and in fact, to the rest of the world, if it only be compatible with the supremacy of the little corner of it from which we come—this classification, New England first and the rest of the world next, we consider a sufficient honor to them:

we only wish we could do better justice to ourselves. And now we have a great deal to admire in what we see before us here and that is an emotion which all can equally share. It needs no mirrors for the display, for each New Englander, looking upon each other New Englander, sees the reflection of the noblest specimens of humanity. Now, it is not at all surprising to us who have studied the subject, that we have these opinions, but it is surprising that the rest of the world is ready to take us at our own words, and that perhaps is the reason we don't think so much of the rest of the world.

New England, I observe, while it retains all its sterling qualities is nevertheless moving forward in the direction of conciliation and peace. I remember, when I was a boy, I travelled 240 miles by stage coach from Boston to New Haven to avoid going to Harvard University, which was across the bridge. It was because of the religious animosities which pervaded the community and I suppose animated my youthful breast; and now here I come to a New England Society and sit between the two presidents of those renowned universities, who have apparently come here for the purpose of enjoying themselves, and of exhibiting that proximity is no longer dangerous to the peace of those universities. No doubt there is a considerable warfare going on between them as to the methods of instruction, but to us who have looked on, we have seen no more obtrusive manifestation of it than that the president on my left, of Yale, in dealing with the subjects that have successively been placed before him, has pursued the method of that university, its comprehensive method, that takes in the whole curriculum; while on my right, the eclectic principle is exercised by my friend, President Eliot, and he has confined himself to the dainty morsels of the repast. I speak of this to show that although an amelioration of climate or an obliteration of virtues is not to be expected in New England, or in New England men, yet there may be an advancement of the sunshine of the heart and that an incorporation of our narrow territory in a great nation, and a transfusion of our opinions, our ideas, our purposes, into the veins of a nation of 40,000,000 of people, may enlarge and liberalize even the views, the plans, and the action of New England.

The quest upon which emigrants from the Old World sought the New, the motives which led their migration, were, as we all know, for the most part to find an abode where they could secure abundant wealth with little labor. But the New Englanders, either by choice or guided by Providence, found a new home which offered them nothing but abundant labor with no wealth at all. And what has come of that? and who possess as much of the wealth, the power, the glory, and the strength of this world as the descendants of the New Englanders who courted labor without wealth? This narrow and barren and weak territory could say to the newcomers only this, " Silver and gold have I none, but such as I have give I thee; " and out of that possession, out of the power of labor, out of the frugality, out of the self-denial, out of the rigorous virtues they bred, they have gone out and possessed and ransacked its wealth.

Now, if there be one trait in the New England character more valuable than another, more admirable and more constant, it is this: That the New Englanders are ready to meet the duties of their time, when those duties are to be performed, and at the sacrifice and the cost that the present discharge of those duties requires. It is easy for philosophers and for scholars, for poets and for people, to warm with the patriotism of ancient Greece and to glow with the enthusiasm of future generations. The New Englanders thought at the time of the first plantation and have thought ever since that this retrospective and prospective enthusiasm and energy were of very little account in the affairs of this world. They have courted always the duties of the present hour; they have not disguised their difficulty; they have not retreated before their danger; they have had but one purpose—to take their share of every conflict and honestly to bear their share of the common result. Now, if these spring-heads of New England virtue, that never will be removed from her soil, can be maintained and defended, the streams of life and prosperity to the rest of the country will never fail. Let us, then, with honest enthusiasm, without form and without ceremony, feel that it is a great thing in our continuing life that we do celebrate that day, and love to celebrate it as the greatest day in our history.

New England in itself to-day, within its own boundaries, is the richest, the best cultivated, the most instructed, and the most energetic portion of the land. In the country of which it forms a part it finds a nation of prodigious energies and of magnificent proportions;

and that nation, take it through and through, with all defects, with all shortcomings, with all difficulties, and all dangers, even a New England judgment, censorious though it is apt to be, could but pronounce a land of which the sternest of our New England ancestors would have been proud to-day. If, then, we look at this nation in its relations to the rest of the world, these few outcasts of fortune, cast upon the New England shore in a December night, being the beginnings and the foundations of the nation, this nation, it is not too much to say, finds every other nation ready to respect its power and confess its justice; so much so that in the preservation of the peace of the world this nation has the readiest and the safest part that ever a nation had. Nobody that is powerful desires to quarrel with it and nobody that is powerless is it possible for us to quarrel with.

Thus all our energies, all our duties, all our labors, dangers, and difficulties are within our own borders; and the New England of to-day, placing itself in present relations to things as they are, must determine what line of duty, what path of honor, what purposes, and what results it proposes to follow in the current questions of the day. Its duty, its temper, are not necessarily the same as they have been heretofore. The same principles are to guide, but the action may be different. We have finished a struggle that has made permanent and general in the constitution, in the laws, in the arrangements of society, a complete admission of the equality of man, of the safety of citizenship, and of the duty of mutual love. Now, after a great civil war, greater than any nation has ever endured separately without disintegration or injury to its integrity, there are duties that do not belong to the condition either preparatory to the strife or when the strife was in progress. We have found out what bayonets mean in this country; and you remember what Hosea Biglow says on that subject:

" Lord ! didn't I feel streaked,
    The first time I found out why bayonets were peaked."

And you will observe that their utility is of a somewhat demonstrative character. But I think it is Bismarck who is credited with the *mot* that bayonets are not an institution to sit down on. And so the American people, as adverse as any people could be to the use or the administration of bayonets, is the last nation of the world that would wish to sit down on that institution.

When, therefore, we have come to a time when, having secured every purpose of war; when, having enlisted the law and the institutions of society in furtherance of New England virtues, that justice and duty and right should prevail throughout this land, let us accept at once what we shall be recreant and faithless to our inheritance if we do not accept,—that New England opinions, New England ideas, and New England results are to make their way in this country by moral and intellectual methods. And when we talk of reactionary influences and tendencies let us understand that if we are not willing to be patient and faithful laborers in building up the wastes of this land, if we are impatient to precipitate, that we are those that will be the leaders in reaction from the

moral and intellectual processes to the finished methods
of force. Whenever those methods shall become necessary, whenever justice and right shall require that defence, New England will resume her arms. But New
England will not resort to animosities or jealousies in
order to reach the ruder and grosser methods of hostility when moral suasion cannot prevail. I say, then,
that New England will practise in patience and in
faith these methods; and if they be slow it is because
the moral position of the country, the pervasion of the
whole community by character, sentiments, the diffusion of manners, of habits, of systems, is a gradual
and a slow process; and the moral government and
the moral forces of this world are not to be changed
even in honor of our New England ancestry.

Now, there are three questions before the people
of the country to-day and they are all public, all unselfish, all patriotic, all elevated, and all ennobling as
subjects of contemplation and of action. They are the
public peace in this large and general sense that I have
indicated. They are the public faith, without which
there is no such thing as honorable national life; and
the public service, which unless pure and strong and
noble makes all the pæans of free government but
doggerel in our ears.

Now, in regard to the public faith, the same principles which I have indicated as showing that we have
passed the stage of antagonism, of hostility, and must
reach the stage of co-operation, of sympathy, and of
succor, apply to all these great questions of the public
debt and of the nation's burdens. They are great burdens; they do impose great difficulties; they do include

perhaps great dangers. We need no hostilities between North and South, none between East and West, none between debtor and creditor; we need all our resources, all our wealth, all our gold, all our silver, all our industry, and all our thrift. Bear, then, with such differences of opinion as grow out of differences of situation; make the most of brotherhood and the least of dissension; see that great and common burdens rest unequally and are to be borne unequally; see to it that there shall be no failures in that perfect disposition on the part of the wealthy and powerful States of New England and their wealthy distributive share of the country in bearing the burdens that rest more heavily upon others than upon ourselves. Let us remember that generous and wise maxim of Mr. Webster, who in the bitterest of the strifes of his declining years used no words of harshness against disputants, and was ready to say of them, as he did say, "They are not bad men, but bad reasoners."

And now about the public service. Well, on that subject it may be said that one good example teaches more than many precepts, and perhaps in an after-dinner speech the least said is the soonest mended. But nevertheless there should be no step backward in magistrates, in statesmen, in preachers, in teachers, in editors, in the people. We must go on. We do understand as a people the difficulties that we are in; we do understand as a people the methods by which we have reached them; and we do understand, I think, the way out of them. It may be hedged with difficulties and opposed with dangers. It touches the very life of free government; it touches the very sincerity of the public methods of the nation. For such is human nature that, as Mr. Burke has said (and I hope I do not too much misquote his words), "By whatever paths the great places in a State are to be reached by its public men that path will be trod; and if the path be devious, and slimy, and wicked, and horrid with calumnies and jealousies, nevertheless, if that be the only path upward, the statesman will take it." It is for you to say—you as a people to say—whether or no the paths of your public life shall be clean and bright and noble and ever tending upward. I believe there is great good fortune in this people that, to start with, you have a president who has never pursued any devious paths and does not propose to encourage their pursuit by others.

Butler, Benjamin F., a noted American lawyer and soldier, born at Deerfield, N. H., November 5, 1818; died in Washington, D. C., January 11, 1893. He was admitted to the bar in 1841, and began the practice of law in Lowell, Mass., quickly becoming conspicuous for his able conduct of criminal cases. As an active politician he entered the State Legislature as a Democrat in 1853, and served there till the opening of the Civil War. He then received a general's commission, and was a very prominent military leader throughout the four years of conflict. He sat in the lower house of Congress, 1866–79, one term excepted, as a Republican member, and took a most active part in congressional debates. He was defeated as Republican candidate for the governorship of Massachusetts in 1871, and again in 1878 and 1879 as the candidate of the Greenback party. The Democrats elected him governor in 1882, but he was defeated the next year. In 1884 he was the Greenback candidate for the Presidency. His abilities as a lawyer were very marked, and he was a ready, audacious speaker in debate.

CHARACTER AND RESULTS OF THE WAR.

DELIVERED APRIL 2, 1863.

MR. MAYOR,—With the profoundest gratitude for the too flattering commendation of my administration of the various trusts committed to me by the government, which, in behalf of your associates, you have been pleased to tender, I ask you to receive my most heartfelt thanks. To the citizens of New York here assembled, graced by the fairest and loveliest, in kind appreciation of my services supposed to have been rendered to the country, I tender the deepest acknowl-

edgements. I accept it all, not for myself, but for my
brave comrades of the Army of the Gulf. I receive it
as an earnest of your devotion to the country—an
evidence of your loyalty to the constitution under
which you live and under which you hope to die.

In order that the acts of the Army of the Gulf may
be understood, perhaps it would be well, at a little
length, with your permission, that some details should
be given of the thesis upon which we fulfilled our
duties. The first question, then, to be ascertained is,
what is this contest in which the country is engaged?
At the risk of being a little tedious, at the risk, even, of
calling your attention to what might seem otherwise
too elementary, I propose to run down through the
history of the contest to see what it is that agitates the
whole country at this day and this hour.

That we are in the midst of a civil commotion, all
know. But what is that commotion? Is it a riot?
Is it an insurrection? Is it a rebellion? Or is it a
revolution? And pray, sir, although it may seem still
more elementary, what is a riot? A riot, if I understand it, is simply an outburst of the passions of a
number of men for the moment, in breach of the law,
by force of numbers, to be put down and subdued by
the civil authorities; if it goes further to be dealt with
by the military authorities. But you say, sir, "Why
treat us to a definition of a riot upon this occasion? Why, of all things, should you undertake to
instruct a New York audience in what a riot is?"

To that I answer, because the administration of Mr.
Buchanan dealt with this great change of affairs as
if it were a riot; because his government officer gave

22

the opinion that in Charleston it was but a riot; and
that, as there was no civil authority there to call out
the military, therefore Sumter must be given over to
the rioters, and such was the beginning of this struggle. Let us see how it grew up. I deal not now with
causes but with effects—facts.

Directly after the guns of the rebels had turned upon
Sumter, the several States of the South, in convention assembled, inaugurated a series of movements
which took out from the Union divers States, and as
each was attempted to be taken out, the riots, if such
existed, were no longer found in them, but they became insurrectionary, and the administration, upon
the 15th of April, 1861, dealt with this state of affairs
as an insurrection and called out the militia of the
United States to suppress an insurrection. I was called
at that time into the service to administer the laws in
puttting down an insurrection.

I found a riot at Baltimore. The rioters had burned
bridges; but the riot had hardly arisen to the dignity
of an insurrection, because the State had not moved
as an organized community. A few men were rioting
at Baltimore; and as I marched into the State at the
head of the United States troops, the question came
up, what have I before me? You will remember that
I offered then to put down all kinds of insurrection so
long as the State of Maryland remained loyal to the
United States. Transferred from thence to a wider
sphere at Fortress Monroe, I found that the State of
Virginia through its organization had taken itself out
of the Union and was endeavoring to erect for itself
an independent government, and I dealt with that State

as being in rebellion and thought the property of the rebels of whatever name or nature should be deemed rebellious property and contraband of war, subject to the laws of war.

I have been thus careful in stating these various steps, because, although through your kindness replying to eulogy, I am here answering every charge of inconsistency and wrong of intention for my acts done before the country. Wrong in judgment I may have been, but I insist wrong in intention or inconsistent with my former opinions never. Upon the same theory by which I felt myself bound to put down insurrection in Maryland, while it remained loyal, whether that insurrection was the work of blacks or whites—by the same loyalty to the constitution and laws I felt bound to confiscate slave property in the rebellious State of Virginia. Pardon me, sir, if right here I say that I am a little sensitive upon this topic.

I am an old-fashioned Andrew Jackson Democrat of twenty years' standing. And so far as I know I have never swerved, so help me God, from one of his teachings. Up to the time that disunion took place, I went as far as the farthest in sustaining the constitutional rights of the States. However bitter or distasteful to me were the obligations my fathers had made for me in the compromise of the constitution, it was not for me to pick out the sweet from the bitter, and, fellow Democrats, I took them all because they were constitutional obligations, and sustaining them all I stood by the South and by Southern rights under the constitution until I advanced so far as to look into

the very pit of disunion into which they plunged, and
then not liking the prospect I quietly withdrew.

And from that hour we went apart, how far apart
you can judge when I tell you that on the 28th of
December, 1860, I shook hands on terms of personal
friendship with Jefferson Davis, and on the 28th of
December, 1862, you had the pleasure of reading his
proclamation that I was to be hanged at sight.

And now, my friends, if you will allow me to pause
for a moment in this line of thought, as we come up to
the point of time when these men laid down their constitutional obligations, let me ask, what then were my
rights and what were theirs? At that hour they repudiated the constitution of the United States by vote
in solemn convention, and not only that, but they took
arms in their hands and undertook by force to rend
from the government what seemed to them the fairest
portion of the heritage which my fathers had given to
you and me as a rich legacy for our children. When
they did that they abrogated, and forfeited every constitutional right, and released me from every constitutional obligation so far as they were concerned.

Therefore when I was thus called upon to say what
should be my action thereafter with regard to slavery,
I was left to the natural instincts of my heart as
prompted by a Christian education in New England,
and I dealt with it accordingly. The same sense of
duty to my constitutional obligations, and to the
rights of the several States that required me, so long
as those States remained under the constitution, to protect the system of slavery,—that same sense of duty
after they had gone out from under the constitution,

caused me to follow the dictates of my own untrammelled conscience.

So you see—and I speak now to my old Democratic friends that, however misjudging I may have been, we went along together, step by step, up to the point of disunion, and I claim that we ought still to go on in the same manner. We acknowledged the right of those men to hold slaves, because it was guaranteed to them by the compromise of our fathers in the constitution, but if their State rights were to be respected, because of our allegiance to the constitution and our respect for State rights, when that sacred obligation was taken away by their own traitorous acts, and we, as well as the negroes, were disenthralled, why should not we follow the dictates of God's law and humanity?

By the exigencies of the public service removed once more to another sphere of action, at New Orleans, I found this problem coming up in another form, and that led me to examine and see how far had progressed this civil commotion now carried on by force of arms.

I believe, under our complex system of States, each having an independent government, with the United States covering all, that there can be treason to a State and not to the United States; revolution in a State and not as regards the United States; loyalty to a State and disloyalty to the Union; and loyalty to the Union and disloyalty to the organized government of a State. As an illustration, take the troubles which lately arose in the State of Rhode Island, where there was an attempt to rebel against the State government, and to change the form of that government, but no rebellion against the United States. All of you are familiar with the movements of Mr. Dorr; in that matter there was no intent of disloyalty against the United States, but a great deal against the State government.

I therefore, in Louisiana, found a State government that had entirely changed its form and had revolutionized itself so far as it could; had created courts and imposed taxes, and put in motion all kinds of governmental machinery; and so far as her State government was concerned, Louisiana was no longer in and of itself one of the United States of America. It had, so far as depended on its own action, changed its State government and by solemn act forever seceded from the United States of America and attempted to join a new national government,—hostile to us, as one of the so-called Confederate States.

I found, I respectfully submit, a revolutionized State. There had been a revolution, by force; beyond a riot, which is an infraction of the law; beyond an insurrection, which is an abnegation of the law; beyond a rebellion, which is an attempt to override the law by force of numbers; a new State government formed that was being supported by force of arms.

Now, I ask myself, upon what thesis shall I deal with this people? Organized into a community under forms of law, they had seized a portion of the territory of the United States and were holding it by force of arms; and I respectfully submit I had to deal with them as alien enemies. They had forever passed the boundary of " wayward sisters " or " erring brothers," unless indeed they erred toward us as Cain did against his brother Abel. They had passed beyond brotherhood by treason added to murder. Aye, and Louisiana had done this in the strongest possible way, for she had seized on territory which the government of the United States had bought and paid for, and to which her people could advance no shadow of claim save as citizens of the United States. Therefore I dealt with them as alien enemies.

And what rights have alien enemies captured in war? They have the right, so long as they behave themselves and are non-combatants, to be free from personal violence; they have no other rights; and therefore it was my duty to see to it (and I believe the record will show I did see to it) that order was preserved and that every man who behaved well and did not aid the Confederate States was not molested in his person. I held, by the laws of war, that everything else they had was at the mercy of the conqueror. They have claims to mercy and clemency; but no rights. Permit me to state the method in which their rights were defined by one gentleman of my staff. He very coolly paraphrased the Dred Scott decision and said they had no rights which a negro was bound to respect. But, dealing with them in this way, I took care to protect all men in personal safety.

Now, I hear a friend behind me say: "But how does your theory affect loyal men?" The difficulty in answering that proposition is this: In governmental action the government in making peace and carrying on war cannot deal with individuals, but with organized communities, whether organized wrongly or rightly; and all I could do, so far as my judgment taught me, for the individual loyal citizen, was to see to it that no exaction should be made of him and no property taken away from him that was not absolutely necessary for the success of military operations.

I know nothing else that I could do. I could not alter the carrying on of the war because loyal citizens were, unfortunately, like Dog Tray, found in bad company; to their persons, and to their property, even, all possible protection I caused to be afforded. But let me repeat—for it is quite necessary to keep this in mind, and I am afraid that for want of so doing some of my old Democratic friends have got lost in going with one portion of the country rather than the other in their thoughts and feelings—let me repeat that, in making war or making peace, carrying on governmental operations of any sort, governments and their representatives, so far as I am instructed, can deal only with organized communities, and men must fall or rise with the communities in which they are situated.

You in New York must follow the government as expressed by the will of the majority of your State until you can revolutionize that government and change it; and those loyal at the South must, until this contest comes into process of settlement, also follow the action of the organized majorities in which their lot has been cast, and no man, no set of men, can see the possible solution of this or any other governmental problem as affecting States, except upon this basis.

Now, then, to pass from the particular to the general, to leave the detail in Louisiana, of which I have run down the account, rather as illustrating my meaning than otherwise, I come back to the question: What is now the nature of the contest with all the States that are banded together in the so-called Confederate States? Into what form has it come? It started in insurrection: it grew up a rebellion; it has become a revolution, and carries with it all the rights and incidents of a revolution.

Our government has dealt with it upon that ground. When the government blockaded Southern ports they dealt with it as a revolution; when they sent out cartels of exchange of prisoners they dealt with these people no longer as simple insurrectionists and traitors, but as organized revolutionists who had set up a government for themselves upon the territory of the United States.

Sir, let no man say to me, " Why then you acknowledge the right of revolution in these men!" I beg your pardon, sir; I only acknowledge the fact of revolution—that which has actually happened. I look these things in the face and I do not dodge them because they are unpleasant; I find this a revolution and these men are no longer, I repeat, our erring brethren, but they are our alien enemies, foreigners carrying on war against us, attempting to make alliances against us, attempting surreptitiously to get into the family of nations. I agree that it is not a successful revolution and a revolution never to be successful,—pardon me, I was speaking theoretically, as a matter of law,—never to be successful until acknowledged by the parent State. Now, then, I am willing to unite with you in your cheers when you say a revolution, the rightfulness of success of which we, the parent State, never will acknowledge.

Why, sir, have I been so careful in bringing down with great particularity these distinctions? Because in my judgment there are certain logical consequences following from them as necessarily as various corollaries from a problem in Euclid. If we are at war, as I think, with a foreign country, to all intents and purposes, how can a man here stand up and say that he is on the side of that foreign country and not be an enemy to his country?

A man must be either for his country or against his country. He cannot, upon this theory, be throwing impediments all the time in the way of the progress of his government, under pretence that he is helping some other portion of his country. If any local man thinks that he must do something to bring back his erring brethren (if he likes that form of phrase) at the South, let him take his musket and go down and try it in that way. If he is still of a different opinion and thinks that is not the best way to bring them back, but he can do it by persuasion and talk, let him go down with me to Louisiana and I will set him over to Mississippi and if the rebels do not feel for his heart-strings, but not in love, I will bring him back. Let us say to him: "Choose ye this day whom ye will serve. If the Lord thy God be God, serve him; if Baal be God, serve ye him. But no man can serve two masters, God and Mammon."

Again, there are other logical consequences to flow from the view which I have ventured to take of this subject, and one is as regards to our relations from past political action. If they are now alien enemies I am bound to them by no ties of party fealty or political affinity. They have passed out of that, and I think we ought to go back only to examine and see if all ties of party allegiance and party fealty as regards them are not broken, and satisfy ourselves that it is your duty and mine to look simply to our country and to its service, and leave them to look to the country they are attempting to erect, and to its service; and then let us try the conclusion with them, as we are doing by arms and stern arbitrament of war.

Mark, by this I give up no territory of the United States. Every foot that was ever circumscribed on the map by the lines around the United States belongs to us. None the less because bad men have attempted to organize worse government upon various portions of it. It is to be drawn in under our laws and our government as soon as the power of the United States can be exerted for that purpose, and therefore, my friends, you see that next one of the logical consequences that proceed from our theory: that we have no occasion to carry on the fight for the constitution as it is.

Who is interfering with the constitution as it is? Who makes any attacks upon the constitution? We are fighting with those who have gone out and repudiated the constitution, and made another constitution for themselves. And now, my friends, I do not know but I shall speak some heresy, but as a Democrat, and as an Andrew Jackson Democrat, I am not for the Union as it was. I say, as a Democrat, as an Andrew Jackson Democrat, I am not for the Union to be again as it was. Understand me, I was for the Union because I saw or thought I saw the troubles in the future which have burst upon us, but having undergone those troubles, having spent all this blood and this treasure I do not mean to go back again and be cheek by jowl with South Carolina as I was before, if I can help it.

Mark me, let no man misunderstand me, and I repeat, lest I be misunderstood—there are none so slow to understand as those who do not want to—mark me, I say I do not mean to give up a single inch of the soil of South Carolina. If I had been in public life at that time and had had the position, the will, and the ability, I would have dealt with South Carolina as Jackson did and kept her in the Union at all hazards, but now she has gone out, and I will take care that when she comes in again she comes in better behaved, that she shall no longer be the firebrand of the Union —aye, and that she shall enjoy what her people never yet have enjoyed—the blessings of a republican form of government.

Therefore in that view I am not for the reconstruction of the Union as it was. I have spent treasure and blood enough upon it, in conjunction with my fellow citizens, to make it a little better. I think we can have a better Union the next time. It was good enough if it had been let alone. The old house was good enough for me, but as they have pulled down all the L-part, I propose, when we build it up, to build it up with all the modern improvements.

Another of the logical sequences, it seems to me, that follow in inexorable and not-to-be-shunned sequence upon this proposition, that we are dealing with alien enemies, is with regard to our duties as to the confiscation of rebel property, and that question would seem to me to be easy of settlement under the constitution and without any discussion, if my first proposition is right. Has it not been held from the beginning of the world down to this day, from the time the Israelites took possession of the land of Canaan, which they got from alien enemies—and is it not the well-settled law of war to-day, that the whole property of alien enemies belonged to the conqueror, and that it is at his mercy and his clemency what should be done with it?

For one I would take it and give the loyal man who was loyal in his heart, at the South, enough to make him as well as he was before, and I would take the balance of it and distribute it among the volunteer soldiers who have gone—(The remainder of the sentence was drowned in a tremendous outburst of applause.) And so far as I know them, if we should settle South Carolina with them, in the course of a few years I would be quite willing to receive her back into the Union.

This theory shows us how to deal with another proposition: What shall be done with the slaves? Here again the laws of war have long settled, with clearness and exactness, that it is for the conqueror, for the government which has maintained or extended its jurisdiction over conquered territory, to deal with slaves as it pleases, to free them or not as it chooses. It is not for the conquered to make terms, or to send their friends into the conquering country to make

terms for them. Another corollary follows from the
proposition that we are fighting with alien enemies,
which relieves us from a difficulty which seems to
trouble some of my old Democratic friends, and that
is in relation to the question of arming the negro
slaves.

If the seceded States are alien enemies, is there any
objection that you know of, and if so, state it, to our
arming one portion of the foreign country against the
other while they are fighting us? Suppose that we
were at war with England. Who would get up here
in New York and say that we must not arm the
Irish, lest they should hurt some of the English? And
yet at one time, not very far gone, all those English-
men were our grandfathers' brothers. Either they or
we erred, but we are now separate nations. There
can be no objections, for another reason, because there
is no law of war or of nations,—no rule of governmental action that I know of, which prevents a country from arming any portion of its citizens; and if
the slaves do not take part in the rebellion, they become simply our citizens residing in our territory
which is at present usurped by our enemies to be used
in its defence as other citizens are. At this waning
hour I do not propose to discuss but merely a hint at
these various subjects.

There is one question I am frequently asked, and
most frequently by my old Democratic friends: " General Butler, what is your experience? Will the negroes
fight?"

To that answer, I have no personal experience, because I left the Department of the Gulf before they

were fairly brought into action. But they did fight under Jackson at Chalmette. More than that; let Napoleon III answer, who has hired them to do what the veterans of the Crimea cannot do—to whip the Mexicans. Let the veterans of Napoleon I, under Le Clerc, who were whipped by them out of San Domingo, say whether they will fight or not.

What has been the demoralizing effect upon them as a race by their contact with white men I know not, but I cannot forget that their fathers would not have been slaves, but that they were captives of war in their own country in hand-to-hand fights among the several chiefs. They would fight at some time, and if you want to know any more than that I can only advise you to try them.

Passing to another logical deduction from the principle that we are carrying on war against alien enemies (for I pray you to remember that I am only carrying out the same idea upon which the government acted when it instituted the blockade), I meet the question whether we thereby give foreign nations any greater rights than if we considered them as a rebellious portion of our country. We have heretofore seemed to consider that if we acknowledged that this was a revolution, and the rebels were alien enemies in this fight, that therefore we should give to foreign nations greater apparent right to interfere in our affairs than they would have if the insurgents were considered and held by us as rebels only, in a rebellious part of our own country.

The first answer to that is this: that so far as the rebels are concerned, they are estopped to deny that they are exactly what they claim themselves to be, alien enemies; and so far as foreign nations are concerned, while the rebels are alien to us yet they are upon our territory, and until we acknowledge them there is no better settled rule of the law of nations than that the recognition of them as an independent nation is an act of war. They have no right to recognize them, because we say to them, "We will deal with you as belligerent alien enemies," than they would have to treat with them if we hold them simply as rebels; and no country is more sternly and strongly bound by that view than is England, because she claimed the recognition by France of our independence to be an act of war and declared war accordingly.

Therefore I do not see why we lose any rights. We do not admit that this a rightful rebellion—we do not recognize it as such—we do not act toward it except in the best way we can to put it down and to re-revolutionize the country. What is the duty then of neutrals if these are alien enemies? We thus find them a people with whom no neutral nation has any treaty of amity or alliance: they are strangers to every neutral nation. For example let us take the English. The English nation have no treaty with the rebels—have no relations with the rebels—open relations I mean, none that are recognized by the laws of nations. They have a treaty of amity, friendship, and commerce with us, and now what is their duty in the contest between us and our enemies to whom they are strangers? They claim it to be neutrality, only such neutrality as they should maintain between two friendly nations with each of whom they have treaties of amity. Let me illustrate: I have two friends that have got into a quarrel—into a fight if you please; I am on equally good terms with both and I do not choose to take a part with either. I treat them as belligerents and hold myself neutral. That is the position of a nation where two equally friendly nations are fighting.

But again I have a friend who is fighting with a stranger, with whom I have nothing to do, of whom I know nothing that is good, of whom I have seen nothing except that he would fight—what is my duty to my friend in that case? To stand perfectly neutral? It is not the part of a friend so to do between men and it is not the part of a friendly nation as between nations. And yet from some strange misconception our English friends profess to do no more than to stand perfectly neutral while they have treaties of amity and commerce with us and no treaty which they acknowledge with the South.

And therefore I say there is a much higher duty on the part of foreign nations toward us when we are in contest with a people with which they have no treaty of amity than there possibly can be toward them. To illustrate how this fact bears upon this question: the English say, " Oh ! we are going to be neutral; we will not sell you any arms, because to be neutral strictly we should have to sell the same to the Confederates."

To that I answer: You have treaties of amity and commerce with us by which you have agreed to trade with us. You have no treaty of amity and commerce with them by which you agree to trade with them. Why not then trade with us? Why not give us

23

that rightful preference except for reasons of hostility to us that I will state hereafter? I have been thus particular upon this, because in stating my proposition to gentlemen in whose judgment I have great confidence they have said to me, " I agree with your theory, Mr. Butler, but I am afraid you will involve us with other nations by the view that you take of that matter."

But I insist, and I can only state the proposition for want of time—your own minds will carry it out particularly—I insist that there is a higher and closer duty to us—treating the rebels as a strange nation not yet admitted into the family of nations—that there is a higher duty from our old friendship on her part, from our old relations toward Great Britain, than there is to this rebellious, pushing, attempting-to-get-into-place member of the family of nations.

There is still another logical sequence which in my judgment follows from this view of the case. The great question put to me by my friends and the great question which is now agitating this country is, How are we to get these men back? How are we to get this territory back? How are we to reconstruct the nation? I think it is much better answered upon this hypothesis than any other. There are but two ways in which this contest can be ended; one is by re-revolutionizing a portion of this seceding territory and have the people ask to be admitted into the Union; another is, to bring it all back so that if they do not come back in the first way they shall come back bound to our triumphal car of victory. Now when any portion of the South becomes loyal to the North and to the Union,

or to express it with more care when any portion of
the inhabitants of the South wish to become again a
part of the nation and will throw off the government
of Jefferson Davis, erect themselves into a State, and
come and ask us to take them back with such a State
constitution as they ought to be admitted under, there
is no difficulty in its being done. There is no witchery
about this. This precise thing has been done in the
case of Western Virginia. She went out—stayed out
for a while.

By the aid of our armies and by the efforts of her
citizens she re-revolutionized, threw off the government of the rest of the State of Virginia; threw off
the Confederate yoke; erected herself into a State
with a constitution such as I believe is quite satisfactory to all of us, especially the amendment. She
has asked to come back and has been received back and
is the first entering wedge of that series of States who
will come back that way.

But suppose they will not come back?

We are bound to subjugate them. What then do
they become? Territories of the United States—acquired by force of arms—precisely as we acquired
California, precisely as we acquired Nevada, precisely as we acquired—not exactly though—as we acquired Texas—and then is there any difficulty in treating with these men? Was there any difficulty in
dealing with the State of California when our men
went there and settled in sufficient numbers so as to
give that State the benefits of the blessings of a republican form of government? Was there any diffi-

culty in obtaining her beyond our transactions with Mexico?

None whatever. Will there be any difficulty in taking to ourselves the new State of Nevada when she is ready to come and ripe to come? Was there any difficulty in taking into the Union any portion of the Louisiana purchase when we bought it first? Will there be any difficulty when her people get ready to come back to the United States of our taking her back again more than perhaps to carry out the parallel a little further, to pay a large sum of money besides, as we did in the case of California after we conquered it from Mexico? These States having gone out without cause, without right, without grievance, and having formed themselves into new States and taken upon themselves new alliances, I am not for having them come back without readmission.

I feel, perhaps, if the ladies will pardon the illustration, like a husband whose wife has run away with another man, and has divorced herself from him; he will not take her to his arms until they have come before the priest and been re-married. I have, I say, the same feeling in the case of these people that have gone out; when they repent and ask to come back I am ready to receive them, and I am not ready until then.

And now, having gone by far too discursively over many of these points which I desired to bring to your attention, let us return to what has been done in the Department of the Gulf, to which you have so flatteringly alluded, and to which I will answer. While I am very much gratified at the kind expression of your regard, whether that expression is justified can be told in a single word. When I left the Department of the Gulf, I sat down and deliberately put in the form of an address to the people of that Department, the exact acts I had done while in their Department; I said to them, " I have done these things." I have now waited more than three months, and I have yet to hear a denial from that Department that the things therein stated were done.

And to that alone, sir, I can point as a justification of your too flattering eulogy, and to that I point forever as my answer to every slander and every calumny. The ladies of New Orleans knew whether they were safe; has any one of them ever said she was not? The men of New Orleans knew whether life and property were safe; has any man ever said they were not? The poor of New Orleans knew whether the money which was taken from the rich rebels was applied to the alleviation of their wants; has any man denied that it was? To that record I point—and it will be the only answer that I shall ever make; and I only do it now because I desire that you shall have neither doubt nor feeling upon this subject—it is the only answer I can ever make to the thousand calumnies that have been poured upon me and mine, and upon the officers who worked with me for the good of our country.

I desire now to say a single word upon the question, what are the prospects of this war? My simple opinion would be no better than that of another man; but let me show you the reason for the faith that is in me that this war is progressing steadily to a successful termination. Compare the state of the country on

January 1, 1863, with the state of the country on January 1, 1862, and tell me whether there has not been progress. At that time the Union armies held no considerable portion of Missouri, of Kentucky, or of Tennessee; none of Virginia, except Fortress Monroe and Arlington Heights; none of North Carolina save Hatteras, and none of South Carolina save Port Royal. All the rest was ground of struggle at least, and all the rest furnishing supplies to the rebels.

Now they hold none of Missouri, none of Kentucky, none of Tennessee, for any valuable purpose of supplies, because the western portion is in our hands, and the eastern portion has been so run over by the contending armies that the supplies are gone. They hold no portion of Virginia valuable for supplies, for that is eaten out by their armies. We hold one-third of Virginia and half of North Carolina. We hold our own in South Carolina, and I hope that before the eleventh of this month we shall hold a little more. We hold two-thirds of Louisiana in wealth and population. We hold all Arkansas and all Texas so far as supplies are concerned, so long as Farragut is between Port Hudson and Vicksburg. And I believe the colored troops held Florida at the last accounts.

Now, then, let us see to what the rebellion is reduced. It is reduced to the remainder of Virginia, part of North and South Carolina, all of Georgia, Alabama, and Mississippi, and a small portion of Louisiana and Tennessee; Texas and Arkansas, as I said before, being cut off. Why I draw strong hopes from this is, that their supplies come either from Kentucky, Tennessee, Missouri, Arkansas, or Texas, and these are now completely beyond their reach. To this fact I look largely for the suppression of this rebellion and the overthrow of this revolution.

They have got to the end of their conscription; we have not begun ours. They have got to the end of their national credit; we have not put ours in any market in the world. And why should any man be desponding? Why should any man say that this great work has gone on too slowly? Why should men feel impatient? The war of the Revolution was seven years. Why should men be so anxious that nations should march faster than they are prepared to march —faster than the tread of nations has ever been in the Providence of God? Nations in war have ever moved slowly. We are too impatient—we never learn anything, it would seem to me, from reading history—I speak of myself as well as you—I have shared in that impatience myself. I have shared in your various matters of disappointment.

I was saying but the other day to a friend of mine, "It seems strange to me that our navy cannot catch that steamer 'Alabama,' there must be something wrong in the Navy Department, I am afraid," and I got quite impatient. I had hardly got over the wound inflicted by the capture of the "Jacob Bell," when came the piracies of the "Golden Eagle," and the "Olive Jane," and as one was from Boston, it touched me keenly.

He replied: "Don't be impatient; remember that Paul Jones, with a sailing-ship on the coast of England, put the whole British navy at defiance for many months, and wandered up and down that coast, and worked his will upon it, and England had no naval power to contend with, and had not twenty-five hundred miles of sea coast to blockade as we have."

I remember that in the French war, Lord Cochrane, with one vessel, and that was by no means a steamship, held the whole French coast in terror against the French navy. And so it has been done by other nations. Let us have a little patience, and possess our souls with a little patriotism and less politics, and we shall have no difficulty.

But there is one circumstance of this war, I am bound to say in all frankness to you, that I do not like the appearance of, and that is because we cannot exactly reach it. I refer to the war made upon our commerce, which is not the fault of the navy, nor of any department of the government, but is the fault of our allies. Pardon me a moment, for I am speaking now in the commercial city of New York, where I think it is of interest to you, and of a matter to which I have given some reflection—pardon me a moment, while we examine and see what England has done. She agreed to be neutral—I have tried to demonstrate to you that she ought to have been a little more than neutral — but has she been even that? ("No, no no.") Let us see the evidences of that "No."

In the first place there has been nothing of the Union cause that her orators and her statesmen have not maligned; there has been nothing of sympathy or encouragement which she has not afforded our enemies; there has been nothing which she could do under the cover of neutrality which she has not done to

aid them. Nassau has been a naval arsenal for pirate
rebel boats to refit in. Kingston has been their coal
depot, and Barbadoes has been the dancing hall to
fête pirate chieftains in.

What cause, my friends; what cause, my countrymen, has England so to deal with us? What is the
reason she does so deal with us? Is it because we have
never shown sympathy toward her or love to her people? And mark me here, that I make a distinction
between the English people as a mass and the English government. I think the heart of her people beats
responsive to ours—but I know her government and
aristocracy hate us with a hate which passeth all understanding. I say, let us see if we have given any
cause for this. I know, I think, what the cause is;
but let us see what we have done.

You remember that when the famine overtook the
Irish in 1847, the "Macedonian" frigate carried out
the bread from this country to feed the poor that England was starving. When afterward the heir to her
throne arrived here, aye, in this very house, our people
assembled to do him welcome in such numbers that the
very floor would not uphold them, and to testify our
appreciation of the high qualities of his mother and
sovereign, and our love of the English people—we
gave him such a reception as Northern gentlemen give
to their friends, and his present admirers at Richmond
gave him such a reception as Southern gentlemen give
to their friends. What further has been done by us?
No, I have no right to claim any portion of it. What
has been done by the merchants of New York? The
"George Griswold" goes out to feed the starving

poor of Lancashire, to which yourselves all contributed, and it was only God's blessing on that charity that prevented that vessel being overhauled and burned by the "Alabama," fitted out from an English port.

And to-day at Birkenhead the "Sumter" is being fitted out—at Barbadoes the captain of the "Florida" is being fêted—and somewhere the "290," the cabalistic number of the British merchants who contributed to her construction, is preying upon our commerce, while we hear that at Glasgow a steamer is being built for the Emperor of China, and at Liverpool another is about to be launched for the Emperor of China. Pardon me, I don't believe the Emperor of China will buy many ships of Great Britain until they bring back the silk gowns they stole out of his palace at Pekin. And even now, I say that our commerce is being preyed upon by ships in the hands of the rebels built by English builders. And I ask the merchants of the city of New York whether it has not already reached the point where our commerce, to be safe, has to be carried in British bottoms.

Now I learn from the late correspondence of Earl Russell with the rebel commissioner Mason, that the British have put two articles of the treaty of Paris in compact with the rebels: First, that enemies' goods shall be covered by neutral flags, and there shall be free trade at the ports and open trade with neutrals. Why didn't Great Britain put the other part of the treaty in compact; namely, that there should be no more privateering, if she was honest and earnest, and did not mean our commerce should be crippled by rebel piracy?

Again, when we took from her deck our two senators and rebel ambassadors, Slidell and Mason, and took them, in my judgment, according to the laws of nations, what did she do but threaten us with war? I agree that it was wisely done, perhaps, not to provoke war at that time—we were not quite in a condition for it—but I think God, and that always, that we are fast getting in a condition to remember that threat always and every day! Why is it all this has been done? Because we alone can be the commercial rivals of Great Britain! and because the South has no commercial marine.

There has been in my judgment a deliberate attempt on the part of Great Britain, under the plea of neutrality, to allow our commerce to be ruined for her own benefit, if human actions indicate human thoughts. It is idle to tell me Great Britain does not know these vessels are fitted out in her ports. It is idle and insulting to tell me that she put the " Alabama " under $20,000 bonds not to go into the service of the Confederate States. The " Jacob Bell " alone would pay the amount of the bond over and over again.

We did not so deal with her when she was at war with Russia. On the suggestion of the British minister our government stopped, with the rapidity of lightning, the sailing of a steamer supposed to be for Russia, until the minister himself was convinced of her good faith and willing to let her go. We must take some means to put a stop to these piracies and to the fitting out of pirate vessels in English ports. They are always telling us about the inefficiency of a republican government, but as they are acting now, we could stop two pirates to their one. We must in some way put a stop to the construction and fitting out of these pirate vessels in English ports to prey upon our commerce or else consent to keep our ships idle at home. We must stop them—we must act upon the people of England if we cannot secure a stoppage in any other way.

I have seen it stated that the loss to our commerce already amounts to $9,000,000—enough to have paid the expense of keeping a large number of vessels at home and out of the way of these cruisers.

What shall we do in the matter? Why, when our government takes a step toward putting a stop to it (and I believe it is taking that step now, but it is not in my province to speak of it) we must aid it in so doing. We, the people, are the government in this matter, and when our government gets ready to take a step we must get ready to sustain it.

England told us what to do when we took Mason and Slidell, and she thought there was a likelihood to be war. She stopped exportation of those articles which she thought we wanted, and which she had allowed to be exported before. Let us do the same thing.

Let us proclaim non-intercourse, so that no ounce of American food shall ever by any accident get into an Englishman's mouth until these piracies cease. (A voice: "Say that again!") I never say anything, my friends, that I am afraid to say again. I repeat— let us proclaim non-intercourse, so that no ounce of American food shall by any accident get into an Englishman's mouth until these piracies are stopped. That we have a right to do; and when we ever do do it, my word for it, the English government will find out where these vessels are going to, and they will write to the Emperor of China upon the subject. But I hear some objectors say, "If you proclaim non-intercourse England may go to war."

Now I am not to be frightened twice running. I got frightened a little better than a year ago, but I have gotten over it. Further, this is a necessity; for we must keep our ships at home in some form to save them from these piracies when a dozen of these privateers get loose upon the seas. It will become a war measure which any nation, under any law, under any construction, would warrant our right to enforce.

And this course should be adopted toward the English nation alone, for I have never heard of any blockade runners under the French flag, nor under the Russian flag, nor under the Austrian flag, nor under the Greek flag. No! not even the Turks will do it. Therefore I have ventured to suggest the adoption of this course for your consideration as a possible,—aye, not only possible, but, unless this state of things has a remedy, a probable event; for we must see to it that we protect ourselves and take a manly place among the nations of the earth. But I hear some friend of mine say, " I am afraid your scheme would bring down our provisions; and if we do not export them to England we shall find our Western markets still more depressed." Allow me, with great deference to your judgment, gentlemen, to suggest a remedy for that at the same time.

I would suggest that the exportation of gold be

prohibited and then there would be nothing to forward to meet the bills of exchange and pay for the goods we have bought, except our provisions. And, taking a hint from one of your best and most successful merchants, we could pay for our silks and satins in butter, and lard, and corn, and beef, and pork, and bring up the prices in the West, so that they could afford to pay the increased tariff in bringing them forward, now rendered necessary, I suppose, upon your railroads. And if our fair sisters and daughters will dress in silks, and satins, and laces, they will not feel any more troubled that a portion of the price goes to the Western farmer to enhance his gains instead of going into the coffers of a Jew banker in Wall street.

You will observe, my friends, that in the list of grievances with which I charge England, I have not charged her with tampering with our leading politians. So far as any evidence I have, I don't know that she is guilty; but what shall we say of our leading politicians that have tampered with her? I have read of it in the letters of Lord Lyons with much surprise —with more surprise than has been excited in me by any other fact of this war—I had, somehow, got an inkling of the various things that came up in previous instances, so I was not very much surprised at them; but when I so read a statement, deliberately put forward, that here in New York leading politicians had consulted with the British minister as to how these United States could be separated and broken up, every drop of blood in my veins boiled; and I would have liked to have met that leading politician. I do not know that Lord Lyons is to blame. I suppose, sir, if a man comes to one of your clerks and offers to go into partnership with him to rob your neighbor's bank, and he reports him to you, you do not blame the clerk; but what do you do with the man who makes the offer?

I think we had better take a lesson from the action of Washington's administration—when the French minister, M. Genet, undertook even to address the people of the United States by letter, complaint was made to his government and he was recalled, and a law was passed preventing for all future time any interference by foreign diplomatists with the people of the United States.

I want to be understood,—I have no evidence of any interference on the part of Lord Lyons; but he says in his letter to Earl Russell that, both before and after a certain event, leading politicians came to him and desired that he would do what—(I am giving the substance and not words)—desired that he would request his government not to interfere between the North and South. Why? Because it would aid the country not to interfere? No! Because, if England did interfere the country would spurn the interference and be stronger than ever to crush the rebellion.

Mark again the insidious way in which the point was put. They knew how we felt because of the action of England; they knew that the heart of this people beat true to the constitution and that it could not brook any interference on the part of England. What, then did these politicians do? They asked the British minister to use the influence of British diplomacy to induce other nations to interfere, but to take care that Great Britain should keep out of sight, lest we should see the cat under the meal. This is precisely the proposition that they made. You observe that in speaking of these men I have up to this moment used the word politicians. What kind of politicians? They cannot be Democratic politicians.

How I should like to hear Andrew Jackson say a few words upon such politicians who call themselves Democrats! ("He would hang them.") No, I don't think he would have an opportunity to do so; he never would be able to catch them. I have felt it my duty here in the city of New York, because of the interest I have in public affairs, to call attention to this most extraordinary fact—that there are men in the community so lost to patriotism, so bound up in the traditions of party, so selfish, as to be willing to tamper with Great Britain in order to bring about the separation of this country.

It is the most alarming fact that I have yet seen. I had rather see a hundred thousand men set in the field on the rebel side,—aye, I had rather see Great Britain armed against us openly, as she is covertly—than to be forced to believe that there are amongst us such men as these, lineal descendants of Judas Iscariot, intermarried with the race of Benedict Arnold.

It has shown me a great danger with which we are threatened, and I call upon all true men to sustain the government—to be loyal to the government. As you, sir, were pleased to say, the present government was not the government of my choice, I did not vote for it or for any part of it; but it is the government of my country, it is the only organ by which I can exert the force of the country to protect its integrity; and so long as I believe that government to be honestly administered, I will throw a mantle over any mistakes that I may think it has made and support it heartily, with hand and purse, so help me God!

I have no loyalty to any man or men; my loyalty is to the government; and it makes no difference to me who the people have chosen to administer the government as long as the choice has been constitutionally made and the persons so chosen hold their places and powers. I am a traitor and a false man if I falter in my support. This is what I understand to be loyalty to a government; and I was sorry to learn, as I did the other day, that there was a man in New York who professed not to know the meaning of the word loyalty. I desire to say here that it is the duty of every man to be loyal to the government, to sustain it, to pardon its errors and help to rectify them, and to do all he can to aid it in carrying the country on in the course of glory and grandeur in which it was started by our fathers.

Let me say to you, my friends—to you, young men, that no man who opposed his country in time of war ever prospered. The Tory of the Revolution, the Hartford Conventionist of 1812, the immortal seven who voted against the supplies for the Mexican War —all history is against these men. Let no politician of our day put himself in the way of the march of this country to glory and greatness, for whoever does so will surely be crushed. The course of our nation is onward and let him who opposes it beware.

24

" The mower mows on—though the adder may writhe,
Or the copperhead coil round the blade of his scythe."

It only remains, sir, for me to repeat the expression of my gratitude to you and the citizens of New York here assembled for the kindness with which you and they have received me and listened to me, for which please again accept my thanks.

Breckinridge, John C., an American politician and soldier, born near Lexington, Ky., January 21, 1821; died at Lexington, Ky., May 17, 1875. He established himself as a lawyer in Lexington, held a major's commission in the army during the Mexican War, and at its close was sent to the lower house of the State Legislature, where his abilities as a debater became evident. He went to Congress in 1851, and was re-elected two years later. In 1857 he became Vice-President, and in 1860 was one of the four candidates for the Presidency. He was, however, elected to the National Senate that same year, and for a short time advocated there the cause of secession. Resigning his seat, he was appointed a major-general in the Confederate army, and from January to April, 1865, was Confederate Secretary of War. He then went to England, but returned in 1868, and passed the remainder of his life in Kentucky.

ADDRESS PRECEDING THE REMOVAL OF THE SENATE.

ON the 6th of December, 1819, the Senate assembled for the first time in this Chamber, which has been the theatre of their deliberations for more than thirty-nine years.

And now the strifes and uncertainties of the past are finished. We see around us on every side the proofs of stability and improvement. The Capitol is worthy of the Republic. Noble public buildings meet the view on every hand. Treasures of science and the arts begin to accumulate. As this flourishing city enlarges it testifies to the wisdom and forecast that dictated the plan of it. Future generations will not be disturbed with questions concerning the centre of population, or of territory, since the steamboat, the railroad, and the telegraph have made communication almost instantaneous. The spot is sacred by a thousand memories, which are so many pledges that the city of Washington, founded by him and bearing his revered name, with its beautiful site, bounded by picturesque eminences, and the broad Potomac, and lying within view of his home and his tomb, shall remain forever the political capital of the United States.

It would be interesting to note the gradual changes which have occurred in the practical working of the government since the adoption of the constitution; and it may be appropriate to this occasion to remark one of the most striking of them.

At the origin of the government the Senate seemed to be regarded chiefly as an executive council. The President often visited the chamber and conferred personally with this body; most of its business was transacted with closed doors, and it took comparatively little part in the legislative debates. The rising and vigorous intellects of the country sought the arena of the House of Representatives as the appropriate theatre for the display of their powers. Mr. Madison observed, on some occasion, that being a young man and desiring to increase his reputation, he could not afford to enter the Senate; and it will be remembered that so late as 1812 the great debates which preceded the war and aroused the country to the assertion of its rights took place in the other branch of Congress. To such an extent was the idea of seclusion carried that when this chamber was completed no seats were prepared for the accommodation of the public; and it was not until many years afterward that the semi-circular gallery was erected which admits the people to be witnesses of your proceedings. But now, the Senate, besides its peculiar relations to the executive department of the government, assumes its full share of duty as a co-equal branch of the legislature; indeed from the limited number of its members and for other obvious reasons the most important questions, especially of foreign policy, are apt to pass first under discussion in this body,—and to be a member of it is justly regarded as one of the highest honors which can be conferred on an American statesman.

It is scarcely necessary to point out the causes of this change, or to say that it is a concession both to the importance and to the individuality of the States, and to the free and open character of the government.

In connection with this easy but thorough transition, it is worthy of remark that it has been effected without a charge from any quarter that the Senate has transcended its constitutional sphere—a tribute at once to the moderation of the Senate, and another proof to thoughtful men of the comprehensive wisdom with which the framers of the constitution secured essential principles without inconveniently embarrassing the action of the government.

The progress of this popular movement in one aspect of it, has been steady and marked. As the origin of the government, no arrangements in the Senate were made for spectators; in this chamber about one third of the space is allotted to the public; and in the new apartment the galleries cover two thirds of its area. In all free countries the admission of the people to witness legislative proceedings is an essential element of public confidence; and it is not to be anticipated that this wholesome principle will ever be abused by the substitution of partial and interested demonstrations for the expression of a matured and enlightened public opinion. Yet it should never be forgotten that not France, but the turbulent spectators within the hall, awed and controlled the French assembly. With this lesson and its consequences before us, the time will never come when the deliberations of the Senate shall be swayed by the blandishments or the thunders of the galleries.

It is impossible to disconnect from an occasion like this a crowd of reflections on our past history and of speculations on the future. The most meagre account of the Senate involves a summary of the progress of our country. From year to year you have seen your representation enlarge; again and again you have proudly welcomed a new sister into the confederacy; and the occurrences of this day are a material and impressive proof of the growth and prosperity of the United States. Three periods in the history of the Senate mark in striking contrast three epochs in the history of the Union.

On the 3d of March, 1789, when the government was organized under the constitution, the Senate was composed of the representatives of eleven States containing three millions of people.

On the 6th of December, 1819, when the Senate met for the first time in this room it was composed of the representatives of twenty-one States containing nine millions of people.

To-day it is composed of the representatives of thirty-two States containing more than twenty-eight millions of people, prosperous, happy, and still devoted to constitutional liberty. Let these great facts speak for themselves to all the world.

The career of the United States cannot be measured by that of any other people of whom history gives account; and the mind is almost appalled at the contemplation of the prodigious force which has marked their progress. Sixty-nine years ago thirteen States, containing three millions of inhabitants, burdened with debt, and exhausted by the long war of independence, established for their common good a free constitution on principles new to mankind, and began their experiment with the good wishes of a few doubting friends and the derision of the world. Look at the result to-day; twenty-eight millions of people, in every way happier than an equal number in any other part of the globe! the centre of population and political power descending the western slopes of the Alleghany Mountains, and the original thirteen States forming but the eastern margin on the map of our·vast possessions.

See besides, Christianity, civilization, and the arts given to a continent; the despised colonies grown into a power of the first class, representing and protecting ideas that involve the progress of the human race; a commerce greater than that of any other nation; free interchange between States; every variety of climate, soil, and production, to make a people powerful and happy—in a word, behold present greatness, and in the future an empire to which the ancient mistress of the world in the height of her glory could not be compared.

Such is our country; aye, and more—far more than my mind could conceive or my tongue could utter. Is there an American who regrets the past? Is there one who will deride his country's laws, pervert her constitution, or alienate her people? If there be such man, let his memory descend to prosperity laden with the execrations of all mankind.

So happy is the political and social condition of the United States, and so accustomed are we to the secure enjoyment of a freedom elsewhere unknown, that we are apt to undervalue the treasures we possess, and to lose in some degree the sense of obligation to our forefathers. But when the strifes of faction shake the government and even threaten it we may pause with advantage long enough to remember that we are reaping the reward of other men's labors. This liberty we inherit; this admirable constitution, which has survived peace and war, prosperity and adversity, this double scheme of government, State and Federal, so peculiar and so little understood by other powers, yet which protects the earnings of industry and makes the largest personal freedom compatible with public order; these great results were not achieved without wisdom and toil and blood—the touching and heroic record is before the world. But to all this we were born, and, like heirs upon whom has been cast a great inheritance, have only the high duty to preserve, to extend, and to adorn it. The grand productions of the era in which the foundations of this government were laid, reveal the deep sense its founders had of their obligations to the whole family of man. Let us never forget that the responsibilities imposed on this generation are by so much the greater than those which rested on our revolutionary ancestors, as the population, extent, and power of our country surpass the dawning promise of its origin.

It would be a pleasing task to pursue many trains of thought, not wholly foreign to this occasion, but the temptation to enter the wide field must be rigorously curbed; yet I may be pardoned, perhaps, for one or two additional reflections.

The Senate is assembled for the last time in this chamber. Henceforth it will be converted to other uses, yet it must remain forever connected with great events, and sacred to the memories of the departed orators and statesmen who here engaged in high debates and shaped the policy of their country. Hereafter the American and the stranger, as they wander through the Capitol, will turn with instinctive reverence to view the spot on which so many and great materials have accumulated for history. They will recall the images of the great and the good, whose renown is the common property of the Union; and, chiefly, perhaps, they will linger around the seats once occupied by the mighty three, whose names and fame, associated in life, death has not been able to sever; illustrious men, who in their generation sometimes divided, sometimes led, and sometimes resisted public opinion—for they were of that higher class of statesmen who seek the right and follow their convictions.

There sat Calhoun, the senator, inflexible, austere, oppressed, but not overwhelmed by his deep sense of the importance of his public functions; seeking the truth, then fearlessly following it—a man whose unsparing intellect compelled all his emotions to harmonize with the deductions of his rigorous logic, and whose noble countenance habitually wore the expression of one engaged in the performance of high public duties.

This was Webster's seat. He, too, was every inch a senator. Conscious of his own vast powers, he reposed with confidence on himself; and scorning the contrivances of smaller men, he stood among his peers all the greater for the simple dignity of his senatorial demeanor. Type of his northern home, he rises before the imagination, in the grand and granite outline of his form and intellect, like a great New England rock, repelling a New England wave. As a writer, his productions will be cherished by statesmen and scholars while the English tongue is spoken. As a senatorial orator, his great efforts are historically associated with this chamber, whose very air seems to vibrate beneath the strokes of his deep tones and his weighty words.

On the outer circle sat Henry Clay, with his impetuous and ardent nature untamed by age, and exhibiting in the Senate the same vehement patriotism and passionate eloquence that of yore electrified the House of Representatives and the country. His extraordinary personal endowments, his courage, all his noble qualities, invested him with an individuality and a charm of character which in any age would have made him a favorite of history. He loved his country above all earthly objects. He loved liberty in all countries. Illustrious man!—orator, patriot, philanthropist—whose light, at its meridian, was seen and felt in the remotest parts of the civilized world; and whose declining sun as it hastened down the west threw back its level beams in hues of mellowed splendor, to illuminate and to cheer the land he loved and served so well.

All the States may point with gratified pride to the services in the Senate of their patriotic sons. Crowding the memory come the names of Adams, Hayne, Wright, Mason, Otis, Macon, Pinckney, and the rest—I cannot number them—who, in the record of their acts and utterances, appeal to their successors to give the Union a destiny not unworthy of the past. What models were these, to awaken emulation or to plunge in despair! Fortunate will be the American statesman who in this age or in succeeding times shall contribute to invest the new hall to which we go with historic memories like those which cluster here.

And now, senators, we leave this memorable chamber, bearing with us unimpaired the constitution we received from our forefathers. Let us cherish it with grateful acknowledgments to the Divine Power who controls the destinies of empires and whose goodness we adore. The structures reared by men yield to the corroding tooth of time. These marble walls must molder into ruin; but the principles of constitutional liberty, guarded by wisdom and virtue, unlike material elements, do not decay. Let us devoutly trust that another Senate, in another age, shall bear to a new and larger chamber this constitution vigorous and inviolate, and that the last generation of posterity shall witness the deliberations of the representatives of American States still united, prosperous, and free.